Why Design Now?

WHY DESIGN NOW?

National Design Triennial

WITHDRAWN
UTSA LIBRARIES

Ellen Lupton

Cara McCarty

Matilda McQuaid

Cynthia Smith

with contributions by Andrea Lipps

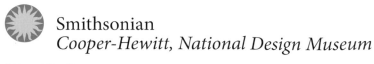

Smithsonian
Cooper-Hewitt, National Design Museum

New York

WHY DESIGN NOW?
NATIONAL DESIGN TRIENNIAL
Ellen Lupton, Cara McCarty, Matilda McQuaid, and
Cynthia Smith, with contributions by Andrea Lipps
© 2010 Smithsonian Institution

Published by
Cooper-Hewitt, National Design Museum
Smithsonian Institution
2 East 91st Street
New York, NY 10128, USA
www.cooperhewitt.org

Published on the occasion of the exhibition
Why Design Now? National Design Triennial
at Cooper-Hewitt, National Design Museum,
Smithsonian Institution,
May 14, 2010–January 9, 2011.

Why Design Now? National Design Triennial
is sponsored by

Generous support is provided by Agnes Bourne,
the Norwegian Consulate General in New York,
the Esme Usdan Exhibition Endowment Fund, the
Ministry of Culture Denmark, and public funds
from the New York State Council on the Arts,
a State agency.

Additional funding is provided by Dr. Leonard
Polonsky and Dr. Georgette Bennett, The Consulate
General of Switzerland in New York, and the
Office of Cultural Affairs, Consulate General of
Israel in New York.

This publication is made possible in part by
The Andrew W. Mellon Foundation.

Museum Editor: Chul R. Kim,
Director of Publications

Design: Michael Bierut and Yve Ludwig,
Pentagram, New York

Printed in China by Toppan Printing Company.

Distributed to the trade worldwide by
Distributed Art Publishers
155 Sixth Avenue, 2nd floor
New York, NY 10013, USA
www.artbook.com

First edition: May 2010
ISBN: 978-0-910503-87-7

Library of Congress Cataloging-in-Publication Data

National Design Triennial (4th : 2010 :
New York, N.Y.)
Why Design Now? : National Design Triennial /
Cara McCarty ... [et al.] ; with contributions by
Andrea Lipps.
p. cm.
Includes index.
"Published on the occasion of the exhibition Why
Design Now? National Design Triennial at Cooper-
Hewitt, National Design Museum, Smithsonian
Institution, May 14, 2010–January 9, 2011."
ISBN 978-0-910503-87-7 (alk. paper)
1. Design--History--21st century--Exhibitions.
2. Industrial design--History--21st century--
Exhibitions. 3. Sustainable design--Exhibitions.
I. McCarty, Cara. II. Cooper-Hewitt Museum.
III. Title.

NK1397.N38 2009
745.409'05110747471--dc22

2010004050

Title page: Jardin Botanico-Orquideorama
(Orchid Botanical Garden), Medellín, Colombia.
Alejandro Bernal, Felipe Mesa, Camilo Restrepo,
and J. Paul Restrepo, Plan B Architects;
additional team members: Jorge Buitrago,
Lina Gil, Carolina Gutierrez, Catalina Patiño,
Viviana Peña. Colombia, 2004–7

Mixed Sources
Product group from well-managed
forests, controlled sources and
recycled wood or fiber
www.fsc.org   Cert no. DNV-COC-000054
©1996 Forest Stewardship Council
FSC

6   Foreword
Caroline Baumann, Deputy Director, and Bill Moggridge, Director
Cooper-Hewitt, National Design Museum

9   Introduction
The Curators

12   **Energy** Cara McCarty

36   **Mobility** Cara McCarty

48   **Community** Matilda McQuaid

68   **Materials** Matilda McQuaid

96   **Prosperity** Cynthia Smith

118   **Health** Cynthia Smith

140   **Communication** Ellen Lupton

168   **Simplicity** Ellen Lupton

186   Authors

187   Selected Index

191   Photographic Credits

192   Acknowledgments

Foreword

Caroline Baumann and Bill Moggridge

The 2010 *National Design Triennial*—entitled *Why Design Now?*, the fourth installation in Cooper-Hewitt's acclaimed series since its inception ten years ago—is global in reach for the first time, showcasing some of the world's most innovative, forward-thinking designs while assessing themes in social change and environmental accountability. We ask questions throughout the exhibition and within this catalogue to engage the viewer and the reader: Why and how is design thinking an essential tool for solving some of today's most urgent problems? Why should business leaders, policy makers, consumers, and citizens embrace design values? How can design promote environmental stewardship, social equity, accessibility, and creative capital? This *National Design Triennial* and its 134 selected projects—from ZenithSolar's Z-10 concentrated solar-power system, which achieves greater efficiency and cost reduction, and David Chavez's Haptica Braille timepiece, which provides time reading without the need for sound, to the Samarth bicycle trailer, which empowers rural Indian women—answer these questions and provoke further discussion. We are proud to present this groundbreaking exhibition of design projects representing the "revolution" taking place within all areas of design practice—not only how products and projects are conceived, but also how goods, services, and ideas are produced, distributed, and used worldwide.

We, and the Board of Trustees, wish to thank Cooper-Hewitt's terrific curatorial team and the entire staff for organizing this stunningly varied survey of contemporary design. Thanks are also in order for Paul Warwick Thompson, the former Director of Cooper-Hewitt and current Rector of the Royal College of Art, who embraced the show's theme and breadth from the start and encouraged the curators to cast the net far and wide to collect the best examples of design.

Why Design Now? would not have been possible without the generosity of GE as our lead sponsor. We thank the entire GE team for their support and promotion of the exhibition, particularly Cooper-Hewitt trustee Beth Comstock, who recognized the importance of the exhibition from the start. We also extend our sincere gratitude to Cooper-Hewitt trustee Agnes Bourne for her continued support of the *Triennial* series since its start in 2000; Agnes was instrumental in the creation of the series and advocates its importance from west to east coasts! Thanks are also in order to the Norwegian Consulate General in New York, the Esme Usdan Exhibition Endowment Fund, the Ministry of Culture Denmark, NYSCA, Dr. Leonard Polonsky and Dr. Georgette Bennett, the Consulate General of Switzerland in New York, and the Consulate General of Israel in New York. Thank you all for making this stellar exhibition possible!

Introduction

The Curators

Why design now? Designers around the world are answering this question by creating products, prototypes, proposals, buildings, landscapes, messages, and more that address social and ecological problems. How can we power the world with clean energy? How can we move people and products more safely and efficiently? How can we shelter communities in safe, sustainable environments? How can we close the open loop of materials extraction and disposal? How can we enable people around the globe to share and generate wealth? How can we improve the quality of life for all people through health-care innovations? How can we communicate ideas more effectively and creatively? How can we discover beauty in simple forms that use minimal resources? Collectively, designers are seeking to enhance human health, prosperity, and comfort while diminishing the conflicts between people and the global ecosystems we inhabit.

Energy is essential to every human endeavor. As we deplete the earth's finite supply of fossil fuels, we are also polluting the atmosphere and catalyzing climate change. Around the world, scientists, engineers, and designers are studying ways to harness energy from the sun, wind, and tides and to create new products and structures that use energy not just efficiently but also self-sufficiently, generating surplus power.

Celebrity wallpaper. Mieke Gerritzen, All Media Wallpaper. The Netherlands, 2009

The human urge for mobility has produced interconnected landscapes where time and distance have progressively collapsed—at a steep environmental cost. Allowing people to travel across town or over a continent while conserving resources requires fresh design solutions, from foldable bicycles, on-demand electric vehicles, and self-propelled trains to new conceptions of how cities work.

Architecture creates the context for community. Built environments shelter the body while inspiring the mind and enabling social life. In response to ever-expanding sprawl in the developed world and escalating urban density in developing areas, architects are creating rooftop villages, urban farms, and mixed-use housing developments that employ local materials and encourage harmonious, energy-efficient living at close quarters.

Products and buildings all consume materials. Chemists, engineers, and designers are inventing everything from biodegradable, petroleum-free plastics to foam insulation that grows in the dark like a mushroom, requiring minimal energy to produce. New information systems are helping consumers find goods with a clean biological record, such as materials made from reclaimed waste, from nontoxic substances, or from rapidly renewable agricultural products.

Prosperity is a state of material well-being that exceeds mere subsistence. Without access to adequate food, hygiene, safety, and protection from the elements, people cannot enjoy social and spiritual life. Nor can they invent solutions to the problems around them. Today, progressive designers and entrepreneurs are building engines of prosperity that enable local communities to use their own resources to create their own wealth as well as to participate in the global economy.

The health of individuals and societies depends on design ingenuity. From creating prosthetic limbs controlled by the human mind to devising new ways to deliver health care to rural populations, designers are improving mental and physical wellness for the rich and poor, young and old, able-bodied and physically challenged.

New ideas have nowhere to go without the tools of communication. Smart phones, digital reading devices, and social networks are changing the way people use and produce information. Designers are helping people understand the world's problems by visualizing complex data and by delivering urgent messages about safety, equality, and the environment.

The design process often involves a quest for simplicity. Many designers seek to create compact, coherent structures that speak clearly to their purpose. Today, as designers strive to simplify production processes and consume fewer materials in smaller amounts, the quest for simplicity is shaping design's economic and ethical values as well as its sense of beauty.

Why Design Now? is the fourth installment in the *National Design Triennial* series, launched by the Smithsonian's Cooper-Hewitt, National Design Museum in 2000. The previous exhibitions focused on work conceived in the United States or created abroad by American designers. The *Triennial* has now gone global, reflecting the growing connectedness of design practices and the need for international cooperation to solve the world's problems.

    Why Design Now? is organized by a team of curators from Cooper-Hewitt, National Design Museum, each of whom represents different areas of expertise, including product design, architecture, textiles, technology, communication, and design for social change. The curatorial team invited nominations from the public and from colleagues in the field and conducted independent research. A long process of internal vetting and discussion yielded the final selection of projects, which we are proud to share with you here.

    Why Design Now? is an open snapshot of contemporary innovation, a sample of what progressive designers, engineers, entrepreneurs, and citizens are doing in diverse fields and at different scales. For each project selected, dozens more could take its place, addressing similar questions from different angles and from different points on the globe. Many of the featured works have influenced other designers by proposing new methodologies or by pioneering new techniques. Included are practical solutions already being implemented as well as experimental ideas designed to inspire further research. A few projects will provoke controversy, answering some questions while raising others. Each one—from a soil-powered table lamp to a post-petroleum urban utopia—celebrates the transformative power of design.

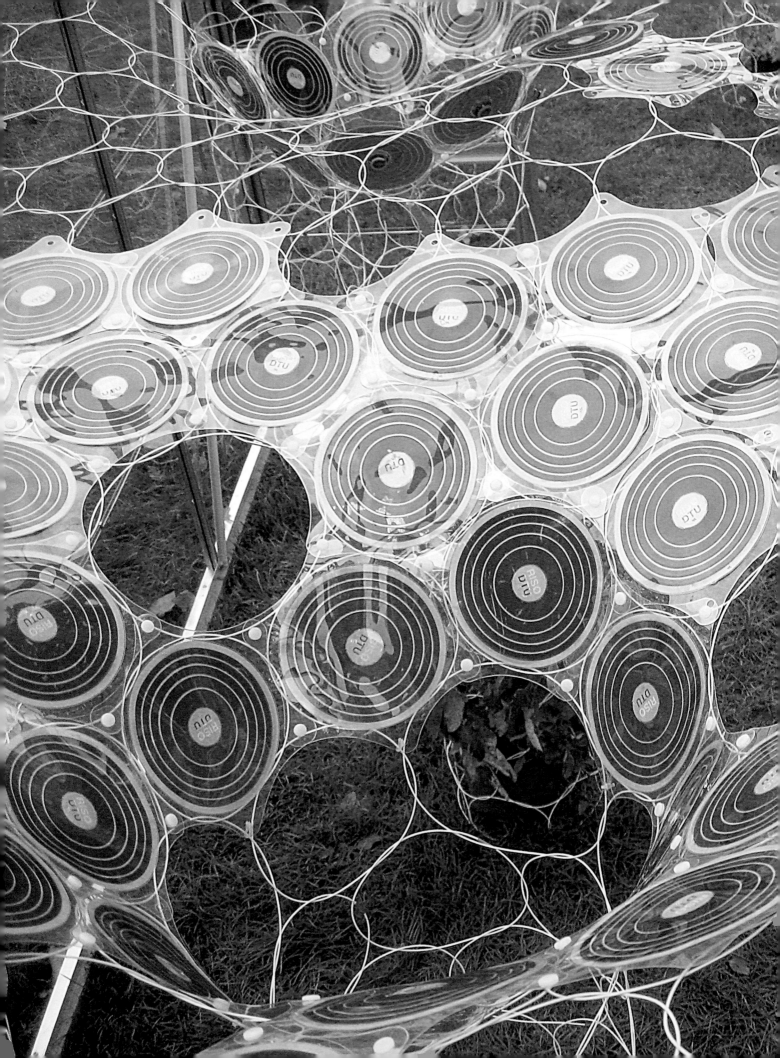

Energy

Cara McCarty

There is now scientific and political consensus that global greenhouse-gas emissions pose a critical threat to the earth's climate, and that this environmental warming is produced by the burning of fossil fuels—by human actions. As about 86% of energy used globally is generated from the use of oil and coal,[1] which produces greenhouse gases, responsive action must be taken through significant cooperation at an international level, balancing the responsibilities of advanced as well as rapidly developing industrial economies. For the United States, which imports about 70% of the oil it consumes and has among the highest carbon-dioxide emissions per capita in the world,[2] the goal must be to make decisive policy, technological, and social changes. Designers, both in this country and elsewhere, can be important contributors to this urgent assignment.

One of the fastest, easiest, and least expensive ways to slow climate change is to use less energy. But efficiency can only take us so far. To achieve more substantial reductions in the production of greenhouse gases, we must replace our current energy supply with clean, renewable energy—a shift which presents countless design opportunities. Fortunately, designers the world over, often in collaboration with scientists and engineers, are innovating solutions that harness such clean

MetaboliCity. Rachel Wingfield and Mathias Gmachl, Studio Loop.pH. Solar cells: Risø DTU, the National Laboratory for Sustainable Energy. Designed United Kingdom, solar cells Denmark, 2008. Composite fiber rods, plants, water growing culture with pumps and irrigation, organic polymer printed solar cells energy sources. Many of the products are at the small, domestic, even microscopic scale, while others are still too expensive, complex, or experimental to be implemented immediately.

Sunlight is the world's largest source of renewable energy. The pressing dilemma is in finding inexpensive ways to store solar energy, for there is no sunlight at night and its output during the day depends on the weather. Vast amounts of affordable storage are needed: one expert calculates that an array of photovoltaic solar panels spread across more than half the land area of California would be needed to meet the daily energy needs of the United States; at present, all panels built to date cover barely ten square miles.[3] Greater efficiency and cost reduction are being achieved by ZenithSolar in Israel, whose Z-10 system concentrates and intensifies sunlight to create heat through the use of simple mirrors and tracking devices, a design inspired by sunflowers (fig. 1). Breakthroughs in nanotechnology are also making solar panels more affordable and efficient, and are alleviating the storage problem by capturing energy in small, decentralized fuel cells. Thin, flexible plastic solar panels resembling rolls of film offer "portable" electricity that can be unfurled and wrapped around structures. One advocate suggests that solar power is doubling every two years; that we are only eight doublings away from meeting 100% of the world's energy needs; and that we have 10,000 times more sunlight than we need to do this.[4]

fig. 1

Wind is another viable source of clean energy. It is growing in popularity primarily through the use of larger and highly engineered terrestrial turbines, especially in Northern and Western European countries, where giant offshore wind farms are becoming common in the North Sea. Wind power requires less land footprint than any other option,[5] but, similar to other forms of renewable energy, conventional wind energy is subject to fluctuations in weather and limitations imposed by the availability of electrical transmission. Alternatively, high altitudes promise to provide more consistent energy from the powerful and more dependable winds aloft, with fewer transmission problems because high-altitude winds are relatively independent geographically. This is spurring designers to experiment with various aerial structures to harness high-altitude winds, such as the wing-shaped kites designed by Makani Power in California (fig. 2).

fig. 2

Ocean wave and tidal power can also be captured to produce electricity, and, according to some scientists, it is the largest unexplored source of renewable energy. It requires no land and is more dependable than solar or wind power, as tides rely on the gravitational forces of the sun, earth, and moon, which are accurately and reliably calculated. However, relatively little is known about the effects large power-generating structures may have on marine life. Nevertheless, it has been estimated that oceans could eventually supply about 10% of the electricity consumed in the United States.[6] Among the designs currently being tested to harness the kinetic energy of ocean turbulence is the bioWAVE ocean-wave energy system, an enormous underwater machine that mimics the swaying motion of seaweed (fig. 3).

fig. 3

The solution to the problems of storage and intermittent clean-energy sources and their integration from geographically dispersed sources lies in the creation of smart power grids. These intelligent networks are energy superhighways that promote optimal electricity distribution and use, similar to what the Internet did for computing. They can connect and combine diverse systems and monitor and measure vast quantities of data to improve reliability and efficiency and to reduce costs. They can even regulate thermostats, meters, and appliances as well as inform consumers about high peaks of energy use. A number of products entering the market, such as the Energy Aware clock or the Power Aware cord, provide real-time ways for consumers to instantly visualize their electricity consumption (figs. 4, 5). At the global scale, an intelligent international grid could help relieve energy shortages throughout the world. Today, one in four people does not have electricity in his or her home, and many of those who do have only a sporadic supply.

fig. 4

fig. 5

Designing systems to conduct our existing business more efficiently and economically must be an adjunct to the organization of new energy sources. The United States is responsible for roughly 50% of the world's carbon-dioxide emissions, and our buildings produce the largest share of this.[7] Tougher building codes are inspiring changes in construction, including more efficient windows, roofing materials, lighting, and heating and cooling systems; proper building orientation and insulation; recyclable materials; and the inclusion of renewable power sources. Green roofs keep buildings warmer in winter and cooler in summer, and they absorb rainfall, slowing the rate of run-off into the city's water system. In addition, they reduce urban heat islands, which absorb heat and radiate it back into the air. The plant-covered, contoured roof designed by Renzo Piano for the California Academy of Sciences is a key component of the building's overall ecological system, making it one of the most sustainable new buildings today (fig. 6).

fig. 6

The average house in America is 45% larger than it was thirty years ago,[8] and requires a commensurately larger amount of energy to run. Designers are countering the increase by creating appliances that consume less energy: for example, most water heaters—the second largest power consumer in the home—are already operating at half the energy consumption of earlier models. Designers can also find ways to make products work together, such as harnessing the heat generated from a clothes dryer, which now goes to waste. Lightbulbs are undergoing major changes and improvements (fig. 7), and an expanded use of low-energy, LED technology not only promises improved color quality and cost-efficiency, but entirely new lighting forms previously unimagined. Design at a much larger scale is also undergoing reconsideration. Using solar energy to light city streets, resulting in significant savings, is being studied in projects such as Jongoh Lee's Invisible Streetlight (fig. 8). The new desert city, Masdar, in the United Arab Emirates, is among the current experiments in which comprehensive changes to urban technologies, policies, and user behavior are being attempted. Designers will hopefully be able to apply lessons learned from this colossal project to many parallel conditions in existing cities.

fig. 7

What is clear is that the current path of industrial societies as inefficient users of energy and producers of intolerable and ugly waste can no longer be sustained. For designers, creating circumstances in which renewable energy is technically and economically feasible, in which resources are cultivated rather than wasted, in which the human environment is enhanced rather than degraded, is both a profound responsibility and a significant intellectual challenge.

fig. 8

1   Budd Steinhilber, "A Look Back…and Forward?" in *Innovation* (spring 2008): 55–57.
2   "Energy Inefficient" editorial, in *The New York Times* (January 19, 2009): A24.
3   Steinhilber, pp. 55–57.
4   Ray Kurzweil, "Going Down the Rabbit Hole," in *GOOD* magazine (spring 2009): 104–5.
5   Mark Z. Jacobson, "Review of Solutions to Global Warming, Air Pollution, and Energy Security," briefing to Senator Jeff Bingaman, Chairman, Senate Energy and Natural Resources Committee, October 8, 2008. In *Energy & Environmental Science* (January 2009): 148–73.
6   Isabel Ordóñez, "Everybody into the Ocean," in *The Wall Street Journal* (October 6, 2008): R6.
7   Peter Miller, "Saving Energy: It Starts at Home," in *National Geographic* (March 2009): 60–78.
8   Ibid.

The author wishes to thank Julian Beinart and Mark Z. Jacobson.

1

bioWAVE Ocean-wave Energy System

The bioWAVE, developed by Australia-based BioPower Systems, is a new device that harnesses the power of ocean waves and converts it into smart grid–connected electricity. Like wind and solar energy, ocean-wave energy is an abundant source of renewable energy, with coastlines awash with untapped clean power. But rather than a visually obtrusive system installed at or near the water's surface, the bioWAVE is an underwater unit mounted on the seabed, imitating the swaying motion of sea plants.

The design is based on biomimicry, which applies evolution's 3.8-billion-year optimization process in the development of a unit that is efficient, lightweight, well adapted, and in harmony with the marine life that inspired its form. The bioWAVE is designed to orient itself to the direction of waves and to lie flat when extreme conditions prevail. The swaying motion activated by the ocean's fluctuations is used to drive an onboard generator that produces electrical power, delivered ashore via a subsea cable. Each unit is expected to generate up to two megawatts of energy, and multiple machines can be deployed as a farm, harvesting enough clean power to meet utility-scale electricity needs.
—*Andrea Lipps*

1 bioWAVE ocean-wave energy system, prototype. Timothy Finnigan, BioPower Systems Pty Ltd. Australia, 2005–9. Computer rendering

2

California Academy of Sciences

The recently completed California Academy of Sciences in San Francisco, designed by architect Renzo Piano, is a vibrant expression of the Academy's mission to explore, explain, and protect the natural world. At over 400,000 square feet, it is the largest public building ever to obtain a LEED (Leadership in Energy and Environmental Design) Platinum rating for its environmental performance. This natural-history museum is organized around a central atrium which leads to three architectural elements retained from the previous museum; and two new ninety-foot-high spheres, one housing a planetarium, the other a rain forest. The atrium is covered by two layers of tensile nets which hold sun, acoustic, and rain shades. Surrounding the building is a solar canopy embedded with 60,000 photovoltaic cells, which produces between 5 and 10% of the building's power and casts a vibrating light shadow on the space below. The steel used for the structure is recycled; parts of the former demolished museum have been reused in a nearby freeway; excavated sand has restored the nearby coastal dunes; a large part of the building's insulation is from recycled denim (San Francisco is home to Levi's jeans); and water from the nearby Pacific Ocean is filtered and piped directly into the museum's aquarium, which features the world's deepest live coral-reef exhibit.

Another distinguishing feature is the museum's 2.5-acre roof, landscaped with seven verdant mounds covered by nine indigenous plant species that provide habitat for butterflies, bees, hummingbirds, and other creatures. The roof's eco-friendly design is a living environment and outdoor laboratory for students and scientists. The green roof also helps regulate temperatures throughout the building and absorbs 98% of all storm water, thus lowering its impact on San Francisco's sewage system. The roof plants are carried in specially designed bio-trays made from coconut-husk fiber, lined with fungi to supply nutrients; the trays disintegrate within three years.

2–5 California Academy of Sciences, San Francisco, CA. Renzo Piano Building Workshop with Stantec Architecture; design team: M. Carroll and O. de Nooyer (senior partner and partner in charge) with S. Ishida (senior partner), B. Terpeluk, J. McNeal, A. De Flora, F. Elmalipinar, A. Guernier, D. Hart, T. Kjaer, J. Lee, A. Meine-Jansen, A. Ng, D. Piano, W. Piotraschke, J. Sylvester, C. Bruce, L. Burow, C. Cooper, A. Knapp, Y. Pages, Z. Rockett, V. Tolu, A. Walsh. CAD Operators: I. Corte, S. D'Atri, G. Langasco, and M. Ottonello. Models: F. Cappellini, S. Rossi, A. Malgeri, and A. Marazzi. Consultants: Ove Arup & Partners, engineering and sustainability; Rutherford & Chekene, civil engineering; SWA Group, landscaping; Rana Creek, living roof; PBS&J, aquarium life support systems; Thinc Design, Cinnabar, Visual-Acuity, exhibits. General contractor: Webcor Builders. Designed Italy and United States, 2000–8

6 Energy Aware clock, prototype. Loove Broms and
Karin Ehrnberger, with Sara Ilstedt Hjelm, Erika
Lundell, and Jin Moen, Interactive Institute AB.
Sweden, 2007. Epoxy, polyamide, acrylic, electronic
components

6

7

Energy Aware Clock

Electricity is invisible, and for many of us, it is something we take
for granted. To provide people with better knowledge of, and
control over, their energy consumption, designers are conceiving
of in-home solutions that are more appealing than electricity
meters. The Energy Aware clock, designed by Loove Broms and
Karin Ehrnberger, in collaboration with Sara Ilstedt Hjelm, Erika
Lundell, and Jin Moen for the Interactive Institute in Sweden, is
intended to resemble an ordinary kitchen clock in form and use,
drawing a parallel between the rhythms of energy and of time. The
clock shows electricity use in real time: if the dishwasher is turned
on, the energy surge appears immediately on the clock's display.
It also tracks energy consumption over a twenty-four-hour period
and compares usage over several days through overlaid graphic
visualizations. Energy Aware also functions as an ordinary clock.
It is wirelessly connected to an energy meter and can be integrated
into portable objects, serving as an ambient display.

GreenPix Zero-energy Media Wall
and SolPix™

Using building façades as canvases for advertising or public art
is not new, but today, LED lighting can be embedded into glass
curtain walls, transforming them into interactive, programmable
spectacles. New York–based architect Simone Giostra pushes this
technology in his site-specific installation, SolPix, an animated
media wall that runs on solar energy. This project is based on
Zero-energy Media Wall, a carbon-neutral LED display he created
for the Xicui Entertainment Complex in Beijing. Referred to
in Beijing as GreenPix, it consists of 2,292 energy-efficient lights
distributed across the massive 24,000-square-foot façade,
making it the largest color LED display in the world. For the first
time, polycrystalline photovoltaic cells were placed with varying
density in the building's skin, laminated within the entire glass
envelope of the building. Since there are windows in the building,
the cells were clustered in patterns that allow natural light
to penetrate where needed. In addition to the digital displays,
the wall also serves as a type of weather report: sensors placed
between the glass panels register variations in wind pressure
and solar exposure, and use embedded software to create
real-time interactive animations that transform the building
façade into a responsive environment. These sustainable digital-
media spaces offer many new possibilities for integrating media,
art, and architecture in an urban context.

8

7 SolPix™. Simone Giostra, Simone Giostra and
Partners. Manufactured by Permasteelisa, Zahner,
and Scheuten Solar. System specifications: Ove
Arup. Media art content: Jeremy Rotsztain.
Designed United States, manufactured United
States and Germany, 2008–10. Computer rendering.
Courtesy of Simone Giostra and Partners

8 GreenPix Zero-energy Media Wall, Beijing, China.
Simone Giostra, Simone Giostra and Partners.
Lighting design and façade engineering: Ove Arup.
Manufactured by Suntech and Thorn Lighting.
Client: Jingya Corporation. Designed United States
and United Kingdom, manufactured and installed
China, 2005–8

9

Hope Solar Tower

Solar towers are among the more ambitious attempts being made to capture solar energy more effectively than through photovoltaic panels. The Australian company EnviroMission is currently commercializing solar-tower technology, originally conceptualized by the German structural engineering firm Schlaich Bergermann and Partner. The Hope solar tower operates by collecting the sun's radiation to heat a large body of air under an expansive collector zone, which acts as a giant greenhouse. Based on the principle that heat rises, this air flows towards the center of the collector through electricity-generating turbines and up and out of the tower, like a chimney. A single 200-megawatt solar tower is estimated to produce enough electricity to power approximately half a million households, preventing more than one million tons of greenhouse gases from entering the atmosphere. To offset the drop in energy production once the sun sets, heat-retention systems can be incorporated to store heat during the daytime and release it at night to power the tower's turbines.

10

9–10 Hope solar tower. EnviroMission Ltd. Concept: Jörg Schlaich, Schlaich Bergermann & Partner. Designed Australia, to be constructed United States, 2011. Computer renderings

11

HydroNet: San Francisco 2108

San Francisco–based designers IwamotoScott created HydroNet as an experimental project in response to the design challenge of conceiving the city one hundred years in the future. Predicated on the belief that future circulation networks in cities will be more connected but also more self-sufficient, the project proposes a citywide, multi-scale transportation network that collects, distributes, and stores fresh water, geothermal energy, and hydrogen fuel. For areas along the San Francisco Bay impacted by a five-meter water level rise predicted as a result of global climate change, algae ponds occupy a new aquaculture zone that provides the raw material for the production of hydrogen fuel. The Hydro-Net's tunnels form an underground circulation infrastructure that stores and distributes the fuel for hydrogen-powered hover cars, which reduce the number of cars on the streets. High-density housing coexists with the aquaculture zone as a forest of sinuous "algae towers." The network taps the vast underground reserves of water and power from freshwater aquifers and underground geothermal energy stores below San Francisco. HydroNet also links to an array of "fog flowers" that harvest fresh water. The entire network forms a super-system that resembles seaweed and chanterelle mushrooms in form, while allowing much of the character of above-ground San Francisco to be preserved and to evolve organically.

12

11–12 HydroNet: San Francisco 2108, concept. Lisa Iwamoto and Craig Scott, IwamotoScott; project team: Cassiano Bonjardim, Sean Canty, Chris Chalmers, Andrew Clemenza, Manuel Diaz, Ryan Golenberg, Wei Huang, Christina Kaneva, John Kim, Charles Lee, Stephanie Lin, Dan Sullivan. United States, 2008. Computer renderings

13

Invisible Streetlight

Imagine walking through a forest at night and seeing small bursts
of light, like fireflies, magically scintillating among the branches.
Such is the concept behind Korean designer Jongoh Lee's Invisible
Streetlight: artificial leaves that can be wrapped around tree
branches and other natural surroundings. During the day, these
thin, delicate leaf structures, invisible as they mingle with the
tree's natural leaves, harness and store sunlight. At night, they
provide a poetic alternative to most streetlights, which are strictly
functional and designed for fixed, pre-determined heights.

The body of Invisible Streetlight is made by the double
injection of silicon and aluminum. These lightweight materials
ensure flexible movement. Silicon's high thermal conductivity
protects the leaves from water, and its semi-transparency diffuses
the fixture's LED light as it shines in the dark. Using a "photo-
capacitor" that converts solar energy into electricity, which is
then stored in a nano-wire battery, the Invisible Streetlight is able
to utilize indirect sunlight on cloudy or rainy days and release
electricity at any time.

14

13–14 Invisible Streetlight, prototype. Jongoh Lee.
South Korea, 2007. Computer renderings

15

M10 Kite-power System

Wind is a promising source of renewable energy. California-based Makani Power Inc. was founded with the goal of producing low-cost, renewable energy using tethered airfoils, or kites. The M10 kite-power system is a fundamentally new way of harnessing the energy of the wind, using a tethered wing to fly at altitudes where the wind is both stronger and more consistent. At these altitudes, the wing sweeps through a vast amount of area, accessing a tremendous amount of wind energy. The wing is similar in size to a single wind-turbine blade of the same power rating, but without the costly tower and nacelle of a wind turbine. Small turbines on the wing extract power from the wind as it rushes across, converting it into electrical power. Because the kite is moving many times faster than the wind, these turbines capture the same amount of power as a full-size wind turbine. The tether carries the traction force of the wing and transmits electrical power to the ground, where special conditioning hardware connects the system to a power grid. Successful development of the Makani technology would enable large-scale wind energy generation over 80% of the United States' land surface, as well as deployment in offshore locations, allowing wind to be developed closer to demand centers.

15 M10 kite-power system. Damon Vander Lind and Becker Van Niekerk, Makani Power Inc. United States, 2008. Carbon fiber, glass pre-preg (pre-impregnated composite fibers)

16

Masdar Development

Masdar is a brand-new, self-contained, sustainable city of forty thousand residents currently being built on the desert outskirts of Abu Dhabi, in the United Arab Emirates. A vast experiment, its design pushes ideas of alternative energy, aiming to be the world's first car-free, carbon-neutral, zero-waste city powered by renewable energy sources. To achieve this, its master planner, the London-based firm of Foster + Partners, is applying new approaches to architecture and engineering on an urban scale. The project is expected to be completed by 2018. The Masdar headquarters building, designed by Adrian Smith and Gordon Gill, will be completed by the end of 2010.

    With global warming and rising temperatures, people will be living increasingly in interiors. Buildings will be just seven to twelve meters apart—close enough to shade each other—with thick insulation to reduce the need for air conditioning and electric light. The only source of water will be produced through a solar-powered desalination process in which sea water is converted to fresh water. Water usage will be reduced from a national daily average of 143 to about 21 gallons per person by recycling waste-water and by using low-flow fixtures, waterless urinals, and a leak-detection system. The sun will be the primary source of energy, captured in thin-film solar panels in the largest solar plant in the Middle East; and supplemented by wind turbines and waste-to-power plants, which use garbage retrieved from a garbage-collection network as fuel.

Masdar development, Abu Dhabi, United Arab Emirates

16 Masdar headquarters. Adrian Smith and Gordon Gill, Adrian Smith + Gordon Gill Architecture. Client: Masdar Initiative. Designed United States 2008–9, construction 2009–present. Computer rendering

17–18 City master plan and transportation modules. Foster + Partners. United Arab Emirates and United Kingdom, 2007; expected completion 2018. Client: Masdar - Abu Dhabi Future Energy Company. Computer renderings

17

18

19

20

19–20 Sunflower umbrellas. Chris Bosse, Tobias Wallisser, and Alexander Rieck, Laboratory for Visionary Architecture. Engineering: SL Rasch. Designed Germany and Australia 2008–9, expected construction 2011. Computer renderings

21

MetaboliCity

According to designers Rachel Wingfield and Mathias Gmachl of Loop.pH, MetaboliCity is "biomimetic architecture modeled on molecular structures and metabolism in living cells." The project was inspired by their collaboration with Nobel Prize–winning scientist Sir John E. Walker, whose work has greatly contributed to the understanding of energy conversion in the living world. For Loop.pH, the convergence of design and science and, ultimately, the emulation of nature can serve to address some of today's most urgent problems by promoting energy independence, human nutrition, and "metabolic thinking."

MetaboliCity is an urban ecosystem that supports modular farming systems. A lightweight textile structure, whose form is based on non-Euclidean geometry and molecular biology, is woven from millimeter-thick fiberglass rods and serves as the scaffold on which plants are grown. Organic, dye-sensitized solar cells, made from the dye of berries by researchers at the National Laboratory for Sustainable Energy in Denmark, are clad to the woven structures to harvest the sun's energy, powering a pump system that monitors and feeds the plants as well as micro LEDs for ambient light at night. These energy-harvesting canopies mimic the process of photosynthesis, wherein the dye, replacing chlorophyll, absorbs energy from sunlight to produce an electrical current in the solar cells.

—*Andrea Lipps*

22

21–22 MetaboliCity. Rachel Wingfield and Mathias Gmachl, Studio Loop.pH. Solar cells: Risø DTU, the National Laboratory for Sustainable Energy. Designed United Kingdom, solar cells Denmark, 2008. Composite fiber rods, organic polymer printed solar cells

23 Ninety Light. Shawn Littrell, Gensler. Manufactured by Luxo. Designed United States, manufactured Norway, 2008. Aluminum, steel, LEDs

24 Philips LED Replacement for the Common Lightbulb. Philips Bright Tomorrow Team. United States, the Netherlands, and China, 2009. Printed circuit boards, LEDs, metal reflectors, thermal pads, heat sink, insulator, plastic shell, caps containing phosphor

23

24

Ninety Light

The recent introduction of small LED lights to replace the ubiquitous and highly inefficient incandescent lightbulb has provided designers with the opportunity to create new lamp designs. The versatility of LEDs has alleviated the size and shape constraints of traditional bulbs and inspired designers to reconceive the lamp, as exemplified by the Ninety Light task lamp. Designed by American Shawn Littrell for the Norwegian lighting company Luxo, it is a contemporary successor to the firm's classic L-1 task light. The Ninety Light uses four high-power, 1.5-watt LEDs, which consume a total of only 6 watts to distribute twice as much light as the original. In addition to expending very little energy, LEDs produce high lumen outputs with greater color quality than incandescent bulbs, and can last as long as twenty-five years. This sleek lamp, described as "the world's most efficient task light," is distinguished by its minimal L-shaped profile, thin lamp head, 90° bend in its spring-balanced arm, and rotating base. Because of the low power consumption of the LEDs, the lampshade remains cool to the user's touch.

Philips LED Replacement for the Common Lightbulb

There have been numerous attempts to improve the efficiency of lightbulbs, but with the new energy standards that go into effect in 2012, designers must come up with an alternative to the incandescent bulb, which will be outlawed. In May 2008, the U.S. Department of Energy announced the L Prize competition for the design of an LED lightbulb to replace the ubiquitous 60-watt incandescent bulb. It is estimated that more than 425 million such bulbs are sold every year in the United States alone—about 50% of the domestic market. The LED replacement would save enough electricity in one year to power the lights of 17.4 million American households, and would avoid 5.6 million metric tons of annual carbon emissions.

Philips, a Dutch electronics corporation, asserts that its entry meets all the criteria of the contest, which requires the bulb to reproduce the equivalent amount and color of light made by the 60-watt incandescent bulb, using only 10 watts of power. The competition also requires that the new bulb last for more than 25,000 hours—about twenty-five times longer than the standard incandescent lightbulb—and that at least 75% percent of the bulb be manufactured in the United States. One of the great advantages to Philips's design is that it fits into the same socket as incandescent bulbs, which means people will not need to replace their current light fixtures. Philips claims that eventually it can reduce the price of the LED lightbulb to between $20 and $25.

25 Power Aware cord, prototype. Magnus Gyllenswärd and Anton Gustafsson, Interactive Institute AB. Sweden, 2007. Silicon, epoxy, acrylic, electronic components, PVC plastic, copper, ZnS, silver

26 Soil Lamp, prototype. Marieke Staps. The Netherlands, 2008. Glass, soil, copper, zinc

25

26

Power Aware Cord

Most people have little sense of their energy usage until they receive their monthly utility bill. The Power Aware cord helps make the invisible visible. Designed by Anton Gustafsson and Magnus Gyllenswärd at the Interactive Institute in Sweden, it is a simple, poetic gesture that signals the amount of energy that flows to an appliance through glowing pulses and intensity of light. For instance, the effect of changing the volume on stereo equipment becomes immediately visible, as does the silent drain of electricity from appliances on standby. The design is based on our intuitive notion that light symbolizes energy use, and gives people direct feedback and the feeling of both seeing and interacting with electricity. Energy use can therefore be understood from both a technical and an aesthetic point of view, integrating the often separate areas of design and engineering. The light in the Power Aware cord is produced by electroluminescent wire.

Soil Lamp

A number of designers today are integrating objects with alternative means of clean power to create self-contained, self-sustaining systems. For Dutch designer Marieke Staps, the power source is mud. Her Soil Lamp makes use of the metabolism of biological life in dirt to produce enough energy to power a small LED light. The soil, enclosed in cells containing zinc and copper, acts as an electrolyte—an electrically conductive medium—and requires only a simple splash of water to keep it from drying out. The more cells there are, the more electricity can be generated.

Staps's design and naming of the Soil Lamp celebrates the transparency and simplicity of its process: the earth battery is housed in a clear bulbous base, with power carried along a thin conductor leading to a bare bulb. Exposing the possibilities of another source of abundant, renewable energy, the lamp serves to invigorate future innovation for small, contained power systems.
—*Andrea Lipps*

27

Solar Lilies

Nature continues to be an inspiration for designers seeking optimized, sustainable solutions for harvesting energy. Solar Lilies,
designed by the Scottish firm ZM Architecture, are biomimetic
solar collectors whose form is modeled on the plant that inspires
their name. Initially conceptualized for the River Clyde in
Glasgow, the solar lily pads take advantage of open and underused
space along waterways to convert solar energy to grid electricity.
Circular discs made from steel and recycled rubber float on
rivers. The discs are mounted with motorized solar arrays that
rotate to track the sun throughout the day, angling themselves
for maximum exposure to gather the sunlight that is intensified
by the water. The giant Solar Lilies range in diameter from
fifteen to forty-five feet, with "stems" tethered to the river bed
for easy maneuverability.
—*Andrea Lipps*

28

27–28 Solar Lilies, prototype. Peter Richardson,
ZM Architecture. United Kingdom, 2007. Computer
renderings

29

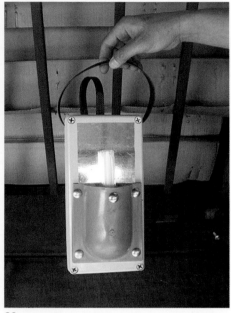

30

Solar Rechargeable Battery Lanterns

Industrial societies take electricity and lighting for granted, but in most rural areas of the developing world, people rely on inefficient fuels such as kerosene that are both dangerous and pose serious health problems. Designed by Nishan Disanayake from Sri Lanka and Simon Henschel and Egbert Gerber from Germany for Sunlabob Renewable Energy, a Laotian energy firm, the solar rechargeable battery lantern provides a safe, competitive electrical lighting alternative to the conventional use of kerosene by reducing greenhouse gases and offsetting fossil fuels, while providing a service-oriented solution for rural electrification. Villagers rent these portable, rechargeable lanterns from a solar charging station set up in the center of the village. There are microeconomic opportunities as well. The stations are rented by village entrepreneurs, who receive technical assistance and training from Sunlabob but undertake the operation and management, empowering communities and fostering a sense of ownership. Each lantern has an embedded microprocessor, an "identification" tag that monitors and safeguards its battery. During recharging, the central station collects data on the use and status of the lantern; the data are analyzed to ensure high efficiency of all equipment and for reliable carbon trading. The lanterns are also being used in Afghanistan and Uganda.

29–30 Solar rechargeable battery lanterns, demonstration stand. Nishan Disanayake, Simon Henschel, and Egbert Gerber, Sunlabob Renewable Energy Co. Ltd. Designed Laos, deployed Laos, Uganda, and Afghanistan, 2009. Plastic, battery, cigarette lighter socket, LED light, recycled "flip-flop shoes," recycled polypropylene lamp cover made of prosthetic limb cut-offs, mirror foil

31 Solé Power Tiles. SRS Energy. United States, 2009. Clay, multilayer photovoltaic laminate on proprietary engineering polymer

32–33 SunShade, prototype. Lianne van Genugten, Lianne van Genugten Product Design. The Netherlands, 2007. Computer renderings

31

32

Solé Power Tiles

With the increasing use of solar power, more engineers and designers are seeking alternatives to traditional flat solar panels, and Solé Power Tiles, produced by Pennsylvania-based SRS Energy, are an attractive new option. Instead of being an extraneous addition placed on top of roofs, they are integrated into the roof system itself. The Solé Power Tile is an electricity-generating, "barrel-style" tile that can be installed alongside traditional terra-cotta tile roofing. Made of lightweight plastic and molded together with a flexible silicon cell, the technology within the tile is cadmium-free, nontoxic, and can be safely recycled. The arch-shaped tile allows air to circulate freely, preventing overheating. The tiles can be installed on an entire roof or be incorporated into an existing roof, and labor costs are reduced because, unlike most solar panels that require specialized installation, the work can be done by regular roofers. In addition to their aesthetic and environmental benefits, solar tiles provide financial benefits as well. Solé Power Tiles are lighter than clay tiles, saving cost and impact during shipping. At present, the tiles are only available in blue, but other color options are being pursued.

SunShade

Increasingly, designers are finding ways to use solar cells in all areas of everyday life. The SunShade, created by Dutch designer Lianne van Genugten, is a giant outdoor floor lamp that provides shade during the day and light at night. With solar cells acting as sensors, the umbrella opens and closes automatically, performing like a real flower in relation to the shifting sun. During the day, the SunShade opens and extends like a parasol, collecting energy from the sun through flexible solar cells embedded in the canopy. As the sun goes down, the parasol contracts, transforming into a lamp shade that glows at night. The parasol is made of polypropylene, a durable plastic polymer that holds up to the repetitive stress of being opened and shut.

33

34

Z-10 Concentrated Solar-power System

In order for solar power to compete with fossil fuels and become a more widespread alternative, the mechanisms that capture the energy must be more affordable and efficient. One recent solution is the Z-10 concentrated solar-power system, designed by Ezri Tarazi and Ori Levin from Tarazi Studio, for the Israeli firm ZenithSolar. What distinguishes this solar technology is its use of simple mirrors to gather and focus diffused light onto a small, fifteen-square-inch "generator" that converts sunlight into electrical and thermal energy. The overall system is a parabolic optical dish, which serves as a tracker, following the sun from dawn until dusk, much like a sunflower. Moreover, the Z-10 harnesses 70% of the solar energy that hits the dish, making it five times more efficient than conventional flat photovoltaic panels. This solar collector serves a dual purpose by capturing heat from the generator to provide hot water. In April 2009, the first field of thirty-two concentrated solar dishes was installed in Kibbutz Yavne, a community of 1,100 inhabitants near Tel Aviv, where it is expected to generate one-third of the kibbutz's electricity needs and all of its hot water. This innovative technology is already being considered for use in India and several other countries due to its efficiency and affordability. Its relatively simple materials are easy to assemble—1,200 flat mirrors mounted to a curved, plastic surface—and, compared to conventional flat panels, the Z-10 system uses only a limited amount of polysilicon and Germanium, which are expensive and in relatively short supply globally.

34 Z-10 concentrated solar-power system. Ezri Tarazi and Ori Levin, Tarazi Studio. Manufacturer and client: ZenithSolar. Israel, 2009. Polypropylene, mirror glass, stainless steel, photovoltaic components, ceramics, copper

Mobility

Cara McCarty

The history of human settlement has always involved the
overcoming of distance, for the movement of human beings
or for the goods they have needed for their well-being.
Today, mechanized transportation has resulted in massive,
interconnected modes of movement by land, air, and water,
allowing us to travel farther in less time than ever before and
creating unimagined social and economic benefits. Half the
planet now congregates in cities, many of vast population size
and spatial spread. But the specifics of how, where, when,
and why we travel also result in significant negative impacts
that undermine the benefits. The key components of personal
transportation are the mode, the number of trips and miles
traveled, the efficiency, fuel type, and route selection. There
are several major shifts currently underway, and designers are
taking on the task of redefining mobility—its future patterns
and components—to effect positive changes on our world.

   Transportation in America relies on a seemingly endless
supply of inexpensive fossil fuels. Among the eighteen economies surveyed by the International Energy Agency, the United
States uses the most energy per passenger mile,[1] and transportation is the fastest growing producer of carbon emissions in
the country.[2] As one expert put it, "It's not that we are almost

NYC Hoop Rack. Ian Mahaffy, Ian Mahaffy
Industrial Design, and Maarten de Greeve, Maarten
de Greeve Industrial Design. Client: New York
City Department of Transportation. Designed
Denmark, manufactured United States, 2008–9.
Galvanized cast ductile iron

out of oil ... we are running out of air to put the CO_2."[3] The many amenities of the low-density American city were achieved through the availability of cars—inexpensive, individual transportation to and from work as well as for pleasure. Communal transportation within cities, especially by rail, generally requires higher aggregations of people within walking distance than the seven minutes that an American suburbanite will walk. Regional high-speed rail transportation between cities, however, is being implemented or upgraded in many parts of the world. Among the forefront of very-high-speed trains is France's recently designed AGV (*automotrice à grande vitesse,* or "high-speed self-propelled train"), which consumes less energy, uses lightweight, recyclable materials, and employs more advanced technology to travel more safely and economically up to 225 miles per hour (fig. 1).

fig. 1

Major efforts are now underway to produce emission-free vehicles through hybrid gas-and-battery or battery-electric technology alone. According to one theory, the United States could replace all of its cars and trucks with electric vehicles powered by wind turbines whose footprint would take up less than three square kilometers.[4] Because most American driving trips do not exceed forty miles, and a vehicle battery can travel for at least that distance on a single charge, recharging could be done easily from a standard home outlet or while vehicle owners are shopping or working, helping to reduce commuter gas consumption by 94%.[5] We have become accustomed today to plugging things in to recharge them, which might help facilitate the acceptance of electric vehicles. Hybrids and other plug-in vehicles could recharge at a broad network of charging stations connected to the energy grid and installed in public and private lots, like the ChargePoint™ Networked Charging Station proposed by Coulomb Technologies (fig. 2). And short trips could be made on foot or bicycle if sidewalk infrastructure were made safer and more pleasant; in small, on-demand electric vehicles like CityCar, designed at MIT (fig. 3); or on portable bicycles like the IF Mode folding bicycle (fig. 4).

fig. 2

fig. 3

In dense metropolitan areas, increasing the cost of using roads has become a new disincentive for using cars, especially if the driver is alone. In London, congestion pricing imposed on vehicles entering the city center has reduced traffic by 15%, the time drivers spend in gridlock by 30%, greenhouse emissions by 16%, and, just as important, allowed buses more clear road space than before.[6] Today's digital technology substitutes body movement with virtual methods of communication, offering options for reducing travel. Telepresence technology, tele-banking, and purchasing goods on the Internet are changing how meetings

fig. 4

are conducted and reducing shopping trips. In addition, rapid-production digital manufacturing processes will reduce waste and the need for long-distance shipping. But there is still much to be learned about the replacement of face-to-face communication with virtual alternatives to travel and methods of contact.

The examples of cities like London and Singapore, which combine road management with sustainable mass transport systems, underscore the importance of seeing transportation as a system of interconnected components that can be accessed easily and conveniently. Mesh networking uses the capabilities of current wireless communication technology to create a "smart," integrated transportation infrastructure: enabling vehicles to communicate with one another or to a central network, employing sensory devices that monitor and regulate traffic by recording location, speed, direction, and time, and having vehicles interact with toll gates and traffic lights.[7]

The need for more sustainable cities requires the next generation of urban transportation to be expansive and multi-purpose. Imagine seamless transfers from automobiles—owned, short-rented, or shared—to trains or buses, bikes or rickshaws, or to walking, all scheduled and combined into a single door-to-door travel experience, with the help of electronic multi-modal journey and integrated fare payment on cell phones or at kiosks, as well as through ubiquitous transfer points.[8] Barriers to such an experience—separated hubs, complex multi-level transfers, carrying shopping goods over distances, the psychological and physical non-accommodation of small children, the elderly, travelers with disabilities—could be eliminated or alleviated through accessible design combined with aesthetic sensibility.

Human welfare depends not only on the mobility of people. In the current system of food transportation around the globe, it takes ten calories of heat for every calorie of food put on a dining-room table.[9] Moving freight by truck poses major issues of truck design and fuel use due to vehicle weight and aerodynamic drag; at fifty-five miles per hour, half of an average car's energy is used to push air out of the way. Recently, Wal-Mart, the world's largest retailer, worked with the Rocky Mountain Institute to determine how it could double by 2015 the fuel efficiency of its fleet, which currently averages about six miles per gallon. This dramatic increase is being achieved by improving the vehicles' aerodynamics and by installing low-rolling-resistant tires.[10] For short trips, designing lightweight commercial and government electric-vehicle fleets is an obvious energy-saving opportunity, as exemplified by IDEA, Bright Automotive's aerodynamic, full-size, plug-in hybrid electric van (fig. 5).

fig. 5

Container ships are a less familiar but major mode of long-distance goods distribution that presents significant health, pollution, and efficiency challenges. According to one authority, a giant container ship emits almost the same amount of cancer and asthma-causing chemicals as fifty million automobiles; fifteen ships may now produce as much pollution as all of the world's cars combined.[11] Yet oceangoing ship pollution remains one of the least regulated parts of the global transportation system. Policies are being implemented to reduce particulate emissions from ships, and companies are becoming more creative about eliminating empty backhauls. The concept cargo carrier, the *E/S Orcelle*, for example, is not fueled by oil, relying instead on multiple alternative energy generators: fuel cells, solar, wind, and wave power (fig. 6).

fig. 6

The role for designers in rethinking our mega-mobile world is tremendous. Nearly every section of today's newspapers contains articles describing new mobility initiatives prompted by environmental concerns and the shift to alternative fuels. Some are micro-technological innovations that are easier to achieve than major changes in people's behavior or in the intrinsic form of cities. Already, the growing demand for more livable cities is inspiring citizens to push for more walkable and bikable communities. And the transformation from independent single-system vehicles to a vast and efficient inter-related mobility network presents enormous opportunities, both in the developed and developing worlds, for designing rural and urban infrastructure coupled with new forms of mobility by land, sea, and air.

1 "Energy Inefficient" editorial, in *The New York Times* (January 19, 2009): A24.
2 Jacob Gordon, "Don't Kill Your Car," in *GOOD* magazine (spring 2009): 82–88.
3 Nathan Lewis, The Art Center Summit 2009: Expanding the Vision of Sustainable Mobility, Pasadena, CA, February 17, 2009.
4 Mark Z. Jacobson, "Review of Solutions to Global Warming, Air Pollution, and Energy Security," briefing to Senator Jeff Bingaman, Chairman, Senate Energy and Natural Resources Committee, October 8, 2008. In *Energy & Environmental Science* (January 2009): 148–73.
5 Ben Jervey, "Batteries Not Included," in *GOOD* magazine (spring 2009): 70–71.
6 Elizabeth Quill, "Unclogging Urban Arteries," in *Science* (February 8, 2008): 750–51.
7 Both IT infrastructure and hardware design are currently being developed and applied in cities around the world through Cisco Systems' Connected Urban Development (CUD) initiative, in partnership with the Clinton Initiative (Sue Zielinski, email correspondence, August 17, 2009).
8 This type of "open-source transportation," applied through New Mobility Hub Network systems, is being piloted in partnership with various cities around the world by the University of Michigan's SMART program, with the support of Ford Motor Company and other business and government leaders (Sue Zielinski, email correspondence, August 17, 2009).
9 Budd Steinhilber, "A Look Back . . . and Forward?" in *Innovation* (spring 2008): 55–57.
10 RMI MOVE (Mobility + Vehicle Efficiency), "Wal-Mart's Truck Fleet." © 2009 Rocky Mountain Institute. http://move.rmi.org/markets-in-motion/case-studies/trucking/wal-mart-s-truck-fleet.html, last accessed February 1, 2010.
11 John Vidal, "Health Risks of Shipping Pollution Have Been Underestimated," in *The Guardian* (April 9, 2009). http://www.guardian.co.uk/environment/2009/apr/09/shipping-pollution, last accessed February 1, 2010.

The author wishes to thank Julian Beinart, Robin Chase, and Sue Zielinski.

1

AGV (*Automotrice à Grande Vitesse*)
[High-speed Self-propelled Train]

Trains are among the most sustainable forms of transportation, and currently there is great international interest in replacing air and automobile regional travel with fast trains. The AGV, designed in France by Alstom Transport's Design and Styling Studio, is at the forefront of high-speed, energy-efficient trains being produced for fast and reliable medium-distance service between major cities. In 2011, the new, privately owned Italian train company Italo will introduce the AGV and provide rail service between Naples and Turin. The 350-mile trip will last about three hours, and the train will travel at speeds of up to 225 miles per hour.

The AGV's design differs from those of conventional trains in a number of respects. Ninety-eight percent of the train is built from recyclable materials, such as aluminum, steel, copper, and glass. Its low weight and efficient traction systems make for a 15% reduction in energy use compared to current trains. The AGV is the first train powered by compact and energy-efficient permanent-magnet synchronous motors, which create electricity and minimize energy loss. It also produces its own electricity from a regenerative braking system: while the train is slowing down, up to eight megawatts of unused electricity is returned to the train's power network. The train's architecture offers both energy savings and improved safety: by locating the bogie between, rather than under, cars, there is no accordion effect in case of derailment.

1 Italo high-speed service on AGV (*automotrice à grande vitesse*), model. NTV and Alstom Transport Design and Styling Studio. Italy, 2009. Resin

2

2 ChargePoint® bollard. Peter H. Muller, Interform. Manufactured by Coulomb Technologies Inc. United States, 2009. Aluminum, molded plastic, power measuring system, modem, ground-fault protection circuitry

3 E/S Orcelle cargo carrier, concept. No Picnic AB. Client: Wallenius Wilhelmsen Logistics. Sweden/Norway, 2005, to be completed 2025. Computer rendering

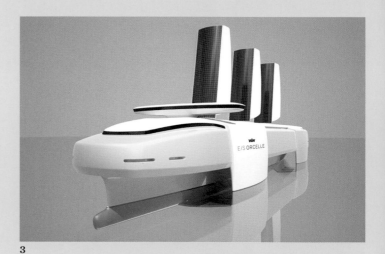

3

ChargePoint® Networked Charging Station

One of the challenges of plug-in and electric vehicles is recharging the battery. The finite driving range of electric car batteries means that replenishing points need to be readily available. California-based Coulomb Technologies has developed the ChargePoint Network, a system of smart charging stations that provides curb-side charging for plug-in electric and hybrid vehicles. Since the majority of daily car trips are less than forty miles, drivers do not have to worry about "range anxiety," as their cars can be conveniently recharged in parking spaces at home or at work, or while the owner is shopping. And by linking Coulomb's stations to smart energy grids, the flow of electricity can be managed.

The first charging stations have been installed in San Jose, San Francisco, Houston, Detroit, and Chicago; and the ChargePoint Network has been deployed in Amsterdam, as part of the city's two-year trial project with plans to fuel ten thousand electric cars by 2015. Electric power distributed by these charging stations is obtained from utility grids, some of which, as in Chicago, Florida, and San Diego, is partly supplied by solar panels. The ChargePoint Network communicates via Wi-Fi with the charging stations in order to provide driver authentication, owner management, and utility real-time control. A home-based ChargePoint system can supply cheaper electricity rates and a safer, more secure, and faster service than standard wall outlets. The charging stations can be mounted on walls, streetlight poles, or as stand-alone bollards.

E/S Orcelle Cargo Carrier

Shipping and air travel have been challenging to regulate in terms of new environmental standards. A dramatic step forward is the E/S Orcelle (E/S stands for environmentally sound; orcelle is French for an endangered type of dolphin), a sustainable vessel proposed by the Swedish/Norwegian transportation company Wallenius Wilhelmsen Logistics. The concept is based on zero emissions and the premise that by 2025 ships will be propelled without oil. The E/S Orcelle would have an optimum cargo capacity of up to 50% more space than today's modern car carriers and could transport ten thousand cars. This increase is achieved by the vessel's five-hull shape along with its use of lightweight materials and energy from renewable sources.

The carrier would be made of aluminum and thermoplastic composite materials, which offer greater high-tensile strength, less maintenance, and are more recyclable than the traditionally used carbon steels. The stability provided by the boat's hull and fin design, combined with the new propulsion systems, eliminates the need for the vessel to take on and release ballast water, which often contains invasive species that cause environmental damage. The E/S Orcelle's primary energy sources can be obtained at sea—dorsal fin sails contain photovoltaic cells that capture solar energy and self-adjust to harness wind energy; and twelve underwater fins capture wave energy, which can be transformed into hydrogen, electricity, or mechanical energy.

4

IDEA Plug-in Hybrid Electric Fleet Vehicle

Reducing wind resistance and vehicle weight are the two keys to improving battery performance and reducing costs in electric vehicles. A recent start-up, Bright Automotive, took these objectives to task with the IDEA, its concept plug-in hybrid electric van designed for light-duty commercial and government fleets. The all-wheel-drive IDEA demonstrates breakthrough vehicle efficiency by operating in all-electric mode for the first forty miles and then switching to a hybrid mode achieving forty miles per gallon. For commercial customers with an eighty-mile daily urban route, the IDEA uses about one gallon of gasoline. By lowering the vehicle's weight, using low-rolling resistant tires, and maximizing its aerodynamic potential, Bright Automotive expects each vehicle to reduce fuel consumption by 1,500 gallons per year and carbon-dioxide emissions by up to sixteen tons per year over competing vehicles. This light truck is constructed of aluminum and sustainable materials, and is manufactured using environmentally friendly methods. Designed as a multipurpose utility van, the vehicle incorporates a 70/30 easy-access split rear door, wide side cargo door, integrated bulkhead, interactive touch-screen computer, and patent-pending passenger seat that converts to a mobile office.

4 IDEA plug-in hybrid electric fleet vehicle. David Busch, Bright Automotive Inc. Assisted by Rollin Nothwehr and Art Center College of Design interns Michael Churchill, Noah Hammersten, Nikita Kalinin, and Nathan Wills. Manufactured by Bright Automotive, Inc. United States, 2009; expected production 2013. Computer rendering

5

5–6 IF Mode folding bicycle. Mark Sanders, MAS
Design, and Ryan Carroll and Michael Lin, Studio
Design by Pacific Cycles. Manufactured by Pacific
Cycles. Designed United Kingdom and Taiwan
2008, manufactured Taiwan 2009. Aluminum,
leather, rubber

6

IF Mode Folding Bicycle

The IF Mode is a full-size folding bicycle designed to make urban
bicycling a more appealing transportation option. Folding bicycles
have typically been heavy to carry, difficult to collapse, and look
disproportionate with their small wheels. By contrast, British
designer Mark Sanders and Ryan Michael Carroll and Michael
Lin of Pacific Cycles, based in Taiwan, conceived of the IF Mode
as portable luggage with a handle to push it around. The bicycle
is made of lightweight materials with simple, elegantly designed
components. It successfully eliminates oily chains, complex tubes,
hidden dirt traps, and much of the clutter of conventional bicycles.
Unlike most folding bikes, it has full-size wheels and should be
seen as a "personal transporter," offering a new image to people
who previously thought of bikes as only for enthusiasts or for
recreation. According to Sanders, "Instead of looking at the bike
and thinking of how to fold it, it began with the folded shape and
thinking of how to turn it into a bike." Furthermore, as mobility
systems become increasingly interconnected, portable designs
like these will facilitate transfers between different modes of
transportation. Like laptops, they might eventually become a
standard piece of one's luggage.

7

MIT CityCar

As designers contemplate future urban transportation systems,
the notions of shared use and mobility on-demand appear as
viable alternatives to private car ownership. MIT CityCar is a new
vehicle type that combines the two. Conceived by the Smart Cities
group of MIT's Media Lab, the stackable, two-passenger electric
CityCar will be available at closely spaced intervals in urban areas
where users swipe a card and take the first fully charged vehicle
at any charging station. Vehicles being returned are stacked and
electrically recharged. The critical component of the car is an
omni-directional robot wheel that contains an electric motor,
suspension, steering, and braking. There are no mechanical
linkages connecting the robot wheel to the driver's controls, and
elimination of the traditional engine and drive train enables the
mechanical systems to be modularized, allowing for flexibility
in the design of the body and interior. When folded and parked,
CityCar is only five feet long, and three to four cars can fit into a
traditional parking space. It is designed for start-and-stop urban
traffic, and the wheel robots allow the car to spin on the spot. A
sophisticated electronic information and management system is
envisaged to control the supply and demand of cars in its network
of sites. Although the CityCar must still operate on congested
urban streets, the vehicle provides a non-polluting, noise-free,
energy-efficient, and convenient alternative to current modes
of short-distance travel.

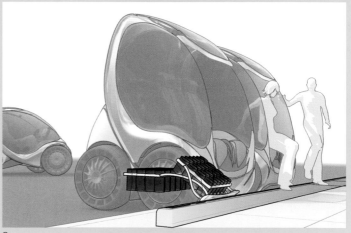

8

7–8 MIT CityCar. William J. Mitchell, Ryan Chin,
William Lark, Jr., Raul-David Poblano, Peter
Schmitt, and Philip Angus Liang, Smart Cities,
MIT Media Laboratory, with Mitchell Joachim and
Franco Vairani, MIT Department of Architecture,
and Andres Sevtsuk, MIT Department of Urban
Studies & Planning. United States, 2003–present.
Computer renderings

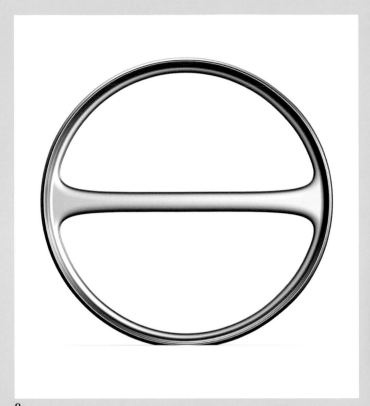

9

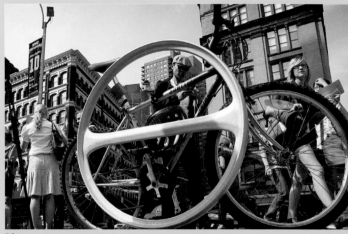

10

NYC Hoop Rack

One simple way to encourage increased bike use in urban areas is to provide bicycle lanes and parking in both commercial and residential locations. A study has shown that a lack of secure bike parking is the main reason why people do not cycle to work. In 2008, New York City's Department of Transportation, in partnership with Cooper-Hewitt and with the support of Transportation Alternatives and Google, organized an international competition for a sidewalk bike rack. The winner was the NYC Hoop Rack, created by two designers in Denmark, Ian Mahaffy and Maarten de Greeve. This elegant, no-fuss, minimal design will become the new standard bicycle rack on the city's sidewalks. Over the next three years, five thousand racks are expected to be installed citywide. The Hoop Rack, a thirty-four-inch circle made of cast metal and bisected by a horizontal bar, can withstand the harsh environment of city streets and is destined to become an iconic member of the urban streetscape.

9–10 NYC Hoop Rack. Ian Mahaffy, Ian Mahaffy Industrial Design, and Maarten de Greeve, Maarten de Greeve Industrial Design. Client: New York City Department of Transportation. Designed Denmark, manufactured United States, 2008–9. Galvanized cast ductile iron. Computer rendering

11

12

13

11–13 *Samarth* bicycle trailer. Radhika Bhalla. Designed United States, deployed India, 2008. Locally sourced bamboo, rattan, iron, jute, coconut fiber, wheels

Samarth Bicycle Trailer

Throughout the developing world, the lack of transportation in rural villages severely restricts many people's ability to access proper healthcare, attend school, receive information, or sell their crops or crafts at markets. The Samarth is a do-it-yourself bicycle trailer that uses local materials and techniques to empower rural Indian women through increasing their mobility. (*Samarth* is the Hindi word for "empower.") Created by Radhika Bhalla, a young Indian designer, the cart responds to the demands of women whose daily routine is spent traveling long distances to transport people and collect water, firewood, or crops. The cart, which can be pushed or pulled or attached to a bicycle, has three configurations: closed like a box, it can carry pots of water or hens or anything that needs to be secured; upright, it can seat two children; and fully opened like a bed, it can carry longer hauls like firewood or crops. The cart requires a structural material like wood or iron for the frame, as well as a soft material, such as jute or coconut fiber, that can be woven, colored, and personalized. Bhalla estimates that the Samarth can provide a woman with five extra hours a day to increase her income by producing handicrafts, take her children to school or to the doctor, or engage in other activities.

Community

Matilda McQuaid

Architecture is a social art, and its collaborative underpinning makes it intrinsically communal. But more than any other time in recent history, architects today are championing a physically and socially responsive architecture that promotes active civic engagement. Whether a rooftop village, urban farm, performance hall, hotel, or library, each project in this section has at its core a social agenda, set by both client and design team, to add to and transform the community it serves.

Foreign Office Architects gives hope to the affordable housing market with its remarkable project in Carabanchel, Spain (fig. 1). Responding to the climate as well as the inhabitants, their energy-efficient apartment building with private garden and balconies offers an alternative vision to the bland housing blocks often identified with social housing. When Snøhetta won the commission for the Norwegian National Opera and Ballet, its scheme was predicated on the idea that it should be a social, rather than physical, monument (fig. 2). The new building not only hosts artistic performances, but is also open for everyone to congregate and enjoy the waterfront, previously off-limits to the public. With a sloping public plaza that also functions as the roof of the opera house, the building speaks to the interconnectedness between the natural and built environment, and the

Didden Village, Rotterdam, the Netherlands. Winy Maas, Jacob van Rijs, and Nathalie de Vries, MVRDV; structure: Pieters Bouwtechniek; stairs: Verheul Trappen; blue finish: Kunststof Coatings; construction: Formaat Bouw. Client: the Didden Family. The Netherlands, 2007

fig. 1

fig. 2

individual's relationship to both. Michael Maltzan's New Carver Apartments in Los Angeles engage the city in a different way (fig. 3). Commissioned by the Skid row Housing Trust, they house the homeless and disabled elderly. Residents stay connected to their surroundings with views of the city from communal spaces while having a secure place to live and receive medical services. The design helps to support a marginal population that is often ignored or forgotten.

fig. 3

Medellín, Colombia, of 2010 bears little resemblance to the city in the 1980s, when violent drug cartels ruled the community based on violence and fear. With dozens of new and renovated schools, centrally located public libraries and parks, an expanded rail system, and landscaped streets, the city has transformed into a desirable place to live and work (fig. 4). The individuals responsible for this social and physical transformation included the mayor and policy makers, sociologists and urban planners, designers and architects, and social workers and community residents. Their strategy was to rid neighborhoods of drug dealers and traffickers while placing beautiful and sophisticated public buildings that brought much-needed public services into underserved areas. Childcare, job training, and medical services were integrated into public libraries, making them centers of social change. In the first phase, priority was given to the construction of public buildings— an intentional decision by the mayor to focus on projects that encouraged the greatest concentration of social interaction, communication, and networking and where everyone ultimately had a stake in the final outcome. Once public needs were met and a mutual trust instilled, additional projects such as improved public housing further addressed the needs of the community.

fig. 4

Just as there is an important social component in architecture, there is also the need to maintain individuality. A community is not about sameness, but understanding differences, celebrating local traditions, and accepting personal identities. This concept is at the core of MVRDV's VerticalVillage. The architects drew inspiration from do-it-yourself extensions they observed in cities like Beijing and Taipei. Urban dwellers are constantly on the lookout for additional living space, and rooftops provide a site for highly personalized structures and an informal urbanism. With VerticalVillage, MVRDV introduces this as a new typology on which to build a community (fig. 5). Providing a kit of parts from which each dweller can select, it empowers the user by expanding upon an already ingrained model that comes from the users themselves.

fig. 5

Empowerment is key to a financially and emotionally healthy community. John Ochsendorf's study of vaults resulted in several high-tech engineering projects where labor and materials come directly from the community for which the project is designed. The Mapungubwe National Park Interpretive Center (fig. 6), for example, was part of a poverty-relief-program that trained dozens of workers to make bricks out of local soil and use software to design domes that span long distances, combining economic relief with more sustainable building solutions.

fig. 6

Just as important as living in a community is thinking like a community. Architect Thomas Rau employs this approach in his own practice, dubbing it "oneplanetarchitecture." Rau sees the whole planet as his community, where societies are "working and living in the constant awareness that any action ultimately produces significant effects in the world at large—ecologically, economically, and socially." Rooted in sustainable practice for over a decade, Rau believes that one's actions should be driven by future results, and that buildings should produce energy rather than consume it. For instance, his H2Otel is designed to be carbon-neutral and relies on water and solar energy for heating, cooling, and generating electricity (fig. 7). Buildings are a temporary covering on the earth, according to Rau, and thus should leave no residue after demolition or dismantling. This entails more integrated thinking and a system approach to building, which is also how KieranTimberlake envisions architecture. Much of the firm's recent work, including Loblolly House (fig. 8), examines how manufacturing methodologies can transform building construction. Going deeper than prefabrication, Loblolly is built off-site from ready-made components that can be assembled quickly using only a wrench, and also disassembled for recycling or reuse.

fig. 7

fig. 8

A desirable quality for any community is self-sufficiency, and one outcome has been an enormous interest in different proposals for urban farming. Eco-Laboratory, a self-sustaining farm, dwelling, and workplace housed in a single structure, mitigates the need for expanding soil-based agriculture by farming vertically rather than horizontally (fig. 9). Moreover, it allows cities to have local distribution of fresh food grown in a controlled environment, which reduces the threat of disease and pests. Ecology, economy, and equity—the triumvirate in cradle-to-cradle practice—ultimately drive this project and others in this section. Designers and citizens are taking responsibility for shaping the environment, energizing the community, and committing to a pursuit of the common good.

fig. 9

1

Carabanchel Social Housing

The need for affordable housing persists globally, yet effective design solutions must consider the climates, sites, materials, and users in each individual area in need. One of the most beautiful and sensitively designed examples of social housing in the last several years is an eighty-eight-unit complex designed by FOA, located on the outskirts of Madrid. Adjacent to an urban park on one side and its own private garden on another, the building is oriented so that each unit opens onto these two different gardens and has private terraces enclosed with operable bamboo shutters. The constantly changing bamboo skin shields residents from the hot sun, and the floor-through apartments provide flexible living space as well as ample cross-ventilation. Solar water-heating panels on the roof and wind chimneys leading to internal bathrooms and kitchens help make the building more energy-efficient. A green roof above the car park acts as another private garden for tenants.

The architects' goal was to maximize the amount and quality of space for each apartment and to give the building the appearance of being a single volume, with a homogeneous exterior skin that conceals the individuality of each unit and the privacy of its occupants. The appearance of the building, rather than being a frozen frame of the architects' vision, is a result of the inhabitants' choices. In the end, what distinguishes this building is that, rather than a design typical of much social housing, it is a home in which anyone would want to live.

1–4 Carabanchel Social Housing, Carabanchel, Spain. Farshid Moussavi and Alejandro Zaera-Polo, with Nerea Calvillo, David Casino, Leo Gallegos, Caroline Markus, and Joaquim Rigau, Foreign Office Architects (FOA). Client: Empresa Municipal de la Vivienda y Suelo (EMVS). Spain, 2003–7

2

3

4

5

Eco-Laboratory

Increasing food production without negatively impacting the environment is at the heart of vertical farming, a new approach to fresh-food distribution that provides urban centers with healthy, "just picked" food, grown within the controlled environment of a multistory building. One of the pioneers of the vertical-farming concept is Dickson Despommier, a microbiologist and ecologist at Columbia University's School of Public Health. He sees vertical farming as a solution to nutritiously feed a world population— currently at 6.8 billion and, by 2050, approaching nine billion people—while avoiding toxic pesticides and fungicides and controlling the spread of pestilence that kills humans and crops. Small-scale versions of vertical farming already exist: hydroponics and aeroponics grow plants without soil, the first in a liquid nutrient and the second in a nutrient mist. According to Despommier, indoor farming allows crops to be grown year-round and organically. It also has other benefits: it eliminates agricultural runoff, reduces infectious diseases, converts black and gray water into potable water, restores farmland to a natural landscape, and reduces fossil-fuel use by reducing farm equipment and food shipping, to name just a few. Vertical farms can be replicated in any part of the world that has famine caused by crop shortage and natural disasters, they are adaptable and feasible, and the technology currently exists to make them.

Eco-Laboratory is one of the more recent and successful examples of such a system. The program merges a neighborhood market, dwelling units, a vocational training facility, and a sustainability educational center for the public into a financially viable downtown residential development. The project is designed to grow its own food, generate electricity, clean its own air and water, and provide a place and purpose for the underserved population. It is a model for bringing together home, work, shopping, community, food and energy production, and waste disposal under one roof. The designers describe it as technically being off the grid, but contextually, it is completely connected.

6

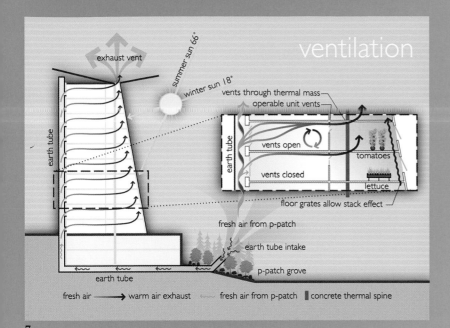

ventilation

exhaust vent

summer sun 66°

winter sun 18°

vents through thermal mass

operable unit vents

earth tube

vents open

tomatoes

vents closed

lettuce

floor grates allow stack effect

fresh air from p-patch

earth tube intake

p-patch grove

earth tube

fresh air ⟶ warm air exhaust ⟿ fresh air from p-patch ▮ concrete thermal spine

7

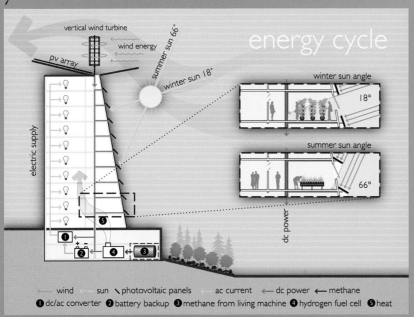

energy cycle

vertical wind turbine

wind energy

pv array

summer sun 66°

winter sun 18°

winter sun angle

18°

electric supply

summer sun angle

66°

dc power

❺

❶ ❷ ❹ ❸

⟵ wind ⟵ sun ⟍ photovoltaic panels ⟵ ac current ⟵ dc power ⟵ methane
❶ dc/ac converter ❷ battery backup ❸ methane from living machine ❹ hydrogen fuel cell ❺ heat

8

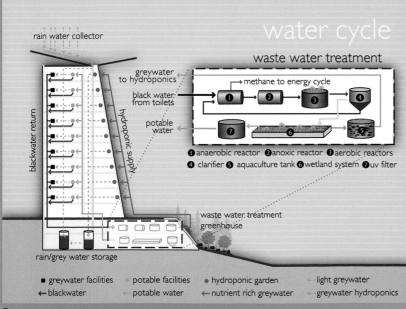

water cycle

rain water collector

waste water treatment

greywater to hydroponics

black water from toilets

methane to energy cycle

❶ ❷ ❸ ❹

potable water

blackwater return

hydroponic supply

❼ ❻ ❺

❶ anaerobic reactor ❷ anoxic reactor ❸ aerobic reactors
❹ clarifier ❺ aquaculture tank ❻ wetland system ❼ uv filter

waste water treatment greenhouse

rain/grey water storage

■ greywater facilities ● potable facilities ● hydroponic garden ⟵ light greywater
⟵ blackwater ⟵ potable water ⟵ nutrient rich greywater ⟵ greywater hydroponics

9

5–9 Eco-Laboratory, concept. Dan Albert, Myer Harrell, Brian Geller, and Chris Dukehart, Weber Thompson. United States, 2009. Computer renderings

10

11

12

10–12 H2Otel, concept. Thomas Rau, Rau. Client:
The Vincent Hotel Group. The Netherlands,
2009–present. Computer renderings

H2Otel

Water is the primary energy source in the H2Otel. Located next
to the Amstel River in Amsterdam with views to the north of
the canals in the city's historic center, the hotel underscores the
Netherlands' geographical affinity with water while utilizing it
for heating, cooling, cooking, and generating electricity. Because
of this comprehensive use of water, the H2Otel is expected to be
named the first carbon-neutral hotel in the Netherlands.

Passive solar energy is also critical in minimizing energy
demands in the building. A dense arrangement of wooden louvers
on the south façade protects the hotel interior during the summer
and from midday sun, while louvers on the north façade are
sparser and offer more panoramic views. Adaptive sensors in each
room monitor and control the temperature in real time by tracking the number of occupants and adjusting the heating or cooling
accordingly. Unoccupied rooms are automatically turned off.

Hydropower is one of the world's largest sources of
affordable and renewable energy, and the H2Otel benefits from
relatively low operating costs and low-tech water-management
solutions associated with hydropower. In fact, while the H2Otel
sounds like a futuristic building, almost all of the design
principles and technical applications used within are already
on the market. Its innovative aspect stems from the architect's
willingness to take responsibility for the long-term impact
of his design.

13

Loblolly House

The Philadelphia architectural firm KieranTimberlake is known for its sustainable practices and intensive research on integrated building. These are brought together in Loblolly House, named for the tall pines that occupy this site on Maryland's Chesapeake Bay.

This 2,200-square-foot house is composed entirely of elements fabricated off-site and readymade components. The timber piles set into a sandy soil are the foundation that supports the four key architectural elements of the house: scaffold, cartridge, block, and equipment. The aluminum scaffold system, coupled with various connectors, provides both the structural frame and the means to join the other three elements, using only a wrench. Floor and ceiling panels, or "smart cartridges," distribute radiant heating, hot and cold water, waste water, ventilation, and electricity throughout the house. Fully integrated bathroom and mechanical room modules, or "blocks," are lifted into position; followed by the exterior wall panels, which contain structure, insulation, windows, interior finishes, and the exterior wood rain screen complete with cladding. The west wall facing the bay is a two-layer glazed system—interior accordion-style folding glass doors and exterior polycarbonate-clad hangar doors—that provides an adjustable awning as well as weather and storm protection. Assembly from the foundation up takes just under six weeks.

The firm's methodology also extends to disassembly. The components can be disassembled as swiftly and in complete parts,

14

13–16 Loblolly House, Taylors Island, MD. Stephen Kieran and James Timberlake, KieranTimberlake. Manufactured by Bensonwood. Onsite construction management: Arena Program Management. Client: Barbara DeGrange. United States, 2006–7

15

after which they can be relocated and recycled or reassembled in new ways. An innovative sustainable model, the Loblolly House is a building that never loses sight of the craft of architecture.

16

17

18

17–20 Mapungubwe National Park Interpretive Center, South Africa. Peter Rich, John Ochsendorf, and Michael Ramage, Peter Rich Architects; additional team members: James Bellamy, Philippe Block, Henry Fagan, Anne Fitchett, Matthew Hodge. South Africa, 2007–9

Community

19

Mapungubwe National Park Interpretive Center

There are many lessons to be learned from studying ancient structures, including how to build with fewer resources. According to structural engineer John Ochsendorf, pre-industrial construction methods can provide fundamental lessons about sustainable design and the environmental impact of our buildings today. For example, his use of the Mediterranean tradition of tile vaulting—thin tile vaults that stretch across large spaces without formwork—is part of a 700-year-old construction method and is sustainable in a number of ways. Masonry's high thermal mass is very energy-efficient, local brick and materials can be used to make the tiles, and the system achieves high structural strength with minimal material. All of these factors have important applications in the developing world, where low cost, efficient construction, and structural durability are model standards for any building project.

The Mapungubwe National Park Interpretive Center in South Africa, part of a UNESCO World Heritage site, uses this type of vaulting exclusively. Locally manufactured tiles replace the more energy-intensive fired-clay bricks, and local workers are trained as masons in order to construct the complex. Each building is designed to operate with very low energy requirements, and most of the construction materials come directly from the site. The largest vault spans sixty feet, and the form of the vaults is determined to minimize the compressive stresses in the weak soil bricks. The project is part of a poverty-relief program that trains local workers and develops new means of livelihood. According to Ochsendorf, had they fabricated concrete panels and transported them to the site, the building would not have changed the area. In the end, masonry surpasses its historic associations and becomes a means of economic empowerment and a catalyst for new sustainable forms.

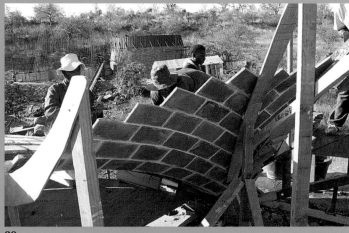

20

59 Why Design Now?

21

Medellín, Colombia

"Our most beautiful buildings must be in our poorest areas": these are the words of former mayor of Medellín, Sergio Fajardo, who led the city's transformation from one of the most violent cities in the world to a vital community whose new architecture carries the powerful message of social and educational inclusion. With a team of architects, urban planners, social workers, community members, and technical and social experts, Fajardo and architect Alejandro Echeverri inserted large-scale public buildings and parks into the most dangerous and desperate neighborhoods. Centrally located libraries, schools, and museums by international architects integrated crucial public services—childcare facilities, job-placement bureaus, and credit services—and made them easily accessible.

A remarkable aspect of this social and physical transformation was the speed with which it was carried out. In just four years, ten new schools were built and 132 more schools were upgraded with state-of-the-art equipment. Also constructed were five library parks and an expanded commuter rail system, including a metro cable car that transports more than 30,000 people a day from the surrounding hillside neighborhoods to the city below. A major north-south avenue was expanded, with grand, beautifully landscaped walkways that accommodate a growing number of street vendors and pedestrians. Parque Explora, an interactive public park for science and technology, connects directly to this main thoroughfare, inviting pedestrians to participate in this creative learning center. Directly across the street, in the Botanical Gardens, is the Orquideorama, a wooden canopy of fourteen tree structures that protect the lush collection of orchids below. The architects wanted the structures to "grow" in the same manner as plants, thriving and popping up next to each other—a reference to the children of Medellín, the ultimate reason for this city's extraordinary transformation.

City master plan: Alejandro Echeverri for former mayor Sergio Fajardo. Colombia, 2004–8

21 Jardin Botanico-Orquideorama (Orchid Botanical Garden). Alejandro Bernal, Felipe Mesa, Camilo Restrepo, and J. Paul Restrepo, Plan B Architects; additional team members: Jorge Buitrago, Lina Gil, Carolina Gutierrez, Catalina Patiño, Viviana Peña. Colombia, 2004–7

22–23 Parque Explora (Explora Park): Alejandro Echeverri; additional team members: John Aristizabal, Juan Carlos Castañeda, Isabel Dapena, Maria Andrea Díaz, Diana Herrera, Edgar Mazo, Sergio Restrepo, Camilo Restrepo Villa, Cesar Rodríguez, Guillermo Valencia. Colombia, 2005–8

24 Parque de los Niños (Children's Park). Alejandro Echeverri Restrepo, Carlos Mario Rodriguez Osorio, and Carlos Alberto Montoya Correa. Client: Alcaldia de Medellín. Colombia, 2004–8

25–26 Parque Mirador, before and after. Alejandro Echeverri Restrepo, Carlos Mario Rodriguez Osorio, and Carlos Alberto Montoya Correa. Client: Alcaldia de Medellín. Colombia, 2004–8

22

23

24

25

26

27

New Carver Apartments

Just south of Los Angeles's rapidly growing downtown, the Skid Row Housing Trust's New Carver Apartments explore how architecture can create new possibilities for a highly vulnerable and underserved population. The ninety-five units provide permanent housing for homeless elderly and disabled residents, offering a place of solace and support amidst the city's chronic homeless problem.

The six-story form emerges from the path of the adjacent Santa Monica Freeway as it traces the site's southern edge. Its spiraling shape encircles a private outdoor courtyard at its center, which provides each unit with natural lighting and views in all directions. Medical and social-services facilities are located at the base of the building, and other communal spaces—kitchens, dining areas, gathering spaces, and gardens—are on the floors above as well as on street level.

The architect, Michael Maltzan, has carefully anchored the design to incorporate the outside world while offering a sanctuary for the tenants. For instance, the laundry and community room on the third floor are at the exact level of the freeway so tenants can watch the passing cars. Other common areas have sweeping views of the skyline and street, emphasizing the strong connection between exterior and interior. In the end, the New Carver Apartments provide both a democratic and architecturally inspiring answer to Maltzan's own question, "How do buildings not shrink from their responsibility of being part of the city?"

28

27–32 New Carver Apartments, Los Angeles, CA. Michael Maltzan, with Peter Erni, Kristina Loock, Wil Carson, Sahaja Aram, Hiroshi Tokumaru, Sevak Karabachian, Steven Hsun Lee, Mark Lyons, Christopher Plattner, and Yan Wang, Michael Maltzan Architecture Inc. Client: The Skid Row Housing Trust. United States, 2007–9

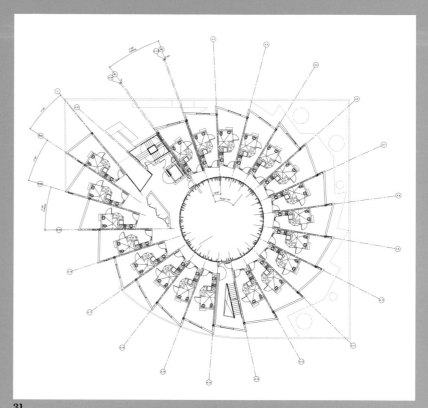

31

29

30

32

33

Norwegian National Opera and Ballet

Monuments to culture, such as museums and concert halls, often exclude one of their essential constituents—the people who will never attend an exhibition or performance, but who nevertheless live and work around the buildings. With the first purpose-built home of the Norwegian Opera and Ballet, Norwegian architects Snøhetta have created an edifice that is as publicly interactive as it is monumental. Its most distinctive feature is a white marble roofscape, which appears like two intersecting ski jumps culminating in the water to the west, yet is really a buzzing public plaza on which one can climb and experience the building without going inside.

The main approach to the building, at the northwest corner, leads into a public foyer where a visitor encounters the Wave Wall, behind which is the main auditorium. One of the three organizing principles for the architects' design, the oak Wave Wall is the threshold between art and everyday life and, in earlier times, the line separating the land from the sea. On the public side is a restaurant, café, shop, and toilets as well as a "street" that runs along the south façade.

The eastern half of the site contains the second principle, the Factory, or production facility, which includes rehearsal studios, costume and scenery workshops, offices, and dressing rooms. These spaces are organized around Opera Street, the main "highway" that runs north-south, dividing the site in half.

The third principle, the Carpet, contains the idea of laying out a public "carpet" that is accessible to all. The white marble roof slopes outward with a decidedly horizontal emphasis that mimics the surrounding landscape and cityscape, and invites the public to explore the architecture.

The last principle pertains to the building's urban context. The Norwegian National Opera and Ballet is the first element in an extensive transformation of the waterfront, which has long been separated from the city by a busy highway. For this reason, the façades closest to the city center are open to the public and city life. From the fjord to the south, there is a clear view inside the fifty-foot-high glass façade. With artists' commissions throughout the public areas, the building is embraced by everyone, acting as both a bridge and anchor for Oslo.

34

35

36

33, 34, 36 Norwegian National Opera and Ballet, Oslo, Norway. Craig Dykers, Tarald Lundevall, and Kjetil Trædal Thorsen, with Bjørg Aabø, Sigrun Aunan, Simon Ewings, Rune Grasdal, Tom Holtmann, Elaine Molinar, Marianne Sætre, Kari Stensrød, and Øystein Tveter, Snøhetta; structure, external walls, and roofs: Veidekke Entreprenør AS; ground works and foundations: Johs. Syltern AS. Client: Norwegian Ministry of Church and Cultural Affairs. Norway, 2001–8

35 MetaFoil theater curtain. Pae White. Belgium and Norway, 2008. Woven wool and cotton

37 before

38 after (proposed)

The VerticalVillage©

Urban density poses challenging questions and investigations for architects who are addressing housing solutions for an escalating global population. Massive, anonymous housing blocks are replacing smaller-scale dwellings, and regional building traditions are yielding to the bland homogeneity that has plagued large-scale housing for years.

MVRDV, a Rotterdam-based architecture firm, has explored various alternatives to multiple-unit housing blocks on a number of different scales. Vital to any of its projects is the integration of local traditions and individual identities. One of these experiments is Didden Village, a rooftop house extension for a family in Rotterdam. The architects created a "mini-village" on top of an existing residence, with bedrooms as individual "houses," connected by a series of mini-plazas and enclosed by a parapet wall. The whole vertical extension has a sky-blue polyurethane coating, giving it a distinctive identity while adding color and life to the neighborhood skyline.

The architects applied the same methodology on a larger scale in VerticalVillage, a temporary installation in Taipei, Taiwan, which uses existing buildings as "hosts" for extensions of different typologies, materials, and forms. The architects observed and used as their model the informal structures built on rooftops in crowded Chinese cities such as Taipei and Beijing. They expand the living space of the occupant in a highly personalized way and provide dense, socially connected communities with an overall diversity of structure and design.

A kit of parts categorized by building, material, typology, landscape, and fence is the organizing principle of VerticalVillage's 3,300-square-meter (35,500-square-foot) site. Within these categories, the intention is to mix and match so that individual expression and spatial requirements become the primary parts of the equation. As colorful as it is charmingly haphazard, VerticalVillage gives hope for an informal and regional urbanism in the future.

39

37–39, 41 TheVerticalVillage,© Taipei, Taiwan. Winy Maas, Jacob van Rijs, and Nathalie de Vries, MVRDV. Client: JUT Foundation for Arts and Architecture. The Netherlands, 2009–present. Computer renderings

40 Didden Village, Rotterdam, the Netherlands. Winy Maas, Jacob van Rijs, and Nathalie de Vries, MVRDV; structure: Pieters Bouwtechniek; stairs: Verheul Trappen; blue finish: Kunststof Coatings; construction: Formaat Bouw. Client: the Didden Family. The Netherlands, 2007

40

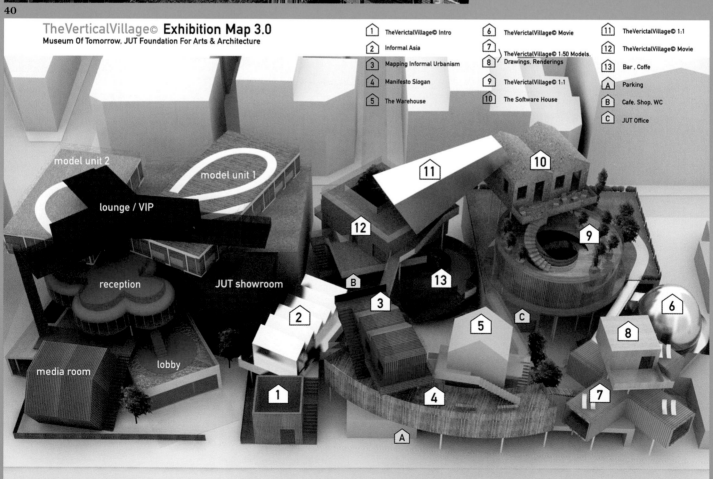

TheVerticalVillage© Exhibition Map 3.0
Museum Of Tomorrow. JUT Foundation For Arts & Architecture

1 TheVerictalVillage© Intro
2 Informal Asia
3 Mapping Informal Urbanism
4 Manifesto Slogan
5 The Warehouse
6 TheVerictalVillage© Movie
7 TheVerictalVillage© 1:50 Models. 8 Drawings. Renderings
9 TheVerictalVillage© 1:1
10 The Software House
11 TheVerictalVillage© 1:1
12 TheVerictalVillage© Movie
13 Bar . Coffe
A Parking
B Cafe. Shop. WC
C JUT Office

model unit 2
model unit 1
lounge / VIP
reception
JUT showroom
media room
lobby

41

Materials

Matilda McQuaid

In any given day, we touch or handle thousands of different materials that are fundamental to our daily lives: a clay pot to hold the food for our dinner, a plastic toothbrush to perform our morning regimen, and a wool sweater to keep us warm and protected. Each culture and region in the world may have its own material solutions, but what we all share is the same earth from which this daily supply of resources emanates. Earth's resources, however, will not last forever. Some statistics state that virgin materials like lead, tin, copper, iron ore, and bauxite will be depleted in less than seventy years.[1] Others note that in the last fifteen years, more new products for buildings have been created than in the entire previous period of architectural history.[2] With this simultaneous decrease in resources and increase in products across all design disciplines, how will we construct our future environment, and with what materials?

There have been great efforts in the last decade to address the need for more sustainable materials, which reduce the amount of energy and fossil fuels used in manufacturing. "Reduce, reuse, and recycle" are the new "three Rs" for the twenty-first century, with the ultimate goal to produce consumer goods that neither pollute the earth in their manufacture or disposal nor exhaust our priceless natural resources.

Kibiso Futsu Crisscross textile. Reiko Sudo, Nuno Corporation. Manufactured by Tsuruoka Fabric Industry Cooperative. Japan, 2008. 62% silk (raw silk and kibiso), 38% cotton; plain weave double cloth

Reduce

Plastic packaging uses an estimated 200,000 barrels of oil per day in the United States, clogs our landfills and oceans, and can take up to a thousand years to break down. There are alternatives to conventional plastics (polyethylene and polypropylene), such as polylactic acid (PLA), which is made from starchy sources like wheat, beets, potatoes, and corn. PLA reportedly uses 75% less energy than conventional plastics, generates up to 68% less greenhouses gases, and breaks down into harmless biomass over time.[3] Kareline has made a PLA reinforced with wood-based pulp fibers to improve technical performance, which can be used for packaging and a variety of other products (fig. 1). The optimal solution is, of course, to eliminate packaging altogether, which would automatically reduce energy consumption. Contour Crafting has the potential to do this for the building industry. A scaled-up version of rapid prototyping, it can "print" a building layer by layer, reducing waste, materials, labor, and energy for transportation and manufacturing (fig. 2).

fig. 1

fig. 2

Reuse

In William McDonough and Michael Braungart's seminal book *Cradle to Cradle: Remaking the Way We Make Things,* one of the authors' guiding principles is the idea that waste equals food. They describe that in nature, the process of every organism contributes to the health of the whole, so that one organism's waste becomes food for another. This same methodology can be applied to design, in which everything should be a potential nutrient. Materials that are biodegradable and can safely return to nature are biological nutrients, and those that can be infinitely recycled while maintaining an equal product are referred to as technical nutrients.[4] This also means that whatever is produced should not only be good for the earth, but the process in which it is produced should either benefit or have zero impact on the environment. An example is Greensulate's insulating panels, which are a superior alternative to polystyrene, commonly used for building insulation (fig. 3). Greensulate's biodegradable panels are composed of rice hulls and cotton burrs in combination with mycelium (the vegetative part of a fungus), and uses a manufacturing process that requires no heat or electricity and, in fact, grows in the dark.

fig. 3

Sometimes our good intentions still result in waste, but this can inspire designers, engineers, and scientists to make something useful out of excess material. The loofah recycled composite panel, for instance, reuses the waste from loofah product manufacturing to insulate panels for the construction of affordable housing in Paraguay (fig. 4). At the same time, it provides a source

fig. 4

of income for loofah growers and is a sustainable alternative to lumber. Carbon dioxide is a waste byproduct of cement manufacturing. With the focus on reducing global greenhouse-gas emissions, there is an incentive to find alternative ways of production that eliminate or reuse these emissions. For example, Calera is developing a new process of producing cement that, rather than emitting carbon dioxide, captures the emissions from existing power plants and converts it into carbonate, which is used to make concrete. As nearly one ton of carbon dioxide is released for every ton of cement produced in conventional cement production, this could have an enormous impact on the environment.

Recycle

Products are increasingly being made with post-industrial and post-consumer recycled content, such as metal, plastic, paper, and glass. The creation of secondary raw materials through recycling expends far less energy in many cases than production based on primary raw materials, and can generate significant financial and energy savings—up to 96% for aluminum cans, 76% for plastic bottles, 45% for newsprint, and 21% for glass.[5] The key factor is the intensity of energy required to extract virgin resources, which is often much higher than that of recovering the same material through recycling. The most recent addition to Coverings Etc's line of eco-friendly products is Bio-Luminum, made of 100% post-consumer recycled aluminum from reclaimed airplane parts (fig. 5). Transformed into sleek and contemporary tiles, they are also 100% recyclable. Similar to aluminum, glass can be recycled infinitely while retaining its strength. IceStone's colorful and durable pre-cast concrete slabs contain 100% recycled glass and can be used for both horizontal and vertical surfaces (fig. 6).

fig. 5

fig. 6

Furniture manufacturers are also becoming active participants in recycling efforts as they consider end-of-use options, namely the recyclability of the goods they produce and the ease and efficiency with which the products can be disassembled for recycling. Steelcase has been one of the leading innovators, and in one of its most recent endeavors, the Cobi chair, worked with McDonough Braungart Design Chemistry LLC to create an object that will earn cradle-to-cradle status.[6] (fig. 7)

Percentages for recycling waste vary widely: in the United States, 33% of municipal solid waste is recycled, compared with 60% in Austria and 10% in Greece (the lowest in the European Union).[7] From the consumer's perspective, one of the biggest disadvantages of recycling is overly complex rules regarding what can be recycled and in what form. If the process were more simplified, efficient, and convenient, recycling rates across the

fig. 7

board would likely be much higher. From a city government's point of view, considerable monies need to be invested to set up a system that has, for example, San Francisco's 70% recycling rate. At the same time, there is money to be earned from recycling. One recent study found that about 90% of the material going to landfills has a market value, a statistic that should motivate any market-driven economy.[8]

In the end, the answer is not to adopt one miracle material or process, but to commit to multiple resources and approaches simultaneously. Preferences should be for rapidly renewable resources that can be safely composted, such as bamboo, linoleum, sustainably harvested wood, and organic cotton and wool. At the same time, consumers should use materials that have a closed-loop recycling system, such as aluminum and glass. As with food, greater transparency of material ingredients should be a requirement so that producers as well as consumers can make informed choices and understand their consequences. Ecolect, for instance, has introduced a "nutrition" label in order to convey information—not pass judgment—on certain sustainable materials and products (fig. 8). This approach speaks to the need for universal metrics and standards in order to quantify benefits and drawbacks, including the cost of alternative materials and energy compared with those of fossil fuels. Crade-to-cradle, LEED (Leadership in Energy and Environmental Design), Blue Angel (Germany), and Flower Label (EU) are just a few of the many programs that aim to do this, but criteria and standards vary. Ultimately, the holy grail of designers is to combine the "big picture" issues—ethics, consumption, environmental impact, and diversity—with details such as function and affordability to make simple, practical, and insightful decisions. Designers will need to rely on their experience and intuition, as well as on science, to set new standards for our material world.

fig. 8

1 Lester Brown, 2007 Earth Policy Institute statistics.
2 Pop!Tech talk by Blaine Brownell, 2006, referring to a conversation with architect James Timberlake.
3 Elizabeth Royte, "Corn Plastic to the Rescue," in *Smithsonian* magazine (August 2006). However, PLA has limitations such as a relatively low melting point, and it only decomposes in a controlled composting environment that is not always accessible to the average consumer.
4 William McDonough and Michael Braungart, *Cradle to Cradle: Remaking the Way We Make Things* (New York: North Point Press, 2002): 104.
5 Alex Hutchinson, "Is Recycling Worth It?" in *Popular Mechanics* (December 2008, http://www.popular-mechanics.com). These statistics are for the United States.
6 To earn this status, products are evaluated within the categories of human health, ecological health, nutrient potential, recycled/renewable content, and embodied energy.
7 EPA Web site statistics and BBC Web site for Greece and Austria statistics, 2007.
8 Alex Hutchinson, "Is Recycling Worth It?"

The author wishes to thank Material Connexion for its assistance throughout her search for materials that contribute to a healthier planet.

1

1–2 AgriPlast. Michael Gass, Biowert Industrie GmbH. Manufactured by aha Plastics, Lakape Plastics, and Biowert Industrie. Germany, 2008. Virgin and recycled thermoplastics with 50% grass fiber

3 AgroResin®. Grenidea Technologies Pte Ltd. Singapore, 2005–present. Networked cellulose fiber and lignocellulosic fiber

3

AgriPlast

AgriPlast is a plastic alternative that can be used for making eating utensils, suitcases, and protective caps. It is made from 50–75% field grass that surrounds the manufacturing facilities of Biowert, AgriPlast's maker, and 25–50% polyethylene, polystyrene, or polypropylene. The company calculates that using AgriPlast reduces petroleum usage by approximately 50–70%, and elements made with AgriPlast are 20% lighter yet have the same greater dimensional stability and abrasion resistance as elements using 100% polyethylene. The injection-molding process is mechanical and the energy comes from biogas, an alternative fuel source. All byproducts and waste from the process of manufacturing AgriPlast are reused or recirculated.

AgroResin®

AgroResin is a sustainable packaging material that can be made from any type of plant fiber—including rice and wheat straw, corn stalk, and residue from cotton and sugarcane harvesting—that would otherwise be incinerated or dumped in a landfill. The material is used for packaging food and other products, and is permeable to air, printable, microwavable, water- and grease-resistant, and can withstand heat up to 356° Fahrenheit. It is manufactured using a molded pulp process, common in the production of packaging materials. AgroResin can be recycled like paper or composted. It is also made into different grades depending upon the use of the product. For example, the PPT200 cavity series is specially designed for ripe fruit and reduces bruising, and the PPT200 prolongs the freshness of mushrooms. The new AgroResin Rainbow series has a range of bright colors that accommodate the need for both a "cool" and sustainable product.

2

4–6 Azha Custom, Indi 002, and Alar 002
wallpapers. Jee Levin and Randall Buck, Trove.
United States, 2008–9. Inkjet on paper

4

5

Alar 002, Azha Custom, and Indi 002 Wallpapers

In the current wallcoverings market, environmentally friendly examples are extremely limited, and papers made with toxic inks, vinyl, and other noxious elements still plague the industry. In 2006, artists Jee Levin and Randall Buck founded Trove, a New York–based company that designs and manufactures commercially rated, environmentally responsible wallcoverings. Trove's products are recyclable, use nontoxic and archival inks, and have a wax-based coating that is washable and durable. All papers are printed to the specific wall height to eliminate waste. Combining digital working methods with imagery inspired from nature, films, and their own paintings and drawings, the duo creates patterns up to twelve feet high and three to six feet wide. Indi is a graphic tribute to Alfred Hitchcock's film *The Birds*, while Alar is inspired by Wim Wenders's film *Wings of Desire*. Azha depicts an array of moths fluttering without direction, and represents how the designers can transform traditional motifs by playing with scale, color, and the image itself. In the end, Trove creates papers that are rich in design, not resources.

6

7

8

9

9 Bananaplac. Pedro Themoteo, Bruno Temer, Thiago Maia, Bernardo Ferracioli, and Claudio Ferreira, Fibra Design Sustentável. Manufactured by GÊ Papéis Artesanais. Brazil, 2008. Banana fibers, vegetable based resin, water

Materials

Alpaca Velvet, Ditto, Gather 006, and Horsehair Striae 003 Textiles

"Reduce, reuse, recycle," or the "3Rs," is the mantra for those practicing environmental sustainability. Over the years, there have been advocates of this approach in the textile industry, which historically has been a major source of environmental pollution. Horsehair Striae 003, Alpaca Velvet, Gather 006, and Ditto are textiles designed and produced by Maharam which exemplify the company's ongoing desire to live by the 3Rs while creating beautiful and high-performing textiles. It uses only natural and undyed fibers for the horsehair and alpaca textiles; chemical processing has been reduced to a minimum while natural color variegation of the animal hair creates a rich color palette. Strict environmental standards at the facility where Gather 006, a wool-and-nylon-blend fabric, is manufactured produces water that is cleaner than when it entered the factory. Ditto uses primarily post-consumer recycled polyester, mainly from plastic bottles, to create a performance textile used primarily by the health sector.

7–8 Alpaca Velvet and Horsehair Striae 003 textiles. Maharam. United States, 2007–9. Alpaca Velvet: alpaca wool; Horsehair Striae 003: dyed cotton warp, horsehair weft

Bananaplac

Bananaplac is an alternative to hardwood and Formica developed in partnership with Brazilian artisans and local communities in need. The material is a veneer produced from banana fiber and nontoxic, vegetable-based resin extracted from castor, soy, and corn oils. Banana fiber is obtained directly from the discarded "stem," which is cut down when harvesting the fruit. The fibers are cooked, rinsed, and broken down into a mixture that is drained through screens into sheets of paper, which are finally pressed with the resin to become Bananaplac. The manufacturing of Bananaplac requires little heat, and the machines that press the fiber and resin into sheets are manually operated. Fibra Design Sustentável, a company that specializes in the development of sustainable materials, was established by students at the industrial-design school at the University of the State of Rio de Janeiro. It developed Bananaplac not only to create a sustainable material, but also to provide job opportunities for impoverished local communities.

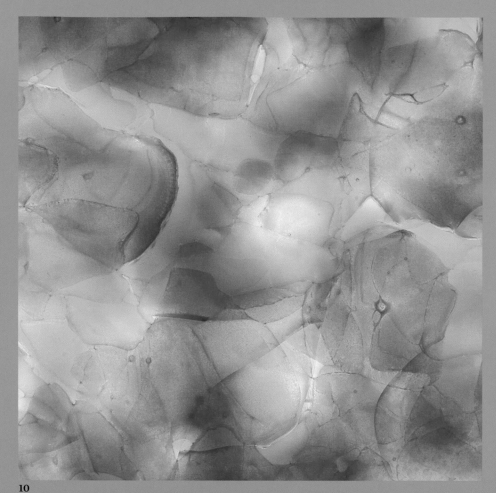

10

11

12

13

Bio-Glass®, Bio-Luminum™, and Eco-Cem

Coverings Etc has expanded its offering of stone and mosaic wall and floor panels to include eco-friendly materials such as post-consumer recycled aluminum and glass in its ECOverings line. Bio-Luminum, the most recent product, uses reclaimed aircraft parts retrieved from abandoned military sites. The parts are melted into blocks and sliced to create a lightweight, utilitarian tile. Bio-Glass is cradle-to-cradle silver certified and manufactured in Europe from recycled stemware and wine, water, and beer bottles. Its colors, which include jade, malachite, fossil amber, aquamarine, and white diamond, derive directly from the bottles themselves. Bio-Glass can be used for countertops as well as vertical walls, while Bio-Luminum can be used for walls and other surface treatments.

Eco-Cem is a blend of 80% cement and 20% cellulose fiber. By increasing the fly ash (a byproduct of the coal industry) content in the cement, Eco-Cem panels are lighter in weight and more durable in application. The cement content is 50% post-industry fly ash, while the cellulose fiber is recycled newspaper. Cement production accounts for almost 6% of human-generated carbon emissions, so reducing the amount of cement and increasing the percentage of postindustrial fly ash can make both a stronger material and reduce the carbon footprint. Coverings Etc's other environmental initiatives include a green roof, purchasing renewable-energy certificates, and remodeling spaces using a greater amount of daylight and recycled materials.

10 Bio-Glass®. Coverings Etc. Italy, 2007. 100% post-consumer recycled glass

11 Bio-Luminum™. Ofer Mizrahi, Coverings Etc. Italy, 2009. 100% post-consumer recycled aluminum from salvaged aircraft carriers

12–13 Eco-Cem. Coverings Etc. Italy, 2002–7. 20% post and 40% pre-consumer recycled content, including wood pulp and fly ash

14 Bioware packaging. Ekapoj Phanunan, House of
Pack Corp. Ltd. Thailand, 2007. Sugarcane fiber

15 Carbon-negative concrete. Brent Constantz,
Calera Corporation. Diagram by Bareket Kezwer.
United States, 2009.

14

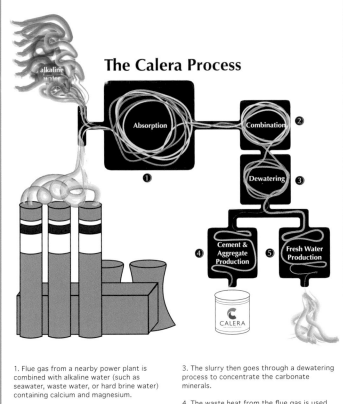

The Calera Process

1. Flue gas from a nearby power plant is combined with alkaline water (such as seawater, waste water, or hard brine water) containing calcium and magnesium.

2. The CO_2 from the flue gas and the alkaline water source combine to form a carbonate slurry.

3. The slurry then goes through a dewatering process to concentrate the carbonate minerals.

4. The waste heat from the flue gas is used for drying the carbonate product, which is used as a cement or aggregate.

5. The resulting water is treated through a desalination process to create fresh water.

15

Bioware Packaging

The need for food packaging and disposable containers will not diminish, and it is imperative that designers discover alternatives that will not consume precious resources or contribute to the rapidly growing landfills. One example is Bioware, a biodegradable packaging material and dinnerware made from bagasse, or the fibrous remains after sugarcane is crushed. This environmentally friendly material is engineered to biodegrade in forty-five days and has an extreme temperature range of –40° to 428° Fahrenheit. Within these temperatures, it is ovenproof and waterproof, microwavable, washable, and has an expected shelf life of up to two years.

Carbon-negative Concrete

Cement is a binder that, together with an aggregate such as sand or gravel and water, makes concrete. Creating it is among the most polluting and energy-consuming industrial processes: for every ton of cement produced, nearly one ton of carbon dioxide is released. Yet concrete is also a highly durable and affordable material, and there is no viable alternative. With demand on the rise—cement production is expected to more than double by 2030—the challenge of creating an environmentally sound, equally effective material to compete with it lies in the production of cement alternatives and aggregates.

Calera, founded by Stanford University scientist Brent Constantz, is developing a new process for producing cement which captures, rather than releases, carbon dioxide into the air. Based on biomineralization, the process is similar to how corals make reefs using seawater minerals to form carbonates. Calera sends carbon dioxide emitted from existing power plants through seawater, effectively converting it into carbonate minerals, which can be used to manufacture cement replacement materials or aggregates. Thus, not only does the process reduce the need to heat cement-making materials in a coal-fired kiln, as with traditional cement production, it sequesters carbon dioxide. In 2009, Calera built a pilot facility attached to a natural gas-power plant, aiming to filter more than 90% of the plant's carbon-dioxide emissions through this process. The company expects to demonstrate its method of sequestration at coal plants in the near future.
—*Andrea Lipps*

16

17

Cobi Chair

Cobi is a new category of seating that promotes collaboration without fatigue in team workspaces while adhering to strict environmental standards in the chair's production process. Steelcase, one of the largest office-furniture manufacturers in the world and a longtime innovator in sustainable practices, has reduced its greenhouse-gas emissions by 49% and its water consumption by 64% since 2001. It has also reduced its waste by 71% and is developing new packaging options, which include no carton for approximately half of its seating products. With the Cobi chair, Steelcase, in collaboration with McDonough Braungart Design Chemistry LLC, achieves cradle-to-cradle standards, which take into consideration the entire lifecycle of the product. The chair is designed to be easily disassembled for recycling or to replace the fabric, and supports a wide range of postures, with only one manual adjustment for seat height. An intuitive weight-activated mechanism automatically responds to the user's movement. The rubber-like top edge gives way and provides comfort as opposed to resistance when users drape an arm over the back of the chair.

16–17 Cobi chair. Tom Lloyd and Luke Pearson, PearsonLloyd, and Bruce Smith, Steelcase Design Studio. Manufactured by Steelcase. United States, 2008. Polypropylene, thermoplastic olefin, steel, aluminum, nylon, polyurethane foam

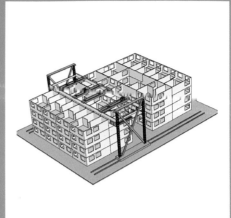

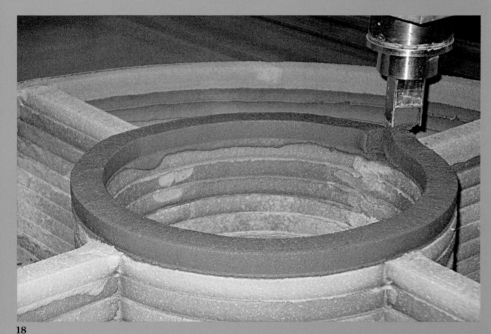

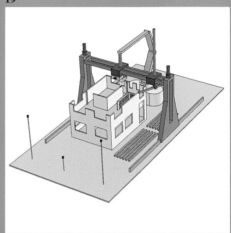

18

19

20

Contour Crafting

Construction has a sizable environmental footprint, accounting for 40% of material use and 33% of carbon-dioxide emissions worldwide. At the University of Southern California, Professor Behrokh Khoshnevis is developing Contour Crafting, a construction technology that has the potential to reduce energy use and emissions. Comprised of robotic arms and extrusion nozzles equipped with trowels, Contour Crafting is essentially a scaled-up version of rapid prototyping, also known as 3-D printing, which automates construction. The computer-controlled gantry system carries a nozzle that moves back and forth, squeezing out inch-thick layers of concrete or other material to additively fabricate a form. Thus, a structure or other component is "printed" layer by layer, eliminating building waste, using less material, reducing transportation of materials, equipment, and labor, and lowering cost and injuries, all while potentially speeding up construction. In a study conducted by Khoshnevis and colleagues in 2009, Contour Crafting resulted in a 75% reduction in total carbon-dioxide emissions and lowered total embodied energy by 50% as compared to standard manual construction using a concrete masonry unit.

The project began in 1996 as a rapid-prototyping process to fabricate large components, but its impact in construction became clear after successful pilot runs with construction materials such as concrete, clay, and plaster. In 2007, the technology reached a significant milestone with the successful prototyping of full-scale, curved walls, which could one day be used as visual and sound barriers, security walls, and flood barriers. The ultimate goal is to "print" a house in a day (doors and windows would need to be manually inserted), with the Contour Crafting machine riding on railroad-like tracks at the construction site, which could revolutionize affordable and emergency housing.
—*Andrea Lipps*

21

Dye Solar-cell PV Window

According to the International Energy Agency, the built environment utilizes over 40% of all global energy. The most credible means to reduce this consumption is with energy efficiency and renewable energy. Dye-sensitized solar-cell (DSC) technology is one example that combines energy efficiency and solar power in building products. Described as artificial photosynthesis, Dyesol's DSC technology uses a dye analogous to chlorophyll to capture the energy from light-releasing electrons, which are trapped and conducted as electricity in a nanoparticulate titanium dioxide (a benign material used in white paint and toothpaste). The dye is sandwiched between two panels, one of which must be transparent like glass, and although one can see through it, the glass becomes like a modern stained glass window due to the dye. Some of the advantages of Dyesol's technology compared with conventional silicon-based photovoltaic technology are lower costs and embodied energy in manufacture. It produces electricity more efficiently even in low-light conditions, and can be directly incorporated into buildings by replacing conventional glass panels, rather than taking up extra roof or land space. Currently, a partnership with Corus (formerly British Steel) is exploring the feasibility of incorporating dye solar cells in prefinished steel roofing materials.

22

21–22 Dye solar-cell PV window, prototype. Marc Thomas and Sylvia Tulloch, Dyesol Inc. United States, 2009. Titanium dioxide, electrolyte, dye, catalyst, glass

Fin spring/summer 2010 collection. Per Sivertsen,
Fin Fashion A/S, Norway, 2009

23 Knitted dress. Organic pima cotton, silk knit

24 Top and pants. Organic cotton voile, organic
cotton poplin

25 Knitted dress. Baby alpaca, silk knit

26 Shirt and skirt. Organic cotton voile, wild
handspun silk

23

24

Fin Spring/Summer 2010 Collection

The trend toward organic goods and ethical trade is spreading in
the fashion world. Fin was one of the first fashion labels to do this
from its inception, with the intent to "run a business and save the
world at the same time," according to one of the founders, Nikolai
Herlofsen. Fin uses organic, fair-trade-certified cotton, which
means no pesticides or harmful chemicals are used by the farmers,
who are guaranteed a minimum income and good working
conditions. Fair-trade certification is an independent regulatory
procedure that enforces ethical production guidelines. In addition
to organic cotton, Fin uses organic bamboo and wool, recycled
polyester, and wild (or "non-violent") silk, handpicked and hand-
spun by Indian artisans that allows the moth to fly free instead of
killing the silkworm, as is the practice in conventional silk production. Fin is also 100% carbon-neutral and buys climate credits
from Clean Development Mechanism, a United Nations–approved
project. The funds are invested in renewable energy projects
in India and Peru, where some of Fin's garments are produced.
Textiles, however, are only part of the story: head designer Per
Sivertsen creates the essence of a slouchy, effortless, feminine
style in the clothing. Timeless classics such as trench coats,
asymmetrical dresses, and pencil skirts are revamped with bold
colors and edgy styling. Silhouettes are sculptural and range
from voluminous shapes to intricate pleating.

25

26

27

FLAKE and Veil Curtains

Environmental concerns play a central role in the production
of Woodnotes's paper-yarn products, which range from elegant
room dividers to scarves, rugs, and furniture. Founded in 1987
by Finnish textile designer Ritva Puotila and her son Mikko,
Woodnotes uses both advanced technologies and handcraftsman-
ship to develop the yarn, which is spun from durable heavyweight
kraft paper that is biodegradable and can be recyclable. Because
of the density of the fibers, paper yarn does not collect dust or
dirt. The white paper is produced without the use of chlorine
gas, and the dyes used to color the yarn contain no heavy metals.
The purity and simplicity of the materials and designs reflect
the Finnish design aesthetic. The hand-knitted paper can be
used for window coverings or space partitions as well as tabletop
textiles. The FLAKE partition, made from Tyvek, a manmade
material that is more durable than paper but has similarities to
paper production, requires the user to create the size and form
of the partition by linking the elements together.

28

29

30

Fuzun™ and RubbRe™

27–28 Veil curtain. Ritva Puotila. Manufactured by Woodnotes Oy. Finland, 2008. Paper yarn

29 FLAKE curtain. Mia Cullin. Manufactured by Woodnotes Oy. Designed Sweden, manufactured Finland, 2007. Tyvek

30 RubbRe™. Dianne Denommee, Aline Denommee, and Robin Gilson, Vulcana® LLC. United States, 2007. At least 30% recycled tires, natural rubber

RubbRe, an ecological alternative to leather, is composed of recycled car tires retrieved from landfills. After fiber and metals have been removed, the tires are ground up into a crumb rubber, which is then compounded with other materials and cured as a non-woven sheet rubber. More recently, Vulcana has developed Fuzun, which bonds the sheet rubber material with woven hemp, a sustainable and durable textile. The finished Fuzun material has a fabric face and a rubber back. The products come in a variety of colors, including burgundy, blue, green, gray, brown, and black, and are currently being used for handbags and other accessories. The company is testing the material for other commercial, industrial, and military applications.

31

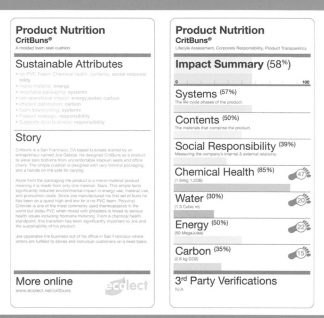

33

32

31–32 GreenBox™. Joe Gebbia, Elizabeth Redmond, and Matt Grigsby, Ecolect Inc. United States, 2008–9. Chipboard, recycled zip-tie, paper, cardboard

33 Product Nutrition Label. Joe Gebbia, Elizabeth Redmond, and Matt Grigsby, Ecolect Inc., and Joep Meijer, theRightenvironment Ltd. United States, 2008–9.

GreenBox™ and Product Nutrition Label

Ecolect, founded by designers Joe Gebbia and Matt Grigsby, is the first materials library to focus solely on eco-effective materials. In 2008, Ecolect introduced the GreenBox, a material subscription service to complement its free online library. Every three months, GreenBox subscribers receive physical samples of innovative, eco-effective materials presented on a die-cut card with an integrated hook, allowing them to be easily hung. The cards include information that synthesizes research, applications, technical attributes, pricing, and manufacturer contact information. The service enables designers to build their own library with a card system designed to be simple, user-friendly, and recyclable, conveying the sustainable attributes Ecolect promotes.

Product Nutrition Labels, developed with partner theRightenvironment, integrate into Ecolect's offerings to convey the sustainability performance of materials and products. The label distills a material's technical lifecycle analysis (LCA) data, presenting them as factors that include embodied energy, chemical health, contents, and social responsibility. The LCA data are presented on a label that employs a similar visual language as that of FDA-mandated nutrition facts labels. This accessible format for visualizing the data brings unprecedented transparency to the life of materials and products and anticipates that one day, such labels will be mandated for all products.
—*Andrea Lipps*

34

Greensulate™

Greensulate is an organic, fire-retardant board made from myce-lium, the "roots" of a mushroom, and other natural byproducts such as buckwheat and rice hulls and cotton burrs. It is an afford-able and environmentally friendly replacement for expanded polystyrene, used in cavity walls and structural insulating panels. Produced without heat and light, the material actually grows in the dark, taking between five and fourteen days for a panel of any size. Its superior strength and insulating properties can reduce the amount of energy used in the home and increase efficiency. The same technology behind Greensulate can also be used to make other products, such as packaging and furniture.

34–36 Greensulate™. Eben Bayer, Gavin McIntyre, and Edward Browka, Ecovative Design LLC. United States, 2007. Mycelium, local agricultural waste including cotton burrs, buckwheat hulls, rice hulls

35

36

37

IceStone Refined Collection

IceStone is the maker of an eponymous material that acts as a highly versatile, nontoxic, sustainable alternative to mined or engineered stone. Each pre-cast slab, made from a mixture of 100% recycled glass, Portland cement, pigment, and proprietary ingredients, can be used for interior and exterior surfaces, including countertops and flooring. The glass and cement are poured into molds and cured in kilns, which increases the strength of the slab. After curing, the slabs are removed from the molds, polished by machine, cut to size, and sealed for the customer by stone fabricators. IceStone incorporates renewable energy and a water-recycling system into its production, and strives for zero waste. They adhere to a triple-bottom-line philosophy that takes into account environmental and social performance as well as financial outcomes. In 2008, IceStone achieved cradle-to-cradle gold certification due to its use of recycled and VOC-free content, its sustainable manufacturing process, and its concern with the welfare of employees. Besides health benefits and living wages, workers receive immigration assistance and life-skill training programs. Monthly town meetings further enhance the culture of inclusion. Employees of the month are celebrated with portraits that are painted by one of the employees and prominently displayed around the factory.

38

37–38 IceStone Refined collection. IceStone LLC. United States, 2009. Recycled glass, concrete, pigments

39–40 Issey Miyake Color Hunting collection, spring/summer 2009. Dai Fujiwara, Issey Miyake Creative Room, Miyake Design Studio. Peru and Japan, 2008.

41 Prism dress. Polyester

42 Rio Drape dress. Polyester, silk

39   40   41

Issey Miyake Color Hunting Collection

In Februrary 2008, Dai Fujiwara and his creative team embarked for the jungles of South America in pursuit of natural colors. They called their project Color Hunting, and with 3,000 color samples, they matched the gentle colors of rivers (which oddly resembled the hues of human skin), leaves, trees, and soil. To test the veracity of their choices, the team hung strips of dyed cloth in open spaces, over rivers, and in front of trees. If the colors "melted away" and blended with the background, they knew they had the correct hue. With these authentic samples from nature, they selected eight to work with for the spring/summer 2009 collection. The colors were distributed randomly in the warp and weft threads, resulting in a wonderfully muted garment with stripes on the garments representing the patterns and colors of life. Artists and designers often look to nature for creative inspiration, and when it is done as directly and creatively as in Color Hunting, it delivers a clear and vital message that we need to preserve its existence.

42

43

44

45

43–45 Suzushi Stripe, Futsu Crisscross, and Kibiso
Bookshelf textiles. Reiko Sudo, Nuno Corporation.
Manufactured by Tsuruoka Fabric Industry
Cooperative. Japan, 2008. 100% raw silk, kibiso

Kibiso Bookshelf, Futsu Crisscross, and Suzushi Stripe Textiles

Nuno, one of the most creative textile companies in the world,
designed a series of uniquely beautiful textiles using *kibiso*, a
previously discarded fiber that forms the outer layer of the silk
cocoon and protects the finer silk underneath. Consisting of sericin
and other amino acids, kibiso is used by various industries as a
natural amino acid in human and pet foods and cosmetics. Nuno's
latest experimentations with kibiso are Kibiso Bookshelf, Futsu
Crisscross, and Suzushi Stripe, which also include raw silk in the
warp (vertical threads) in order to obtain the rich and diverse
texture in each fabric. Used for clothing and interior fabrics, these
textiles have intrinsic natural attributes, such as moisture and
UV filtration.

In its efforts to explore textile applications for kibiso, Nuno
also created an important social network for retired silk weavers,
who are responsible for hand-weaving the kibiso textiles in
Tsuruoka, in northern Japan. Many of these women have spent
their entire life working with silkworms and possess invaluable
knowledge of silk manufacturing. In order to make yarn out of
the very gelatinous kibiso fiber, the weavers split the fiber by hand
into a yarn, which is then machine-loomed.

46 Kraftplex. Well Ausstellungssystem GmbH. Germany, 2009. 100% recyclable cellulose fibers from sustainably cultivated stocks of softwood

47–48 Lin 94 chair, prototype. François Azambourg. Manufactured by Design Composites Solutions. France, 2008. Flax fiber, vegetal resin, aluminum

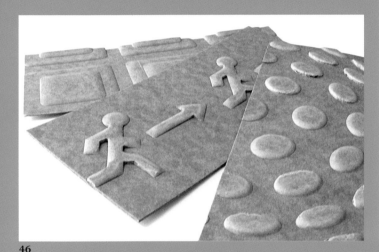

46

47

Kraftplex

Kraftplex is a 100% biodegradable alternative to plastic and metal sheeting. Made exclusively of high-quality cellulose fibers from sustainably harvested soft wood, this flexible fiberboard is manufactured using only water, pressure, and heat, without chemical additives, bleaches, or binding agents. Kraftplex can be laser-cut, perforated, glued, painted, oiled, and waxed. Its surface is printable and can be made three-dimensional through embossing or deep drawing. Uses include furniture, signage, and most any product where flexible sheeting is required.

Lin 94 Chair

Flax is a strong and light natural fiber used to make linen cloth, but in the hands of French designer and inventor François Azambourg, it transforms into high-performing, recyclable furniture. Azambourg has been called a "poet of materials" who constantly pushes the limits of new materials while exploring possibilities for sustainable development. He began working with flax in 2008, trying to develop a natural composite material similar to the lightness and strength of carbon and glass fibers. Flax is lighter than glass fiber and requires less energy to produce than both carbon and glass fibers. Working in collaboration with Design Composites Solutions, Azambourg arrived at a design for the material of the Lin 94 chair, which is made from 94% renewable materials and uses an 80% plant-based epoxy resin in the composite. It retains the natural ecru color and luminosity of the flax, creating a very tactile chair. Still in the prototype stage, the Lin 94 is currently retrofitted with aluminum legs that can be disassembled for shipping or recycling.

48

49

Loofah Recycled Plastic Composite Panel

Lumber is a diminishing natural resource in many parts of the world, and as a result, alternative materials that are local, affordable, and sustainable are being explored for feasibility. In Paraguay, loofah, a cucumber-like vegetable commonly used as an abrading skin sponge, is being combined with recycled plastic to form strong, lightweight building panels. Elsa Zaldívar initiated this use of loofah to improve the lives of rural women by increasing their earning capacity through loofah cultivation. As she developed products with them, she realized that there was an abundance of loofah waste. She teamed up with an industrial engineer to find a use for the waste and discovered a way to construct inexpensive panels for walls and roofing. The lightweight panels are flexible, easy to handle, and will cause less injury in this earthquake-prone area. The panels are competitively priced with wood and, at the end of their lifecycle, can be recycled into new panels or converted into high-energy fuel. According to Zaldívar, "We want to find sustainable housing alternatives for the poor while also discovering new markets for their agricultural products, particularly the loofah. This is a perfect combination."

50

49–50 Loofah recycled plastic composite panel. Elsa Zaldívar and Pedro Padrós. Paraguay, 2007–9. Vegetable fiber plates, thermoplastic material

51

52

Maison Martin Margiela Artisanal Line

Haute-couture fashion is not a likely place to witness the reuse of old and everyday materials, but breathing new life into worn-out, abandoned clothing and found objects is the underlying concept in Maison Martin Margiela's Artisanal line. Known for its penchant for recycling, the Belgian fashion house uses throwaway garments, vinyl records, disco balls, wigs, and other unconventional objects to transform the runway. Its work includes an asymmetrical top of partially cut-up and reassembled trench coats and a dress composed of plastic, tortoiseshell, and horn haircombs fastened together on a metal chain. MMM ultimately gives these pieces a second life so they can be worn again in a different way. The Shoestring dress is 400 shoelaces woven together only at the shoulder and waist, with the remaining strings cascading down the legs. The Plastic Fur jacket consists of 29,000 plastic garment-label fasteners attached to a leather jacket, creating a giant herringbone pattern. Each garment is reworked entirely by hand, and the complexity and specificity of each step make each piece unique.

Maison Martin Margiela Artisanal line. Martin Margiela, Maison Martin Margiela. France, 2009.

51 Plastic fur jacket. 29,000 plastic garment label fastenings, lambskin leather

52 Shoestring dress. 400 cotton or nylon shoelaces, metallic tips

53

54

PLMS6040 Compostable Polymer

Kareline's PLMS is a natural, fiber-reinforced PLA (polylactic acid) that is biodegradable and has applications for consumer electronics, packaging, toys, and other goods. The matrix plastic is PLA, a compostable thermoplastic that is derived from renewable resources such as corn starch and sugar cane. PLA is a sustainable alternative to traditional plastics made from polyethylene, for example, and can be injection-molded and used in the same kind of products as its relative. The fibers that reinforce the PLA are wood-based pulp fibers from a certified forest-stewardship program in Finland, and are manufactured in an environmentally friendly manner. They also improve the technical performance in the injection-molding of the PLA, including the temperature range under which the end products can be used.

53 PLMS6040 compostable polymer. Kareline Oy
Ltd. Finland, 2007. Polylactic acid derived from
corn starch

ProSolve 370e

Allison Dring and Daniel Schwaag, the principals of German-based design firm Elegant Embellishments, created photo-catalytic architectural tiles, called ProSolve 370e, which enable buildings to reduce air pollution in their surrounding environment. The modular tiles are coated with titanium dioxide (TiO_2) that neutralizes oxides of nitrogen (NOx)—a combination of nitrogen oxide (NO) and nitrogen dioxide (NO_2) that causes respiratory problems in humans, ozone depletion, and acid rain—as well as volatile organic compounds and other pollutants when activated by daylight. The photo-catalytic properties of TiO_2, known for their antimicrobial, self-cleaning, anti-fogging, and air-purifying qualities, have been studied since the 1970s and recently been applied in traditional outdoor building materials. But with ProSolve 370e, the technology takes a new, more efficient form.

Designed for absolute material efficiency using computer-generated forms and rapid-prototyping techniques, the tiles maximize the effects of the TiO_2 coating by exposing more surface area to daylight, thereby activating the pollution-fighting technology. The elegant overall pattern has a natural, organic appearance resembling biological growth—in many ways, the sculptural design forms seem inspired by the molecular technology they contain. Yet despite the complexity of the seemingly irregular,

54–56 ProSolve 370e. Allison Dring and Daniel Schwaag, Elegant Embellishments. Germany, 2006–9. Recycled ABS plastic coated in photocatalytic titanium dioxide. Computer rendering (54)

56

five-fold symmetric pattern, the system is composed of only two repeating modules—here, modularity expresses complexity. ProSolve 370e can be installed as a building façade element, a modification that effectively "tunes" existing buildings, according to the designers, by enabling them to perform in new ways.
—*Andrea Lipps*

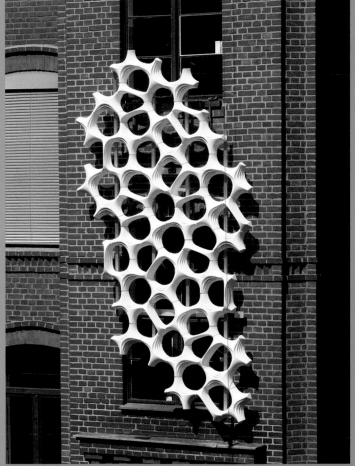

55

57

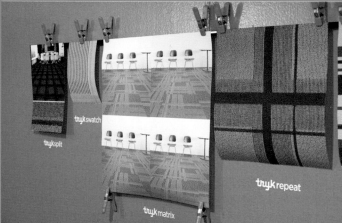

58

59

Tryk Sustainable Sampling Tool

It is estimated that one quart of oil is needed to produce one carpet swatch, and more than 700,000 carpet swatches (or 500 tons) end up in U.S. landfills every year. The founders of Tricycle created Tryk in 2007 to provide an alternative to swatches for the design industry. Tryk is a sampling tool that reduces waste from the very beginning of the design process, as the sample never has to be physically manufactured. Instead, the program produces realistic carpet images using proprietary digital technology that mimics the tufting and weaving processes. Tryk significantly expands an existing program by allowing a greater range of swatches to include woven carpets, wallcoverings, and fabrics, and has greatly improved image quality to be more photorealistic. In addition, Tryk includes a Web platform that is customizable for each client and offers features such as life-size modular tile prints and four simultaneous views of possible installations that integrate the carpet into an interior.

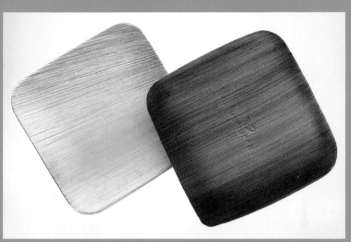

60

VerTerra Tableware

Fallen palm leaves and water are the only ingredients in
VerTerra's disposable dinnerware, a more durable alternative to
plastic and paper plates. The product uses no lacquers or bond-
ing agents, biodegrades naturally within two months, is sturdy
enough to hold hot liquids, and is microwavable and ovenproof for
limited periods. The fallen palm leaves are gathered from planta-
tion owners in India and transported to the company's factory,
where they are sprayed with high-pressure water, steamed, and
UV-sterilized. They then go through a proprietary process which
involves only steam, heat, and cooling. The different leaves are
pressed and dried to make the material that is finally formed into
the products.

57–59 Tryk sustainable sampling tool. Tricycle
Inc. United States, 2007. Digital interface, 100%
recyclable printed paper samples

60 VerTerra tableware. Michael Dwork, VerTerra
Ltd. United States, 2008. Palm leaves

Prosperity

Cynthia Smith

Creative Clusters

I was first struck by the sounds all around, the hum of micro-industries—local artisans clanking and hammering, transforming discarded car parts into devices needed by the community. Metal pounded into bars, welded, and forged into next-generation products: a low-cost vegetable cooler to increase the market life of tomatoes, or a press for the production of local Shea-nut oil. Each summer for the last three years, a diverse group of designers and community partners has converged on the Massachusetts Institute of Technology campus to better understand how to make affordable solutions to help people emerge out of poverty. This year, the summit moved from its regular location in Cambridge to Ghana to facilitate direct collaboration with local villages and master artisans in sub-Saharan Africa's largest industrial cluster, Suame Magazine. This economic engine, like many local businesses and artisans around the world, face extinction unless they can find a way to respond to the changing world market.[1]

These magazines, or industrial artisan clusters, and villages in Ghana embody aspects of what is transpiring in other communities around the world, from Sausalito, California, to Mumbai, India. In a trend that is growing internationally, the Suame artisans work collaboratively. A central workshop designs prototypes based on

Spinner plying yarn at a GoodWeave-inspected factory, Nepal, 2007

ideas and techniques developed at the Kwame Nkrumah University of Science and Technology for direct implementation by small repair shops, workshops, and enterprises in the magazine. Collaborating with NGOs (non-governmental organizations) and local governments, the manufacturers are organizing to create a village of innovation to train an existing pool of young talent in emerging technologies. Suame could prove to be a model for other cluster-based industries in developing countries.

There are differing views as to what constitutes prosperity. Buddhist philosophers might argue that it has less to do with economic well-being and more about a humane approach to living; others may define it as quality of life. To many, prosperity denotes value, an aspiration not merely to survive, but thrive in the world. "Everyone has the right to a standard of living adequate for the health and well-being of himself and of his family," declares the United Nations Universal Declaration of Human Rights.[2] Yet one in four people in the world lives in poverty, barely able to meet basic needs.[3] Designers, architects, and engineers have joined with organizations to find low-cost ways to address the underpinnings of poverty and to improve the quality of people's lives. Focus on this type of work has been building, and collaborative efforts across sectors have produced some of the most effective and economically sustainable solutions. Value is attained not by designing a more efficient machine to help farmers thresh millet (fig. 1) (a staple grain in much of Africa and India), but making it so affordable that they will not only increase their income, but pay for the thresher in the first year. This is a design movement that looks to bring every community out of poverty by applying basic design principles, such as listening to end-users, working in co-creation, using local materials, designing for easy maintenance and repair, and making it affordable for the poorest people.[4]

fig. 1

A growing number of organizations adhere to a new "triple bottom line"—social and environmental impact, along with economic performance—as a measure of a company's progress.[5] This development in business culture has driven many companies to consider bringing additional areas of interest into their portfolio of projects. Anticipating future growth in emerging markets, one multinational, Philips, has focused on the pervasive problem of debilitating interior air pollution from indoor cooking by designing a low-smoke stove manufactured with traditional methods (fig. 2). In New Zealand, architect David Trubridge designs and manufactures a line of furniture inspired by the landscape of this geographically remote island, with the goal to reduce ecological impact (fig. 3). Capitalizing on local resources, the collection is designed with minimal amounts of locally sourced wool and timber, packed flat

fig. 2

fig. 3

in kits to reduce container size and shipping weight for lower fuel consumption. Designers around the world are committing to local manufacture with the global market in mind. In California, two designers, Catherine Bailey and Robin Petravic, have taken over a mid-century pottery studio, Heath Ceramics, and used design to reinvigorate the market for craft products (fig. 4). Made to last, the work consciously embodies a more sustainable aesthetic: combining the studio's classic forms and experimental glazes. To meet one "bottom line," all of the clay is locally sourced, scraps are reused, and defective pieces are recycled by mosaic artists.

fig. 4

Calling on their own experiences, designers are sharing ideas on new best practices,[6] collectively and in their individual companies. Industrial designer Singgih Kartono, witnessing small Indonesian farmers' incomes being decimated by global trade policies, returned to his rural village in central Java to restart the local economy. Combining modern management, traditional craftwork, and sustainable planning, he trained farmers to make small wooden radios for export.[7] (fig. 5) In an effort to preserve artisanal craft, an international rug designer is making heirloom-quality hand-knotted rugs without the use of child labor (fig. 6). To counter the conditions found in Nepal's workshops, she has opened schools and orphanages for young workers. Artecnica, a California-based design producer, partners artisan communities with established designers to create new products for affluent consumers; the community receives a higher premium while preserving local culture and craft (fig. 7). This blending of modern methods with traditional crafts is yielding a new type of product that connects us with our diverse cultural history—a prescient reminder of our humanity in this rapidly changing world.

fig. 5

fig. 6

fig. 7

Questioning their role and responsibility in the creative process, designers co-create with traditional makers and ask clients to consciously participate. With an idealistic urge to better the world and rediscover her pleasure in creative endeavors, Dutch fashion designer Saskia van Drimmelen rejects mass production in favor of returning to a slower pace (fig. 8). The new clothing is made in partnership with Bulgarian needle workers who formerly stitched handkerchiefs for tourists, using nearly forgotten techniques in knitting, embroidery, needlepoint, and lacework.

fig. 8

Cultural sensitivity is at the center of this work. While global trends, such as mass migration and rapid urbanization, are certainly having major impacts, location and culture inform and provide context to these complex subjects. The Finnish telecommunications giant Nokia employs ethnographers for design research, exploring culturally specific aspirations in informal urban settlements with the help of local community groups (fig. 9).

fig. 9

Finding "beauty and value in uncertainty"[8] in these explorations, designers' skills for lateral and deductive thinking can provide the open-ended, innovative, and creative solutions needed for the world's rapidly shifting human geography.

Identifying the drivers of innovation is vital for policy makers and business leaders engaged in the global post-carbon economy. Information designers play a critical role, collapsing large amounts of digital data from disparate sources into accessible visual tools. The World Economic Forum's annual meeting of global leaders employs this visual mapping—locating innovation clusters, displaying sector indices and ideation capacity—to create initiatives to address social and environmental needs and spur a new wave of economic growth (fig. 10). Indicators show that, as talent disperses globally, more ideas will emerge from geographic clusters, open sources, and the developing world.[9]

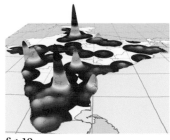

fig. 10

I kept my eye on the two large evergreens rising as guideposts in the midst of the teeming enterprises to help me find my way through Suame Magazine's wandering streets back to the workshop. The chaotic energy symbolized what is possible when local resources, ideas, and communities unite: the sound of prosperity, growing with every mallet swing and cell-phone ring.[10]

1 Field research at the International Design Development Summit 2009, Kwame Nkrumah University of Science and Technology, Kumasi, Ghana, August 4–12, 2009.

2 "Everyone has the right to a standard of living adequate for the health and well-being of himself and of his family, including food, clothing, housing and medical care and necessary social services, and the right to security in the event of unemployment, sickness, disability, widowhood, old age or other lack of livelihood in circumstances beyond his control." Article 25, the Universal Declaration of Human Rights, adopted by the General Assembly of the United Nations, December 10, 1948.

3 "New Data Show 1.4 Billion Live On Less Than US$1.25 A Day, But Progress Against Poverty Remains Strong," August 26, 2008, PovertyNet, The World Bank Web site. http://web.worldbank.org/WBSITE/ EXTERNAL/COUNTRIES/EASTASIAPACIFICEXT/MONGOLIAEXTN/0,,contentMDK:21883042~menuPK: 50003484~pagePK:2865066~piPK:2865079~theSitePK:327708,00.html, last accessed February 3, 2010.

4 Paul Polak, *Out of Poverty: What Works when Traditional Approaches Fail* (San Francisco: Berrett-Koehler Publishers Inc., 2008).

5 John Elkington, *Cannibals with Forks: the Triple Bottom Line of 21st Century Business* (Oxford: Capstone Publishing Ltd, 1999).

6 "The Designers Accord is a global coalition of designers, educators, and business leaders working together to create positive environmental and social impact. Adopters of the Designers Accord commit to five guidelines that provide collective and individual ways to integrate sustainability into design. The Designers Accord provides a participatory platform with online and offline manifestations so that members have access to a community of peers who share methodologies, resources, and experiences around environmental and social issues in design." From The Designers Accord Mission, http://www.designersaccord.org, accessed October 30, 2009.

7 "In principle, New Craft is a manufacturing process that uses traditional craftsmanship as its main means of production and uses modern management techniques in organizing its activities. New Craft is to ensure that every step of the production process contains standard procedures of manufacture, quality standards as well as output and material usage standards. Every new product or design is analyzed first for the purpose of creating a production manual. Based on the manual, the manufacturing activity is then implemented." Singgih S. Kartono, "Magno: The Story Behind," http://www.wooden-radio.com/de/ downloads/magno_-_the_story_behind.pdf, last accessed February 3, 2010.

8 Phone interview with Younghee Jung, Nokia Design Studio research team, May 8, 2009.

9 Innovation 100 meeting report, part of the Geography of Innovation program of the World Economic Forum, Palo Alto, CA, September 3–4, 2008.

10 Opening remarks by Hon. Dr. Anthony Akoto Osei, Ministry of Finance and Economic Planning, Republic of Ghana, at the Workshop on Cluster-based Industrial Development, Accra, Ghana, February 16, 2007. http://www.mofep.gov.gh/cluster.htm, accessed September 29, 2009.

1

Alabama Chanin 2009 and 2010 collections. Natalie Chanin, Alabama Chanin. United States, 2008–9

1 Indigo-dyed and embroidered couched coat. 100% organic cotton, natural indigo plant dye, paint, thread, snaps

2 Fabric sample. 100% organic cotton, paint, thread, couching thread, DMC embroidery thread, beads

2

Alabama Chanin 2009 and 2010 Collections

In 2006, fashion designer Natalie Chanin launched Alabama Chanin in her hometown of Florence, AL, employing local artisans to create limited-edition, hand-sewn garments made from organic, recycled, and new materials. The artisans purchase a sample kit of raw fabrics from the Alabama Chanin factory and then set prices for items they create, which are purchased back by Alabama Chanin. Each garment is numbered and signed by the artisan who creates it.

Textiles have long played a role in this small Alabama town, both economically and in conveying the narrative of place. Alabama Chanin preserves that narrative—Florence employed thousands in local textile manufacture before the jobs were shipped overseas. The company reinvigorates the economy while keeping traditional artisan techniques and practices alive. The pieces from Alabama Chanin's 2009 and 2010 collections are made from organic cotton with quilting, appliqué, and embroidery techniques from the Depression-era South. The garments are imbued with memory and nostalgia, representing a continuum between traditional and contemporary practice.

The company is also building a sustainable, socially-minded business model. The denim used in a number of pieces from the 2009 collection was made in partnership with Goods of Conscience, a venture by a Catholic priest in the Bronx to employ Guatemalan and Salvadoran parishioners to dye indigo in the church's basement. Waste is minimized by limiting production to only the number of garments ordered, and leftover fabric scraps are used for trims, bedding, and pillows. Alabama Chanin's practice signifies a commitment to the process of making and the regeneration of traditional craft in new contexts.
—*Andrea Lipps*

Geographic visualization of cluster level ideation output

Patents granted, 2008

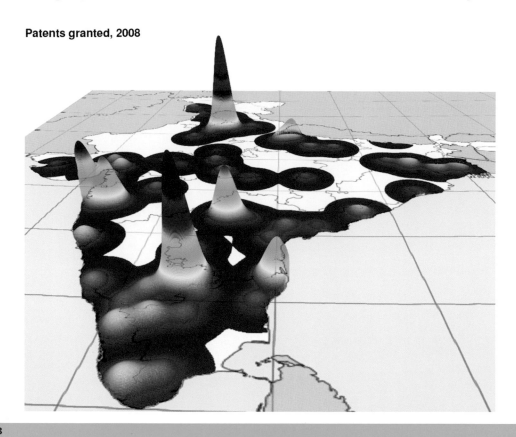

3

Global Innovation Heat Map

Aimed at senior policy makers and industry leaders, the Global Innovation Heat Map aggregates and synthesizes the most relevant data available to visualize where and how "innovation clusters" emerge around the world. The World Economic Forum, in partnership with McKinsey & Co., EMC, SAS, and ESRI, introduced the Heat Map at the 2008 Annual Meeting in Davos, Switzerland.

At the map's core is an extensive repository of more than 700 indicators culled from numerous sources of public and proprietary information. The data cover both "country" and "cluster level" enablers, which include factors such as the quality of local infrastructure, the availability of human and financial capital, the nature of the business environment, and the size and sophistication of local demand. They also measure "innovation ideation," which analyzes a region's ability to create novel concepts; and "commercialization," or a region's ability to implement and disseminate these new concepts.

The Heat Map covers 125 countries and 2,000 cities around the world. Key to the map's utility is its ability to provide detailed city-level visualization of data and sector-specific indexes. Users can navigate through hundreds of these clusters and explore various development phases and factors, such as growth, diversity, sector focus, and bottlenecks to innovation.

These ideas were explored at the 2009 Annual Meeting of New Champions in Dalian, China, known as the "Summer Davos" in Asia, during a session designed to spark insights for the government and business leaders in attendance. This visualized geography of innovation provided the means to explore underlying factors and to discuss the urgent need for creating opportunities for more large vibrant creative ecosystems, called "dynamic oceans"; and fast-growing "hot springs," hubs of innovation, during challenging economic times.

Global Innovation Heat Map. McKinsey & Co.
with EMC, SAS, and ESRI. Client: World Economic
Forum. United States and Germany, 2009

3 Pinpointing ideation output: patents issued in India

4 Tracking the stages of maturity of global
innovation clusters: rate of patents issued and
diversity

Prosperity

Interpreting the geography of global innovation

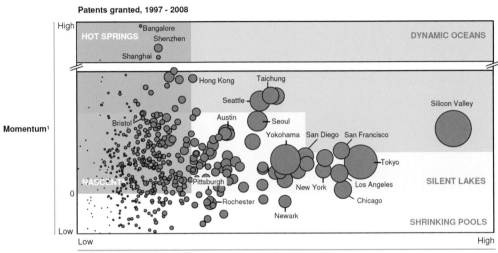

Patents granted, 1997 - 2008

Nascents	Regions with **limited or emerging innovation output** and unclear development path		
Hot Springs	Small but **fast growing** hubs with strong **focus on growth sectors** and a **small number** of innovative companies		
Dynamic Oceans	**Large and vibrant** innovation hubs that **reinvent themselves frequently** through breakthrough innovations		
Silent Lakes	**Slow growing** innovation ecosystems with a **narrow range** of large and **established** companies focused on **incremental innovation**		
Shrinking Pools	**Shrinking** innovation ecosystem based primarily on a **narrow range** of increasingly **commoditized sectors**		

1 Growth of patents in a cluster per year from 1997 - 2008
2 Patents' industry and firm diversity in a cluster in 2008

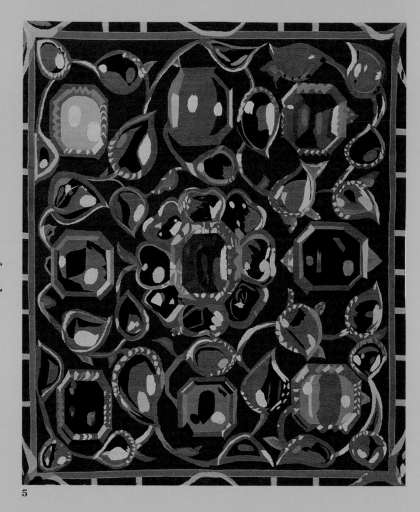

5

6

7

GoodWeave and Odegard Rugs

Tibetan hand-knotted carpets have been in existence for centuries, but it was not until Stephanie Odegard, founder of carpetmaker Odegard, began working with exiled Tibetan carpet weavers in Nepal that they gained popularity in the West. Over twenty years ago, the designer guided the restructuring of wool trading lines and provided weavers with necessary market development and innovative designs, which helped the carpet trade become one of the leading industries in Nepal.

Odegard is also attempting to help end one of the industry's oldest practices—illegal child labor. In South Asia, it is incorrectly believed that the fine knotting of handcrafted rugs requires small hands. According to Odegard, what it really requires is "strong hands." Odegard was the first American company to work with the RugMark Foundation, a global nonprofit that has created an independent labor monitoring program. Carpets sold with the foundation's GoodWeave label are assured to have been made without child labor; surprise inspections by third-party inspectors ensure factories remain compliant. The licensee's sales support educational opportunities provided to children as part of the foundation's mission. Odegard's Navaratna carpet, a richly hued rug whose design depicts the nine gemstones symbolizing celestial forces in Indian culture, carries the GoodWeave label. The yarn is hand-carded, hand-spun, and hand-knotted in Nepal, where the RugMark Foundation inspects seventy-five percent of Nepalese carpet factories annually and has rescued close to two thousand children. Through the production and sale of carpets,

Odegard supports an ethical certification program that embodies the company's commitment to social progress, ensuring that children are safe and educated while promoting traditional crafts as a platform for economic prosperity.
—*Andrea Lipps*

5 Navaratna rug in amaranth red. Stephanie Odegard, Odegard Inc. Manufactured by Ranta Carpets. United States and Nepal, 2007. 100% Himalayan wool, hand-carded, hand-spun, and hand-knotted

6–7 GoodWeave-inspected factories, Nepal, 2000–7

8 Quart bowl and cup with marigold overlap glaze, and quart bowl, cups, and single-stem vase with hibiscus frost overlap glaze

9 Vase collection with fawn exterior and bright yellow interior glazes

10 Quart bowl with bright yellow/fawn overlap glazes

8

Heath Ceramics Tableware

From a small California factory, designers Catherine Bailey and Robin Petravic are building on a tradition started over half a century ago by Edith Heath of Heath Ceramics. Bailey and Petravic, who purchased the company in 2003, continue to create simple, time-less tableware with a commitment to local manufacturing and handcraft technique, showing a reverence for materials and engag-ing in eco-friendly and socially minded practices. They are also introducing new forms and glazing techniques and collaborating with local designers. It is what Bailey calls "a design-led manu-facturer." The close relationship between design and production ensures the holistic integrity and quality of each piece.

The clay used at the Heath factory is locally sourced and is fired using a low-temperature firing technique to reduce fuel consumption that Heath herself developed. Clay scraps are reused and defective products are discounted or recycled by mosaic art-ists, generating little waste. Each step in making an object, from mixing the clay to applying the glazes, is completed in the factory. A few new forms, such as the vase collection, have been added to classic shapes developed by Heath, but still honor the material's simplicity. Updated glazes and color palettes revitalize the classic lines; for the hibiscus frost two-toned glaze bowl, workers scrape off the top glaze to reveal an under-glaze. Double glazes expose the clay, as seen, for example, in vessels with gray exterior and yellow interior glazes, demonstrating the honesty of the material. —Andrea Lipps

9

10

11–14 Improved clay stove. Practical Action Sudan. Concept: Food and Agriculture Organization of the United Nations and the Sudanese National Forestry Corporation. Manufactured by Sudanese women networks. Sudan, 2001–present. Clay, animal dung, millet, sorghum chaff

11

12

Improved Clay Stove

In most of Sudan, cooking has traditionally been done over an open flame. The country's ongoing turmoil has caused large numbers of refugees to crowd into Internally Displaced Persons camps in the Darfur region, leading to several problems: Respiratory illness from cooking smoke is rising in the cramped conditions. The thirst for dwindling firewood supplies has degraded local vegetation. And women—typically the ones responsible for gathering firewood—are forced to travel farther to collect wood, which leaves them more vulnerable to assault.

In 2001, the international non-governmental organization Practical Action introduced an improved clay stove, made only with one brick (cut into three pieces for the stand) and local clay mixture walls molded to fit the women's existing cooking vessel. It is based on a stove first developed in 1986 by the Sudanese National Forestry Corporation, in collaboration with the UN Food and Agriculture Organization, for women in Northern Darfur's El Fashir camp. The stove features an exhaust hole that increases airflow and provides a means for add wood without removing the pot, resulting in a 60% more efficient and affordable stove. Practical Action, standardized the design and taught women from the local potters' association how to make them. But as the war escalated and more people were displaced, the need for additional and more efficient versions grew. In 2003, a step-by-step guide was developed and adopted by one hundred thousand families the first year, but quality remained a problem. The NGO's fundamental philosophy is to engage the stakeholders, and it has continued

to improve the stove's design through "participatory technology development" with users of the stove. Most recently, rather than use a fixed mixture of clay and donkey dung, Practical Action is assessing local clay conditions to control shrinkage and breaking. The improved stove optimizes the space between the pot and the bricks and eliminates gaps, greatly reducing smoke.

13

14

15

Island Seat and Cloud Light, Spiral Islands Collection

New Zealand, a remote island nation 1,250 miles southeast of Australia, provides designer David Trubridge both an opportunity and a challenge. His furniture is informed by this unique location's indigenous culture and land- and seascapes. Aotearoa, the Maori name for New Zealand, translates to "land of the long, white cloud," which is embodied in Trubridge's gossamer Spiral Islands collection Cloud light. The Island Seat's pattern reflects the spiral, or Maori *koru*, the country's national symbol, which represents creation and growth. To begin his design, Trubridge carved a spiral set of wooden bowls from a solid block of timber. The bowls were then scaled up into the seat and light forms, replicating the way in which nature uses the same patterns and structures at multiple scales.

New Zealand's industries have to ship their products long distances, and their inventive solutions for exporting with minimum impact have put this small country at the forefront of environmentally conscious design and business. The government's Better by Design initiative promotes design for export. Trubridge designs, plans, and manufactures many of his designs using flat-packed kit sets to reduce excess space and packing materials. His sculptural furniture combines old-world craft with sustainable materials and the latest technology. The Island Seat uses thin skins in compound curvature to create strong structures with minimal use of material; the supporting seat core is a honeycomb of recycled cardboard. The upholstery is 100% New Zealand wool over foam,

which can be removed for cleaning. The plywood—the least wasteful form of timber conversion since the round log is peeled with knives, leaving no sawdust or half-rounds off the edge—is made with timber from sustainably managed plantations using low voc-and formaldehyde-emitting glues. And manufacture is local, using 70% renewable hydroelectric sources, with all of the factory waste sorted and recycled.

15–17 Island seat and Cloud light, Spiral Islands collection. David Trubridge, David Trubridge Design Ltd. New Zealand, 2008. Seat: plywood, 100% New Zealand wool over foam, recycled cardboard, water-based acrylic sealant, glue; light: PETG plastic, aluminum, low-energy fluorescent tube

16

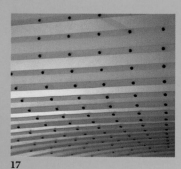

17

18

Magno Wooden Radio

Inspired by the imperfections found in natural materials and informed by a new method of craft manufacture, Indonesian artist turned product designer Singgih Kartono has created a series of tabletop wood radios for the international export market. Seeing that many farmers in his central Java village had lost their small farms to the economics of globalization and were without work, he established a workshop to train the community to make small, functional wooden craft products from locally harvested wood. Adhering to the designer's two basic principles "Less Wood, More Work," and "Cut Less, Plant More"—the workshop replants at least one tree for every one removed. In 2008, Singgih's workshop only cut down one hundred trees, provided livelihoods for thirty people, and planted more than 8,000 new trees.

    The designer intentionally minimizes the radios' form, features, and graphics and provides only a bare oil finish so that the user engages and cares for a high-quality product over many years. Beautiful in their simplicity, the mp3-compatible radios are available in small, medium, and large sizes with AM, FM, and two shortwave bands.

19

18–19 Magno wooden radio, medium and large models. Singgih S. Kartono, Piranti Works. Indonesia, 2007. Wood, fabric, plastic, corrugated paper

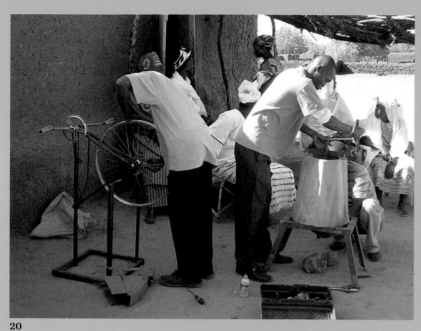

20

21

Mahangu [Pearl Millet] Thresher

Thriving in climates in which most crops fail, *mahangu,* or highly nutritious pearl millet, is produced on small farms in arid parts of Africa and Asia. The cereal is consumed by millions, and demand is increasing as people migrate from rural to urban areas. Women, who traditionally prepare the meals, spend up to four hours at a time threshing and separating the grains from the stem. They first pound off the grain with a mortar and pestle or beat it on the ground, then winnow out the seeds; what remains can be crushed into flour.

While in Namibia designing bike ambulances, Aaron Wieler witnessed the lack of efficient and affordable ways to thresh and clean grain, finding small stones in his *oshifima* porridge. He and his former Hampshire College advisor, Donna Cohn, identified a need for a low-cost threshing machine made from locally available materials. Working in consultation with others familiar with grain production and farming in sub-Saharan Africa, Cohn acquired a supply of pearl millet and began designing a human-powered millet thresher. In 2008, she brought the project to MIT's International Design Development Summit. (IDDS is part of a larger effort at MIT that includes D-Lab, the brainchild of Amy Smith. It focuses on low-cost solutions co-created directly with impoverished communities. The summit brings together students, professors, end-users, and professionals from over twenty countries with a broad range of experience in different disciplines for a month-long intensive workshop.) The IDDS team devised a machine, made from readily available parts. Instead of pounding the stalks, the rotating spoked

wheel effectively knocks off the grain without damaging it, increasing storage life, yield, income, and time.

Women in Mali are field-testing the thresher prototype. The goal is to devise a machine that can be made and repaired locally and produce clean grain faster than the traditional method and would pay for itself in the first year. IDDS team members are designing and testing multi-worker, treadle-driven, and combined threshing-winnowing machines to further improve output.

20–21 *Mahangu* [pearl millet] thresher, prototype. Aaron Wieler and Donna Cohn, Hampshire College, with the MIT International Design Development Summit; team: Francisco Rodriguez; George Yaw Obeng, Technology Consultancy Centre, KNUST; Brian Rasnow, Department of Applied Physics, California State University; Thalia Konaris; and Michelle Marincel in consultation with Jeff Wilson, USDA-Agricultural Research Service, and Rolfe Leary, Compatible Technology International. Designed United States and Mali 2007–8, field tests Mali and Ghana 2008–10. Scrap bicycle, conduit and metal, spring steel, cardboard

22

23

24

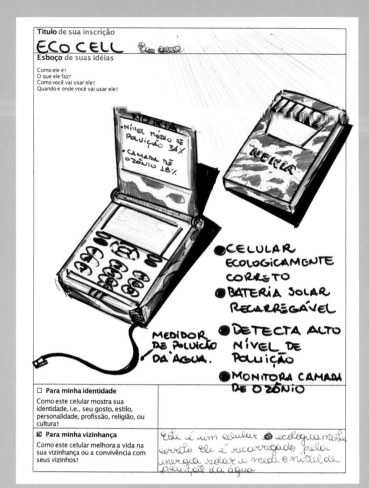

25

Nokia Open Studio

Of the 3.3 billion people who live in urban centers, approximately one billion live in informal settlements, or "slums"—places distinguished by the lack of official land-right recognition—and this number continues to grow. Most of these slums lack clean water, electricity, shelter, healthcare, and education. Nokia's design team, including Younghee Jung and Jan Chipchase, met with local residents in the slums of Dharavi, in Mumbai, India; Favela Jacarezinho, in Rio de Janeiro, Brazil; and Camp Buduburam, in Accra, Ghana, as part of a year-long multicultural study to better understand this rapidly expanding population.

Nokia's interest in these urban communities is a reflection of the informal cities' increasing global relevance. Identifying culturally and locally relevant insights for guiding future product and service development, Open Studio, an exploratory design-research program, actively encouraged residents of the three communities to express their needs and desires by designing a mobile device. The "dream device" acted as a vehicle for the participants to tell stories about the role technology could play in their lives. Approximately 220 designs complemented insights gathered through ethnographic and other research methods.

With limited time (about seven to fourteen days per location) and resources, the program was also organized as a community design competition, enabling the Nokia team to engage individuals to whom they may not have had access otherwise. The researchers provided the framework, including interview and entry forms, for a team of up to twenty local assistants with relevant experience in design, sociology, or journalism, who spoke the language and understood the culture. The assistants promoted the event with radio spots, songs, slogans, and ad campaigns, and facilitated each workshop, guiding and helping those who could not write. The Ghana location, a Liberian refugee settlement, was so popular that a shade space was constructed for the overflow. In Jacarezinho, the second largest *favela* in Rio, gunfire between police and a street gang kept the studio closed for several days. In Mumbai, researchers found that women were motivated to participate as a way to express their ideas and honor their own intellect. Overcoming barriers such as illiteracy and language, culture, trust, and poverty, the Open Studio challenged given assumptions by bringing, according to the researchers, "the very raw voices of people into the corporate context."

Nokia Open Studio. Younghee Jung and Jan Chipchase; additional designers: Indri Tulusan, Fumiko Ichikawa, and Tiel Attar, Nokia Corporation. Designed Finland, research in Brazil, Ghana, and India, 2007

22–23 Participant designing in Ghana

24–25 Participant designs: Peace Cell and Eco-cell, Brazil

27

26

Painted Series

After finding international success with her Van Drimmelen label, Dutch designer Saskia van Drimmelen became disenchanted with the fashion system. Embracing instead the slow process of the handmade, she worked with Desiree Hammen and Margreet Sweerts to form Painted, a Dutch fashion collective dedicated to creating couture formed, layer upon layer, by the hands of designers and artisans. The collective furthers its mission by working closely with clients to create garments of personal value through shared discovery of experiences and desires with clothing. Its Painted series is grown from different signatures (a few of the pieces were made for a Dutch singer and songwriter) inspired by antique Bulgarian clothes to which different generations have added new elements.

Each piece in the collection is built by passing it from one collaborator to the next, and each maker adds his or her talent to shape its story. Cord embroidery, knitting, and bobbin lace all appear in the clothing, as do nearly forgotten techniques of Bulgarian needlepoint lace, performed by Bulgarian artisans. The artisans increase their income while inventively reviving and transforming their techniques into a contemporary context. As a result, the unique pieces evoke the spirit of an heirloom.
—Andrea Lipps

28

Painted series. Saskia van Drimmelen, Desiree Hammen, and Margreet Sweerts, Painted; Bulgarian artisans: Velichka Georgieva, Magdalina Toneva, Rumjana Rakovska. The Netherlands, 2008

26 Flower-volant shirt. Silk organza, cotton thread; needlepoint lace

27 Treasure top. Cotton batiste, silk, cotton thread, sterling silver necklaces, patchwork, embroidery, crochet, needlepoint lace

28 Cocktail dress. Silk organza, linen, cotton thread, beads, needlepoint lace, embroidery

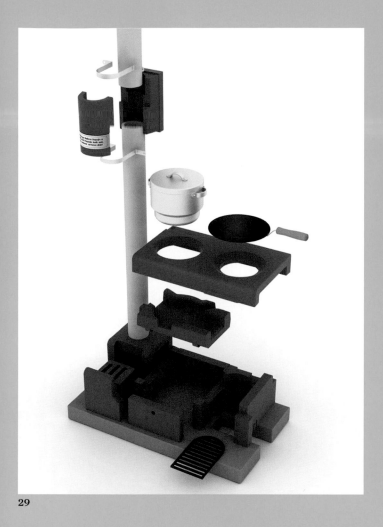

29

29–31 Sampoorna Chulha stove, Philanthropy by Design initiative. Unmesh Kulkarni, Praveen Mareguddi, Simona Rocchi, and Bas Griffioen, Philips Design. The Netherlands and India, 2008. Manufactured by various local non-governmental organizations and entrepreneurs. Partner: Appropriate Rural Technology Institute. Concrete, metal and clay elements, clay, cow dung

30

31

Sampoorna Chulha Stove, Philanthropy by Design Initiative

Most families in rural and semi-urban India cook indoors with biomass fuels, such as wood or cow dung, resulting in respiratory illness and even death. An estimated 1.6 million people around the world die each year due to respiratory sickness caused by burning solid fuels. As part of Philips's Philanthropy by Design program, designers worked in consultation with end users and local stakeholders to develop a more efficient low-smoke stove, which requires less fuel and funnels smoke outdoors to significantly reduce indoor air pollution. Determined to apply their design skills and capabilities for culturally relevant solutions in emerging markets, Philips Design established this new initiative to support non-profit and non-governmental organizations. It aims to leverage local competency to meet social and environmental challenges and focuses on one humanitarian issue a year.

Improving on the traditional stove, the Chulha stove's modular design enables NGOs to establish small traditional-method manufacturing operations without the need for expensive equipment. This eases transport while providing opportunities for local entrepreneurship in its production, enabling community women's groups to sell the low-cost Chulha to their neighbors for a small commission. Willing to invest in the healthier stove the villagers make small payments. The stove is designed so the cooking pots fit more precisely and smoke no longer escapes indoors. In response to the area's culture, the design is flexible—two versions are available—as each location has a different cuisine and cooking requirements. Molded from a concrete mixture with terracotta elements and metal piping for the exhaust, the stove is covered with clay and easily installed and disassembled for part replacement and maintenance. Instead of cleaning the chimney from the roof, a difficult task for the women who cook for the family, a section of the pipe can now be detached for indoor cleaning. The Chulha design and training kit for production and installation is available online to any NGO if the group agrees to train and produce the stove locally, distribute it at a "fair price," and record the results for the Philips design team to assess potential benefits in an effort to support scale-up activities for broader positive impact.

VIET VILLAGE COOPERATIVE URBAN FARM

1 Community Green
2 Grass Paver Parking Lot
3 Market Buildings
4 Public Vehicular Entrance
5 Pedestrian Entrance
6 Community Farm Plots
7 Central Boardwalk

8 Central Bio-Filtration Canal
9 Community Pavilion
10 Central Reservoir
11 Livestock Farm Area
12 Compost
13 Commercial Plots
14 Service Entrance

32

Viet Village Urban Farm

Before Hurricane Katrina, a thriving Vietnamese-American community in East New Orleans grew traditional, locally unavailable Vietnamese fruits and vegetables in home gardens as well as in a thirty-acre communal garden. The growers sold produce they did not consume through informal local markets. Determined to rebuild its community and garden after the hurricane, members of the local Mary Queen of Viet Nam Church, a pillar of the Vietnamese immigrant community, rallied and formed a community-development corporation to recreate their gardens and market in one single location. Working in collaboration with the Tulane City Center, the Urban Landscape Lab at Louisiana State University, and the University of Montana Environmental Studies program, landscape architects Spackman Mossop Michaels met with the community in a series of public meetings to establish project goals, programmatic areas, and the design strategy for the Viet Village urban farm site. The site will be developed as a series of fully functional subprojects that can be funded incrementally yet create a comprehensive system.

The design team and the engineering firm Intuition and Logic assisted the community with the design of the environmental infrastructural systems needed to support an organic urban-farming operation. They aim to be a model for low-tech, sustainable site development by using bio-filtration of water and alternative energy sources such as wind and solar power. The Viet Village integrates pest management, composting, crop rotation, and cover cropping among other organic practices. The twenty-eight-acre farm combines small-plot family gardens, larger commercial plots for New Orleans restaurants and grocery stores, and an area for raising goats and chickens. The market will serve as a community resource and economic catalyst. They expect 3,000 visitors at the Saturday market and more during Vietnamese festival days; and elders will have a place to share traditional skills and culture with Gulf Coast Vietnamese-American families.

The most significant environmental issue for the site is the movement of water; it frequently flooded during storms. A series of sub-watersheds can supply water for irrigation independently if there is a break in the larger system through the use of a portable pumping system. The main power supply for the pumping of water will be a windmill and water tower backed up by electrical pumps.

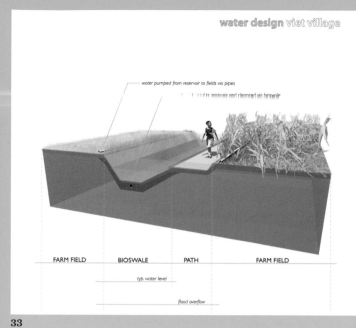

water design viet village

water pumped from reservoir to fields via pipes

FARM FIELD | BIOSWALE | PATH | FARM FIELD

typ. water level

flood overflow

33

32–34 Viet Village urban farm. Elizabeth Mossop and Wes Michaels, Spackman Mossop Michaels, and Dan Etheridge, Tulane University; preliminary research: Len Broberg, Lauren Butz, and Erika Edgely, University of Montana Environmental Studies Program; engineering: Tim Dean and Mark Meyer, Intuition and Logic. Client: Mary Queen of Vietnam Community Development Corporation and New Orleans Food and Farm Network. United States, 2008, expected completion 2012

urban context viet village

New Orleans, LA

01 Central Business District and French Quarter
02 Viet Village- New Orleans East
03 Lake Pontchartrain
04 Mississippi River
05 Site

Viet Village, New Orleans East

34

35

Witches' Kitchen Collection, Design with a Conscience Series

Renowned design producer Artecnica partnered with the nonprofit organizations Aid to Artisans and the British Council to identify artisan communities around the world with which to pair internationally respected designers such as Hella Jongerius and Stephen Burk to create viable products for the global design market. Faced with a dwindling market for local artisan work, the Design with a Conscience collaboration successfully combines fair-trade practices, sustainable and recycled materials, and design insight to increase work and revenue for these impoverished communities. A true partnership, the designer's work is influenced by the artisans' materials, methods, environment, and culture.

Witches' Kitchen, a handcrafted kitchenware collection, is the most recent project in Artecnica's ongoing campaign. Inspired by the darker side of Western fairytales, industrial designer Tord Boontje worked with Brazil's Coopa-Roca women's cooperative to make an all black, hand-sewn selection of kitchen couture; with Guatemalan artisans to make hand-carved, double-ended wooden utensils; and with Colombian potters for a group of hand-formed black ceramic cookware. At the center of Artecnica's series are the people who sustain the traditional crafts, building ongoing relationships with each group. The Coopa-Roca women's cooperative, which previously made a Boontje-designed chandelier, makes the hand-sewn Witches' and Wizards' Apron and Glove collection. Boontje introduced a natural pattern from the forest as a new graphic addition to traditional Colombian black pottery. Leaves

are pressed into the wet clay and burn away when fired, leaving an imprint. Made without glazes, the cookware—a casserole and saucepan—are naturally lead- and toxin-free. Each of the carved Guatemalan utensils is made from sustainable and reforested wood sourced locally.

36

37

Witches' Kitchen collection, Design with a
Conscience series. Tord Boontje, Studio Tord
Boontje. Client: Artecnica. Designed France,
manufactured Brazil, Colombia, and Guatemala,
2008

35 Stacked edition multi-leaf. Manufactured by
Colombian potters. Hand-molded ceramic

36 Assorted wooden utensils. Manufactured by
Guatemalan artisans. Sustainably harvested wood

37 Witches' and Wizards' apron. Manufactured
by Coopa-Roca (Brazil) Women's Cooperative.
Hand-sewn cotton

Health

Cynthia Smith

Citizen Health

"Health is a state of complete physical, mental, and social well-being and not merely the absence of disease or infirmity."
—*Preamble to the Constitution of the World Health Organization*[1]

The World Health Organization has not changed its definition of health in more than sixty years, and this expansive view challenges designers around the world to give form to new ideas for health-care solutions and systems. They can be found not only in countries with the highest standards of living, but also in remote regions with limited resources. And designers are responding, with products ranging from a low-cost incubator made from car parts to sophisticated devices that radically improve mobility for injured veterans and aging populations, bringing unimagined hope and progress to people of all ages and income levels.

Technological advancements are dramatically changing the medical field. Robotics makes surgery more precise and enables remote work on battlefield soldiers.[2] Research-and-development designers are applying what they learned from making robots walk to the Bodyweight Support Assist exoskeleton, enabling workers to perform demanding

Ripple Effect water vessel. IDEO and Acumen Fund. Partner: Naandi Foundation. United States and India, 2008–9. Plastic tasks for longer periods of time (fig. 1). Government agencies, universities, and private industry are collaborating internationally to revolutionize prosthetics with a thought-controlled mechanical arm that restores function and sensory perception. Remote medical consultation and monitoring of patients via telemedicine are helping to improve service, reduce costs, and provide the means for people to track their own health. More transparent information and easier access afforded by digital records are creating an emboldened era of "citizen patients."

fig. 1

The most striking shift bubbling up from the crowd is peer-to-peer mobile applications, which give people new tools to connect—and act—in the developing world. A World Economic Forum council noted that mobile communication is "the fastest growing technology in the history of mankind."[3] Mobile devices are poised to be the "next printing press,"[4] according to MIT Media Lab's Professor Sandy Pentland, who has observed demand growing rapidly from the bottom up rather than from the top down, heralding a structural shift in society. A group working out of the Media Lab, the Next Billion Network, is designing a broad range of mobile health technologies, known as mhealth, to be deployed in isolated locations (fig. 2). In Zambia, one application allows doctors on other continents to analyze uploaded cell-phone images to diagnose and treat local women for cervical cancer.

fig. 2

The flow of health information is becoming more democratized. Some of the most popular sections of social-networking sites are where patients support each other by sharing medical data and treatments. For the global public-health community, disease outbreaks are visualized in real time online from sources both traditional and informal. The H1N1 "swine flu" virus's earliest accounting was not by the Centers for Disease Control and Prevention or the WHO, but from a Web-crawling site, HealthMap, designed by an epidemiologist and software developer that posted an early report about the flu in a Mexican village.[5] (fig. 3)

H1N1 Case Reports
News media sources

Official sources

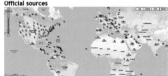

fig. 3

With institutions and infrastructure in poorer countries often being nonexistent or immature, deployment of medical devices is hindered. But this can also mean fewer barriers to innovation and opportunities to leapfrog ahead of countries with more established systems. Visionary design educators are seizing the opportunity where economic constraints meet talent. Stanford University, partnering with the Indian government, opened a Biodesign Center in New Delhi, encouraging effective, low-cost medical design. Alternatively, Design that Matters, along with a doctor at Boston's Center for Integration of Medicine and Innovative Technology, exploits a preexisting system, the network of car mechanics throughout the global south that services aid-agency vehicles, to make and repair infant incubators made from car parts (fig. 4). "Organically resourced"[6]—locally available material drives the design— is emerging as a viable method to ensure a product is easily implemented and maintained.

fig. 4

Even international institutions, notorious for their slow bureaucracy, are seeking lateral changes. United Nations agencies convene hackers, bloggers, humanitarian and development agencies, and designers at an annual conference, Web4Dev,[7] to induce strategies to solve global health threats and development challenges. Designers create additional value by combining institutional and crowd-source data for real-time tracking of events on the ground. Transparent tagging, rapid communication, and information visualization empower those working in the field to make critical decisions, whether it is texting requests for more medication or making sense of erupting conflicts to better target aid and save lives.

Successful implementation, a primary goal in humanitarian design, provides real solutions to real-world challenges. A Norwegian non-governmental organization, Design Without Borders, is collaborating with industrial designers on societal issues, such as post-conflict mine removal (fig. 5), and applying

fig. 5

design methodology and knowledge of manufacturing to bring a life-saving product to the "aid market." Increasingly, designers of all types are placing people directly at the center of the design process, gaining insight on implicit and explicit emotional needs through empathy for others. One California-based designer, Stuart Karten, uses "mode-mapping" to chart tasks and motivations, with the aim of better understanding user experience. Realizing that people consider a hearing aid as a weakness and disability,[8] Karten designed a state-of-the-art device that is nearly invisible when worn (fig. 6).

fig. 6

As the world faces looming social challenges from shifting demographics, changing working environments, and resource constraints, designers are crossing boundaries among different sectors to design the next generation of public services. In the United Kingdom, a cross-disciplinary group, Participle, applies business thinking to make a social enterprise more economically sustainable, and is using design methodology to develop a service to bring together isolated seniors, a growing phenomenon in industrialized countries (fig. 7).

Design plays a critical role in public health, bringing solutions to the growing epidemics of obesity, diabetes, and asthma.

fig. 7

Design Corps' Bryan Bell's emphatic claim that "no issue is not a design issue"[9] encourages lawmakers to include designers and planners in conversations that determine public policy and long-term strategy. Planning for green markets, sidewalks for walking, lanes for biking, and affordable housing with entry stairs instead of elevators are thoughtful remedies to this country's debilitating health concerns.

fig. 8

Determined to bring clean water to people, a respected Bay-area design firm, IDEO, is collaborating with a venture-capital organization to design numerous prototypes (fig. 8). Beginning in India with local partners that have established distribution networks, then expanding into East Africa, the team co-creates with regional groups to be geographically and culturally sensitive. They plan to scale up and transform the way clean water is delivered around the world[10]—in an escalating ripple effect.

1 Preamble to the Constitution of the World Health Organization, as adopted by the International Health Conference, New York, June 19–July 22, 1946; signed on July 22, 1946, by the representatives of sixty-one states (*Official Records of the World Health Organization*, no. 2, p. 100) and entered into force on April 7, 1948. The definition has not been amended since 1948.

2 "Medicine Goes Digital," in *The Economist* magazine (April 18, 2009): 15–17.

3 "Discussion Highlights on the Future of Mobile Communications," the Summit on the Global Agenda, Dubai, United Arab Emirates, November 7–9, 2008, World Economic Forum's Network of Global Agenda Councils.

4 Interview with Prof. Alexander Pentland, Massachusetts Institute of Technology Media Lab, Cambridge, MA, March 12, 2009.

5 John S. Brownstein, Clark C. Freifeld, and Lawrence C. Madoff, "Influenza A (H1N1) Virus, 2009: Online Monitoring," in *New England Journal of Medicine* (2009) 360: 2156.

6 Madeline Drexler, "Looking Under the Hood and Seeing an Incubator," in *The New York Times Magazine* (December 16, 2008).

7 Web4Dev is a community focused on applying Internet-related technologies toward the achievement of the Millennium Development Goals. Created by the World Bank in 2003, it brings together practitioners and experts in the field of Web communication and information management to maximize the effectiveness of Web resources within the UN system. Members come from UN system organizations, civil society, and government and development agencies. http://www.web4dev.org/index.php/History_ Web4Dev, accessed August 2, 2009.

8 Phone interview with Stuart Karten about the Zōn hearing aid's development and design, June 26, 2009.

9 Bryan Bell, Expanding Architecture: Conversations on Design as Activism forum, organized by Metropolis magazine, at Steelcase Inc., New York, NY, November 13, 2008.

10 Design for Social Impact Symposium, organized by IDEO, the Acumen Fund, and the Rockefeller Foundation, New York, NY, June 2, 2008.

1

2

4:Secs Condom Applicator Generation II, Modular Traffic Light System, and Snuza Halo Baby Breathing Monitor

The South African industrial design studio Dot Dot Dot Ex Why Zed Design (...XYZ) is engaged at every step of the design development process, from ideation, concept development, engineering, and tooling for manufacture to brand management. This method has enabled the interdisciplinary team to design a range of products, such as ergonomic applications for medical devices and safer rugged industrial goods, in Africa and for the international market.

Designed for easy and rapid condom application in less than four seconds, the 4:Secs condom applicator generation II aims to reduce the spread of sexually transmitted diseases. HIV/AIDS continues to be a global concern; more than 10% of South Africa is infected with the virus. The first version of the applicator used "hooks" which easily tore the condom's latex if used incorrectly. Generation II houses the condom in a molded channel that prevents tension. ...XYZ also devised thoughtful packaging and suggestive product branding to help attract young consumers.

The result of more than a decade of research in bio-feedback systems ...XYZ's Snuza Halo baby monitor prevents SIDS (sudden infant death syndrome). Instead of the typical under-mattress monitor, this small, portable vital-sign device clips to a baby's diaper for use not only when sleeping in the crib, but also in transit or anywhere the baby sleeps. Incorporating the latest sensing technology, Snuzu Halo tracks the baby's breathing; if breathing stops, the monitor sounds an alarm and vibrates, stimulating the baby into consciousness.

...XYZ and MTLS claim their modular traffic-light system is the world's safest configurable traffic light. A traffic-light pole consisting of stackable tubular plastic or polymer sections held in place with a tensioned cable, the system is designed to collapse if a car collides with it, minimizing vehicle damage and passenger injury. The system requires little maintenance and has low replacement costs. Due to its modularity, MTLS can be repaired quickly and retrofitted with new developments in LED technologies, wireless communication, and advancements in traffic monitoring.

1–2 4:Secs condom applicator generation II. Roelf Mulder, Byron Qually, and Richard Perez, Dot Dot Dot Ex Why Zed Design (Pty) Ltd. South Africa, 2007. High-density polyethylene, PVDC (polyvinylidene chloride), polyester, aluminum, cardboard, surlyn

3

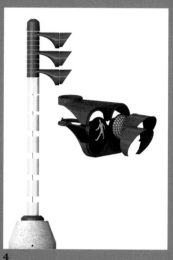

4

3–4 Modular traffic-light system. Barry Geer, MTLS, Roelf Mulder, Byron Qually, Richard Perez, and Ryan Fowler, Dot Dot Dot Ex Why Zed Design (Pty) Ltd. South Africa, 2007. Glass-filled polypropylene, precast concrete foundation, PCBA

5–6 Snuza Halo baby breathing monitor. Roelf Mulder, Byron Qually, Richard Perez, and David Wiseman, Dot Dot Dot Ex Why Zed Design (Pty) Ltd. Manufacturer: Biosentronics. South Africa, 2007. Monprene, polycarbonate, acetyl, PCBA

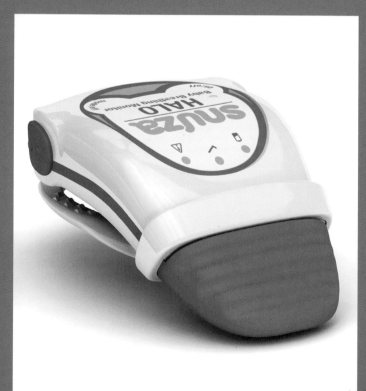

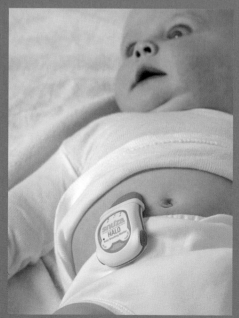

6

5

7

8

AdSpecs

The World Health Organization estimates that over half a billion people around the world need vision correction, but have minimal access to trained eye-care specialists and affordable eyeglasses. The majority of these people live in the developing world, on less than two dollars a day. The educational and economic impact of uncorrected vision is profound, limiting people's ability to read, write, learn, work, and participate actively in daily life. In 1996, Joshua Silver, a physicist at the University of Oxford, created AdSpecs to offer low-cost corrective eyewear to under-served patients, who can "fill" their own prescription without the need for expensive optical equipment. A few years later, Silver introduced a prototype of his self-adjustable glasses, which he developed for small-scale mass production. In 2007, he added a lens power scale, an important feature to allow a user to know their prescription.

The glasses' technology is simple: as the curve of the lens changes, so does its refractive power. Silver created fluid-filled lenses—a clear, circular sac of silicone oil, which has a high refrac-tive index, is sandwiched between two clear and durable plastic membranes. The lenses are connected to a tube and a small syringe fitted with a dial, which wearers use to adjust the amount of liquid in each sac, custom-forming each lens's curvature to their prescription. Once adjusted, the sacs are sealed off with a small valve and the syringes are removed. The technology can correct nearsightedness and farsightedness, but not astigmatism, and the lenses can only be circular. Currently priced at $19 a pair,

the glasses demonstrate how a low-tech solution can bring costs down and allow for easy deployment of a health device. Silver hopes that with his self-refraction approach, half a billion people will be wearing the eyeglasses they need by 2020.
–*Andrea Lipps*

7–8 AdSpecs. Joshua Silver, Adaptive Eyecare Ltd. and Oxford Centre for Vision in the Developing World. Distributed by the Education Ministry of Ghana, US Military Humanitarian and Civic Assistance Program. United Kingdom, initiated 1996, gauged version 2007. Plastic tubing, aluminum rings, silicone fluid, polyester thin film, polycarbonate covers

9

10

Armadillo Body Armor and Facemask

Kode Design met the design challenge posed by the Norway-based non-governmental organization Design Without Borders to improve the existing personal protective equipment (PPE) currently used for humanitarian de-mining in more than eighty countries and on every continent. De-miners were loosening or removing their protection because it was heavy and uncomfortable—with fatal consequences. Combining advanced lightweight materials, ballistic physics, sportswear ergonomics, and physiological science, Kode drastically improved the PPEs' wearability. Field tests of the Armadillo have demonstrated a 10–15% increase in de-miners' efficiency and concentration, leading to safer conditions.

The vest is outfitted with strong plates that move with the user; distributes weight between shoulders and hips to improve balance and mobility and reduce muscle strain; and increases ventilation, which reduces body heat and dehydration. The redesigned mask is 75% lighter and 50% stronger, providing better protection against blasts and direct sunlight. Its efficient valve system of overlapping shells expels exhaled air, and the replaceable visor is positioned closer to the eyes to reduce visual distortion. The Armadillo is currently used in twenty countries and is informing international standards for safer and stronger protective gear.

9–10 Armadillo body armor and facemask. Leif Steven Verdu Isachsen, Kode Design. Manufactured by Rofi Industrier. Client: Norwegian Form Foundation through Design Without Borders, The Norwegian Ministry of Foreign Affairs, and The Norwegian People's Aid. Designed Norway, manufactured Norway and Italy, 2008. PURE® composite, aramid fibers, cordura

11

Bodyweight Support Assist

Honda is traditionally known for automobiles, but for years the company has been conducting research to develop technologies that enhance the broader theme of human mobility. The Bodyweight Support Assist is a recent prototype that assists workers who spend extended periods of time on their feet standing, climbing or descending stairs, or maintaining semi-crouched positions, such as assembly-line workers. The device may also help the elderly get around easier. It is a next-generation product for Honda, based on studies of human walking that resulted in ASIMO, the company's humanoid robot.

The Bodyweight Support Assist, an exoskeleton for the lower body, reduces the load and stress on legs, hips, knees, and ankles. The device's simple form consists of a seat, frame, and shoes. To use it, a person straddles the slender frame, slips on the shoes, and puts the seat into position. Two computer-controlled motors obtain information from sensors in the shoes to determine the support needed based on the bending and stretching of the user's knees. The assist force is directed towards the person's center of gravity, just as with human legs, enabling the device to provide help in various movements. Weighing less than fifteen pounds, the Bodyweight Support Assist is powered by a lithium-ion battery that lasts two hours.
—Andrea Lipps

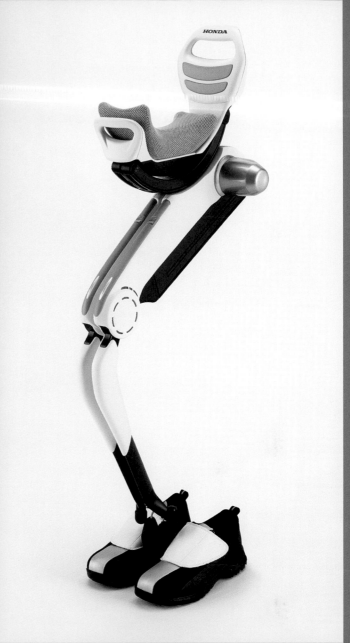

12

11–12 Bodyweight Support Assist, prototype. Fundamental Technology Research Center, Honda R&D Co., Ltd. Japan, 1999–2010. CPU, hip angle sensors, brushless motors

OMEGA INSTITUTE FOR SUSTAINABLE LIVING
RHINEBECK, NY

BUILDING SECTION PERSPECTIVE 1 PHOTOVOLTAIC COLLECTORS: Strategically located throughout the facility, the photovoltaic collectors provide all of the buildings electricity. 2 METAL ROOF: Made from recycled metal, the reflective properties keep the interior spaces cooler and mitigate the "heat island" effect. 3 CONSTRUCTED WETLANDS: Here the water flows through the root structure of wetland plants. The plants remove nitrates and reduce the Biological Oxygen Demand and suspended solids in the water. 4 AERATED LAGOONS: Additional wetland plants are suspended in an Aerated Lagoon. In a symbiotic relationship, the plant roots act as a habitat for microbial populations that further scrub the water. 5 GREEN ROOF: This living roof system provides additional thermal insulation. 6 WOOD RAINSCREEN SIDING: Made from reclaimed cypress lumber, this wall system allows the building skin to "breathe" and eliminates the need for painting. 7 SOLAR TRACKING SKYLIGHTS: These maximize the sunlight available for the plants and people working in the greenhouse. 8 SUNSHADE: The sunshade serves two purposes. First, it works to bounce sunlight onto the ceiling of the greenhouse, more evenly distributing the light. Secondly, it shades the lower portion of the window wall from direct solar exposure during the summer. 9 MECHANICAL AND ELECTRICAL ROOM: Located here are the PV system inverters, and equipment for the Eco Machine and rainwater collection. Windows between this room and the Lobby expose the inner workings of the building systems. 10 INTERIOR FINISHES: Wherever possible, the structural materials and other elements of the building are exposed. With extra care given to making these elements attractive, fewer redundant materials and finishes were used for the project. 11 WOODLANDS RESTORATION: Future projects will restore the woodlands surrounding the OCSL and elsewhere on campus to their natural state.

13

Eco-Machine at the Omega Center for Sustainable Living

Since the 1970s, John Todd has been designing Eco-Machines— wastewater-treatment systems that use natural processes with no hazardous chemicals. His latest is at the Omega Center for Sustainable Living in New York, designed by BNIM Architects, that brings together the most current Eco-Machine technology with green architecture and clean energy. The building houses the primary Eco-Machine cells and is designed with so many sustainable strategies—solar orientation, natural ventilation, photovoltaics, and much more—that it is slated to become the first certified "living building" in the United States by the Cascadia Green Building Council.

At OCSL, the Eco-Machine reclaims and purifies all of the wastewater from the Omega Institute's 195-acre campus, more than five million gallons annually. The wastewater is collected in a 10,000-gallon anaerobic (oxygen-free) tank. Microbial organisms in the water digest the sludge, and the wastewater travels "down-stream" (designed to reduce the need for energy-intensive pumps) to four constructed wetlands. There, plants such as bulrush and cattail help cleanse the water by trapping particles in their roots and ingesting nitrates and other impurities. The water is then pumped into two lagoons divided into cells inside the building, where plants are suspended above water level while their roots serve as a habitat for microbes, fungi, and algae that further scrub the water, converting the waste into energy and nutrients for their small ecosystem. The last cell contains fish, illustrating that the water from the Eco-Machine is clean enough to sustain life. After a final trip through a recirculating sand filter where microorganisms remove any residual waste, the water is ready for non-potable use, flushing toilets, and irrigating the campus's gardens.
—*Andrea Lipps*

13–14 Eco-Machine at the Omega Center for Sustainable Living, Rhinebeck, NY. John Todd, John Todd Ecological Design. Omega Center for Sustainable Living: Brad Clark, Laura Lesniewski, and Steve McDowell, BNIM. Client: Omega Institute for Holistic Studies. United States, 2008–9

14

15

16

17

15–17 Ergon GR2 bike grips. Peter Ejvinsson,
Thomas Nilsson, Anna Carell, and Mårten Andrén,
Ergonomidesign. Manufactured by Ergon. Client:
RTI Sports GmbH. Designed Sweden, manufactured
Germany, 2006–7. Injection molded plastic core,
Kraton rubber, forged magnesium

Ergon GR2 Bike Grips, NioxMino Asthma Monitor, and Spot Guide Cane

The Sweden-based design consultancy Ergonomidesign studies
our physical, cognitive, and emotional capabilities and limitations
to better design objects that are intuitive and inclusive. Whether
continuing to refine its products for enhanced usability or experi-
menting with how new technologies can augment our lives, the
firm focuses on the role of human-centered design in improving
well-being.

The Ergon GR2 bike grips were first introduced in 2006 to
alleviate the numb palms caused by most bicycle handles. After
thorough user research, Ergonomidesign optimized the shape and
texture of the grip to evenly distribute pressure on the palm and
provide maximum control. The firm revised the design in 2009
to include a bar end (the part that mounts and secures the grip
to the handlebar) made of plastic and rubber for increased comfort, integrated transition with the grip, and more cost-effective
manufacturing.

The NioxMino is a medical device for asthma detection that
allows doctors to fine-tune medication dosage while increasing
patient compliance, particularly among children. The mechanism,
which measures airway inflammation via nitric-oxide levels,
accommodates both adults and children and is intended for use in
patients' homes as well as medical facilities. Its non-threatening
appearance and recently redesigned user interface is playful and
intuitive. As the user exhales into the device, the cloud on the
interface grows, indicating the extent of the patient's asthma.

18

19

Spot, a conceptual device for people with impaired vision, integrates artificial intelligence and a GPS system in a wheel-driven guide cane. Mimicking a guide dog, Spot gradually "learns" the behavior and routines of its users and guides them through their environment. The cane's design is approachable, with sensor "eyes" that convey an alert intelligence and color differentiation to denote the cane's protective and tactile elements.
—*Andrea Lipps*

18–19 NioxMino asthma monitor. David Crafoord, Martin Birath, Daniel Höglund, and Elisabeth Ramel-Wåhrberg, Ergonomidesign. Manufacturer and client: Aerocrine AB. Sweden, 2004–8. Nitric oxide sensor, electronics, LCD display, PCBs, ABS plastic

20–21 Spot guide cane, concept. Marcus Heneen, Ergonomidesign. Sweden, 2001–present. Plastics, aluminum, leather, optic sensors, cameras

20

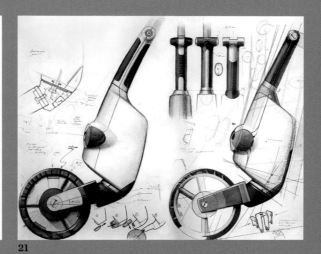

21

The cards shown read:

Current Affairs Group

Quiz

Details
Take part in a fun and exciting quiz

Group numbers
This is a new group looking for new

Mr Welch W9 No. 3351

I Like...
The reading about history of this area and visiting places. I also watching National Geographic.

I'm interested to talk... about l

Stan W9 No. 3350

Phone Groups

To Join
1. Call the operator on...
0800 122 3441
2. We'll arrange a time and date
3. We'll call you at the arranged time
4. Talk as long as you want
To leave the World War Two room just hang up. To get reconnected call the operator

All Calls are free

I Like...
to listen to records, the old stuff - Bing Crosby, Doris Day and Glen Miller. There is nothing like a nice tune. And I like to watch soaps, quizzes, games and football - I support Chelsea

I'm interested to talk... about War and different things you did, and about dogs and horses.

I would like to go to... the Serpentine in Hyde Park, cafes in my area, shopping in Selfridges or a historical tour by scooter!

A little bit about me... I was in a landing squad and went to Corsica, Rome and to Asia. My squad was based in Swansea. After the war, I worked as a manager of a men's clothes shop.

Things I do... I lend my 40s & 50s records and I occasionally meet with John or George for a coffee.

People Call 0800 122 3441 to get connected P.T.O.

22

Get-Together

In the United Kingdom, more than three million people over the age of sixty-five do not see a friend, neighbor, or family member in any given week. The World Health Organization rates social isolation as a greater health risk than smoking. The UK-based public-service design firm Participle was asked by a local authority to design and prototype new services to combat social isolation and loneliness amongst the elderly. Participle is implementing public-sector services by engaging key players in government agencies, working with end users to gain insight, and rapidly testing ideas with a series of prototypes. It is applying design thinking to the challenges of shifting demographics, cultural changes, and constrained resources, with sustainable results.

Get-Together introduced isolated, like-minded individuals to each other via a familiar technology, the telephone. A social network emerged and flourished, with weekly group meetings and activities planned around shared interests. The program is based on the earlier success of Southwick Circle, a rural pilot project, and further developed for an urban location, London, with the intent to implement it nationwide. Created as a sustainable enterprise, it is designed to reap financial returns while saving a significant amount of money on health care and social services.

23

24

22–24 Get-Together. Hilary Cottam, Hugo Manassei, and Michael Tolhurst, Participle Ltd. Design team: Daniel Dickens, Emanuel Farkhar, Hermeet Gill, Michele Lee, Jonas Piet, Emma Southgate, Chris Vanstone, Jennie Winhall. United Kingdom, 2008–present

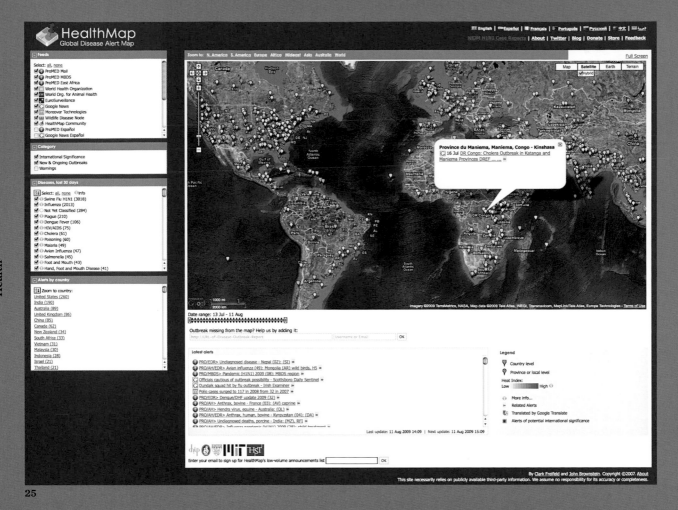

25

HealthMap

Global surveillance of public health has traditionally been the purview of health ministries, public institutions, and multinational agencies, but Internet sites have emerged as valuable alternatives, offering open and accessible platforms and information on disease and treatment. Perhaps more than finding patterns to suggest epidemics, these sites can lead to greater democratization and empowerment in the health field.

Launched by John Brownstein and Clark Freifeld of Harvard Medical School and the Children's Hospital Informatics Program in Boston, HealthMap is a near-real-time, global disease-surveillance and visualization system that is freely available on the Web. The site combs 20,000 global news and health Web sites and blogs each hour to collect reports in English, Spanish, French, Portuguese, Russian, and Chinese. It uses text-mining algorithms to aggregate and sort this information by disease, location, relevance, and duplication clustering. The validated data are overlaid on a Google Map with pushpin-type markers, customary of Web mash-ups, or hybrid applications that combine a number of Web sources into a single platform. The markers are color-coded yellow to red to reflect HealthMap's "heat index," a tool for assessing alerts—the redder the marker, the more relevant and recent the outbreak alert. By clicking on a pushpin marker, a user can access the original news story.

The site currently receives up to 150,000 visitors a day, including many from the Centers for Disease Control and the World Health Organization, who can tailor the view according

to disease, location, date, and news source. By visualizing surveillance data in a user-friendly manner, HealthMap not only facilitates early disease detection, but provides a tool for public awareness and involvement.
—*Andrea Lipps*

25 HealthMap. Clark C. Freifeld, Children's Hospital Boston at the Harvard-MIT Division of Health Sciences and Technology and MIT Media Laboratory, and John S. Brownstein, Children's Hospital Boston at the Harvard-MIT Division of Health Sciences and Technology and Harvard Medical School. United States, 2007

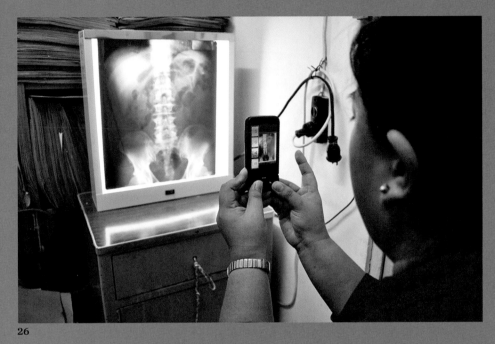

MIT Next Billion Network. Concept: Jhonatan
Rotberg, MIT Engineering Systems Division.
Partners: Fundación Carlos Slim (Javier Elguea),
Telmex (Andrés Vázquez del Mercado), MIT Media
Lab (Luis Sarmenta, Luis Blackaller, Rich Fletcher,
Sandy Pentland, Frank Moss, Mitch Resnick, John
Maeda), MIT HST (Gari Clifford, Leo Celi), MIT
Center for Transportation and Logistics (Edgar
Blanco, Jen-Hao Yang), NextLab student teams
(spring 2008, fall 2008, spring 2009). Conceived
Mexico 2006, launched United States 2007

26 Mobile Care (Moca). Leo Anthony Celi, Gari
Clifford, Jhonatan Rotberg, and Luis Sarmenta,
with Alvin Marcelo, National Telehealth Center,
University of the Philippines-Manila. Partners:
Asia Pacific College, Click Diagnostics, Dimagi,
Google SOC, IEEE, MIT Corporate Relations,
MIT Industrial Liaison Program, MIT Public
Service Center, National Telehealth Center of
the Philippines, OpenMRS, Partners in Health,
Regenstreif Institute. Designed United States
2008–9, deployed Philippines 2009–10

27 Interactive Alerts for Childhood Pneumonia.
Aamir Khan, Rich Fletcher, Gari Clifford, Jhonatan
Rotberg, and Luis Sarmenta. Partners: Nokia,
Johns Hopkins University, PATH, Indus Hospital.
Designed United States and Pakistan 2008–9,
deployed Pakistan 2009

26

MIT Next Billion Network

Within the next three years, another billion people, mostly in the developing world, will have access to cell phones, unleashing a revolution in communications and information access. Recognizing the potential of this transformation, the Next Billion Network at the Massachusetts Institute of Technology is creating innovative mobile technologies to meet the needs of low-income people in developing countries, expanding opportunities for self-reliance in health, personal finance, education, and citizenship. It promotes bottom-up, sustainable, and scalable business models that enable new forms of peer-to-peer collaborations. Sponsored by the Carlos Slim Foundation, the Next Billion Network partners with local non-governmental organizations with which they provoke students to design and deploy mobile technologies to meet real-world needs.

Mobile Care (Moca), an open-source, customizable tele-health platform, is one example of a project generated from the Next Billion Network. Moca enables cell phones to become medical diagnostic devices for health workers in remote areas of the world, connecting them to medical professionals in urban areas. Using Moca, a worker collects data about a patient by following a series of questions or prompts; takes pictures and records voice or video tags if needed; and uploads the information to OpenMRS, a free medical-record system, where a doctor grabs a case from the queue and reviews it. The doctor then replies via Moca with a diagnosis, allowing for same-day treatment or

referral—important in areas where patients often travel great distances for health care.

Interactive Alerts, a system using mobile phones to track childhood pneumonia in Pakistan, is yet another project. Six-week-old infants are given an RFID (radio frequency ID) tag in the form of a traditional bracelet. When a child becomes ill, the RFID-tagged bracelet is scanned by a participating health practitioner using a mobile phone to retrieve pertinent immunization, clinical, and health information. Health workers are then able to effectively track and treat pneumonia, the leading cause of childhood death in a country with high mortality rates of children under the age of five.
—*Andrea Lipps*

27

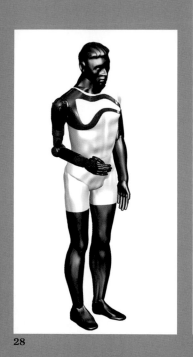

28   29

Modular Prosthetic-limb System

The design and function of prosthetic arms have lagged behind lower-limb prostheses, not evolving much beyond simple hook-and-cable technologies. But with greater numbers of U.S. soldiers returning from Iraq and Afghanistan with missing limbs (fatalities were down thanks to improved armor and medical care), the U.S. Defense Advanced Research Projects Agency sponsored the Revolutionizing Prosthetics 2009 program, aimed at developing a fully articulated, neutrally integrated artificial arm. Dubbed by the media as the "Manhattan Project for Prosthetic Limbs," it consists of a multidisciplinary team from more than thirty organizations across the United States, Canada, and Europe, led by the Johns Hopkins University Applied Physics Laboratory.

The Modular Prosthetic Limb System is the team's latest bionic-arm prototype. Made of lightweight carbon fiber and high-strength alloys, the arm has twenty-five degrees of freedom, or joint motions (the human arm has about thirty), closely mimicking the speed and dexterity of a natural limb. A wide range of neural-integration strategies are being tested to control the arm and restore sensory feedback, from injectable myoelectric sensors—wireless devices the size of a grain of rice implanted in muscles of the remaining limb, which integrate directly with the nervous system to transmit signals instructing the prosthetic's movement—to more near-term methods such as targeted muscle reinnervation, which allow for "thought-controlled" prostheses. This approach reroutes nerves that once controlled the lost

limb to unused muscles nearby, sometimes using chest muscles; when the brain tells the arm to move, the rerouted nerves create a contraction that provides an electrical signal interpreted by the prosthetic limb, making it move in a natural manner. The prototype is modular and configurable to a patient's injury, and cosmeses, or skin coverings, feature simulated pores and hair to mimic the natural appearance of the native limb.
—*Andrea Lipps*

28–29 Modular prosthetic-limb system. Stuart D. Harshbarger, Johns Hopkins University Applied Physics Laboratory and Orthocare Innovations, Thomas Van Dore, HDT Engineering Services, Richard Weir, Rehabilitation Institute of Chicago, and John Bigelow, Johns Hopkins University Applied Physics Laboratory; additional designers: Robert Armiger, James Beaty, Michael Bridges, James Burck, Michelle Chen, Steven Clark, Chad Dize, Harry Eaton, Eric Faulring, Ezra Johnson, Matthew Kozlowski, Niranjan Kumar, Courtney Leigh Moran, Tom Moyer, Aseem Raval, Julio Santos, Grace Tran, Matthew Van Doren, R. Jacob Vogelstein, Douglas Wenstrand, Michael Zeher. Manufactured by Orthocare Innovations and HDT Engineering Services. United States, 2009–present. Computer renderings

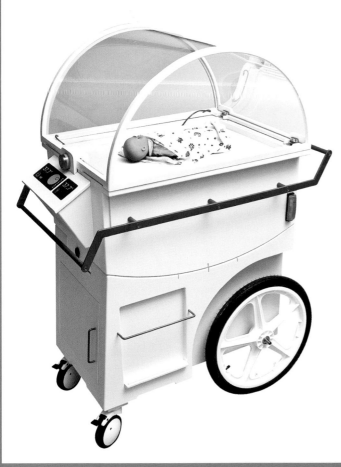

30

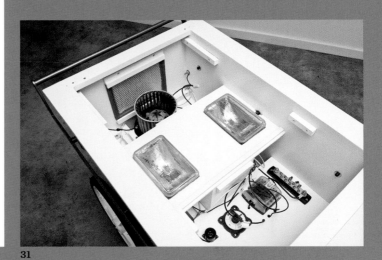

31

Neonurture Car-parts Incubator

Four million babies, mostly from the world's poorest regions, die within a month of birth every year. Many of these deaths could be prevented if a working incubator were available. Currently, neonatal incubators donated to developing countries last less than five years, some due to electrical surges or brownouts, others from lack of training on how to use them. The nonprofit organization Design that Matters teamed with the Center for Integration of Medicine & Innovative Technology, a global-health consortium, to address this urgent need to produce Neonurture, a durable, low-cost neonatal incubator and isolation unit.

Understanding the system in which the incubator would be produced, used, maintained, and distributed was fundamental. Doctors in the field noted that the small trucks, cars, and motorcycles used by aid agencies could be found in the remotest of locations, along with distribution chains for replacement parts and the mechanics to repair them. A modular prototype incubator was developed using these vehicle parts: headlights to generate heat, filters for clean air convection and filtration, alarms to alert caregivers, and a motorcycle battery for power. Plans are to train mechanics to be medical technologists and to conduct clinical trials with the next-generation model, with the ultimate goal to create regional manufacturing systems to build local infrastructure and clinical skills.

30–31 Neonurture car-parts incubator, prototype. Timothy Prestero, Tom Weis, and Emily Rothschild, Design that Matters Inc. Preliminary research: Kris Olson, Center for Integration of Medicine & Innovative Technology. United States, Nepal, India, Bangladesh, Vietnam, Cambodia, Laos, and Indonesia, 2008–9. MDF, Lexan, aluminum, car parts

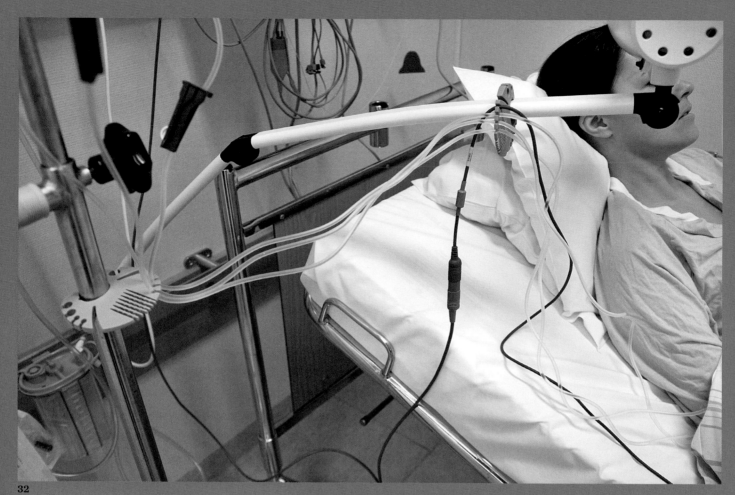

32

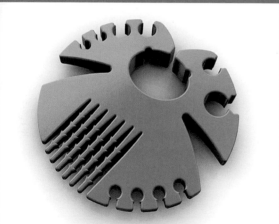

33

32–33 Orio medical-cord organizer. Martin O. Fougner and Jørgen Leirdal, Hugo Industridesign AS. Manufactured by Norplasta. Client: Inora AS. Norway, 2008. Dryflex plastic

Orio Medical-cord Organizer

A simple, elegant solution to the wire chaos found next to most hospital beds, the Orio medical-cord organizer acts as the collection point to prevent tangles, mismanagement, and kinks in tubes that could lead to a critical medicine or fluid being cut off to the patient. Tubes and wires easily snap on or release from the three-inch disc, which can be attached to any pole, rail, or equipment surrounding the patient, eliminating the need to tape cables together. Made from rubber developed especially for hospital use, it is 100% recyclable and can be washed and sterilized repeatedly without losing its effectiveness. Its light-blue color sets it apart from other clinical instruments and allows staff to write on it with a marker.

The Orio is designed by Martin Otto Fougner, a specialist in ergonomics, and Jørgen Leirdal, an expert in interaction design, both of whom were educated at the Oslo School of Architecture and Design. The product was commissioned by Inora, a company developing innovative and functional products for people, from patients with health challenges to those working in hospitals. The organizing lifesaver was quickly brought to market in less than a year, winning two prestigious awards, and is now distributed in Norway, Sweden, Denmark, Holland, Belgium, Luxembourg, Italy, Spain, Portugal, and France, and soon in America and Asia.

34

35

Ripple Effect. IDEO and Acumen Fund. Partners: Jal Bhagirathi Foundation, Naandi Foundation, Piramal Water, Water and Sanitation for the Urban Poor, WaterHealth International, Maji na Ufanisi, Kentainers, PureFlow, and Umande Trust. United States, India, and Kenya, 2008–10

34 Business service model. Partner: Jal Bhagirathi Foundation

35 Water vessel. Partner: Naandi Foundation. Plastic

36 Marketing system model. Partner: WaterHealth International

36

Ripple Effect

Over 1.3 billion people worldwide drink unsafe water. Even when safe water is available, people spend significant time and effort transporting it, with a high risk of contaminating the water in the process. Ripple Effect, a collaboration between the Acumen Fund, IDEO, and local Indian and Kenyan water organizations, is a project to improve access to safe drinking water for underserved people, stimulate innovation among water suppliers, and build development capacity for the entire water sector.

IDEO and Acumen led a workshop of entrepreneurs in India to brainstorm, prototype ideas, and develop concepts for each organization's strategy. Five pilot studies each received funding and design and business support to develop their products, services, and systems. The project team also engaged multiple water organizations in Kenya following the same process.

The Naandi Foundation, which provides clean water from a local source for a nominal fee to Indian villagers with the Ripple Effect team, replaced the typical heavy five-gallon container with a newly designed water vessel that would allow for easy cleaning and use, not just by the men who currently carry the water, but also by women and the elderly. Smooth contours allow the women to carry it on their hips, customarily how they transport pots. An optional wheel kit permits rolling across uneven terrain. An integrated handle reduces the likelihood of contamination while pouring.

The Ripple Effect team and the Jal Bhagirathi Foundation designed a microenterprise for low-cost distribution of clean water to people in the Thar Desert region of Rajasthan, India, where there are major water shortages and poor water quality. Their collaboration created a new business model for JBF's water purification plant, which was having trouble convincing communities to purchase treated clean water. Now, investment in infrastructure delivers water to village depots; local women's groups form microenterprises to sell and distribute water within the villages; and community awareness is raised with rallies and community events, such as theater. As a result, JBF has gone from selling 1,050 gallons to over 4,200 gallons of safe water per day.

Ripple Effect and WaterHealth International designed a safe-water awareness campaign in India. WHI's water-purification plants in the Andhra Pradesh region have trouble convincing people that its water is safer to drink than other available sources, such as ponds and wells, which are often contaminated by bacteria, natural metals, and chemical contaminants. The campaign centers on creating entertainment-based community events throughout the region that culminate with a live clean-water demonstration—bacteriological contaminants from the local sources are exposed under a microscope projected for the entire community to see. Customer registration for WHI's clean water has skyrocketed since the educational events were implemented.

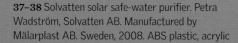

37

38

37–38 Solvatten solar safe-water purifier. Petra
Wadström, Solvatten AB. Manufactured by
Mälarplast AB. Sweden, 2008. ABS plastic, acrylic

Solvatten Solar Safe-water Purifier

A portable ten-liter (approx. 2 5/8 gallon) Solvatten solar safe-water purifying unit, devised with the United Nations Millennium Development Goals in mind, uses solar energy (UV and heat) and a built-in filter to make contaminated water drinkable. After two to six hours, treated water is clean enough to meet the World Health Organization's guidelines for safe water. A key attribute of the unit is the unique indicator that lets the user know when the water is ready.

Solvatten, meaning "sun water" in Swedish, was developed by a Swedish microbiologist turned designer for use in the developing world, where sun is abundant and electricity is often scarce. The more hygienic heated water is intended for personal hygiene and for use by midwives to reduce child mortality. The unit could save women countless hours spent collecting potable water, freeing time for education and economic activity; and reduces deforestation and pollution, since no fire is needed to boil and purify water.

39

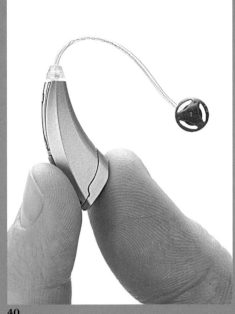

40

Zōn Hearing Aid

No longer classified as a medical appliance, the Zōn hearing aid
was designed by employing empathy-based research to discover
unmet end-user needs. Combining functionality and aesthetics,
this "receiver-in-canal" combats the stigma associated with
hearing aids. A sleek, sculptural form is possible due to manufacturing innovations that allow for assembly without parting lines
or screws. Its small size, selection of colors to match skin and
hair variations, and geometry for a secure, comfortable fit make
it virtually invisible behind the ear. These criteria are important
elements for an aging population—thirty-five million people in
North America suffer from hearing loss—many of whom equate
a hearing aid with disability and weakness.

 The 1.3-inch gadget locates the microphone ports horizontally along the aid's spine for improved clarity, directionality,
and speech audibility. It also incorporates a large, accessible push-
button control for those with limited dexterity.

39–40 Zōn hearing aid. Stuart Karten, Eric
Olson, Paul Kirley, and Dennis Schroeder, Stuart
Karten Design. Manufacturer and client: Starkey
Laboratories Inc. United States, 2008. Injection-
molded nylon housing, chrome microphone port
cover, high-gloss metallic paint

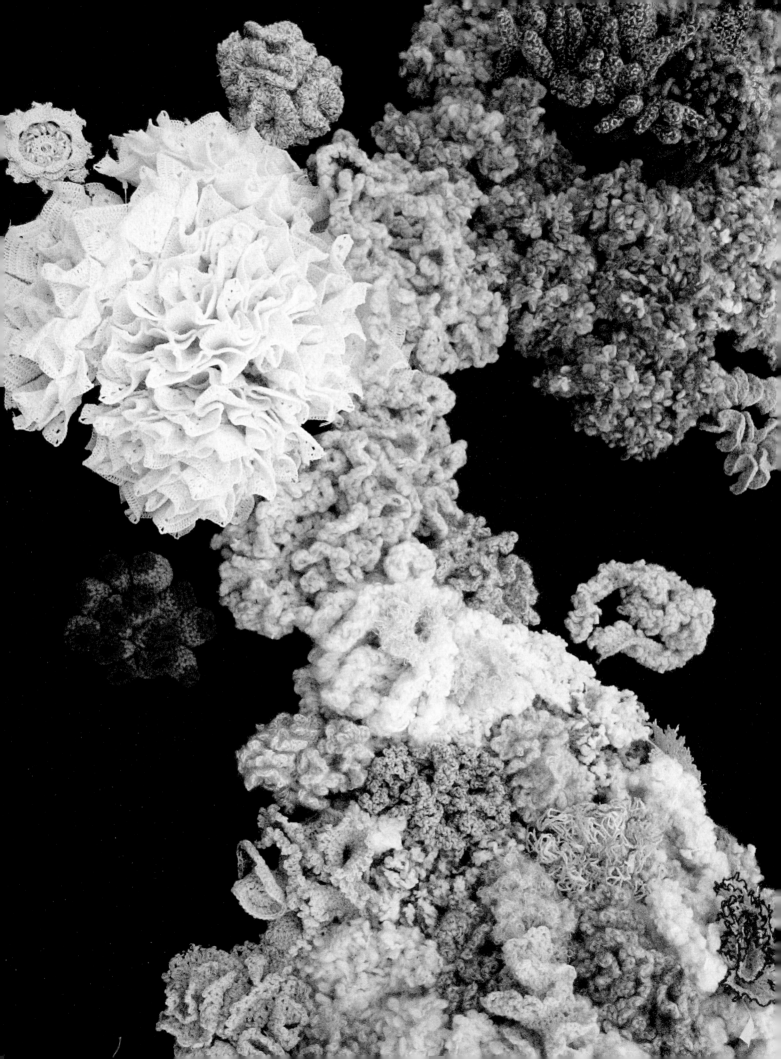

Communication

Ellen Lupton

Nearly every form of communication must be invented, created, tested, and shared. In other words, it must be designed. Today, we communicate with an evolving set of tools, from books, print, and posters to mobile phones, the Internet, and beyond. They enable people to participate in the world economy and live a rich cultural life that embraces experiences both local and distant. Access to communication enhances the lives of all people—rich and poor, young and old, able-bodied and physically challenged.

Any object we use communicates in some way. The familiar anatomy of a chair joins it to the language of other chairs. The buttons on an appliance or a Web page invite users to engage and interact. Some items disappear into the texture of daily life, while others push themselves into our consciousness, surprising us with an unexpected function, an unusual form, or a new solution to an old problem. Objects convey different values over time, shifting in status from edgy to ordinary or from worthless surplus to precious antique.

In the modern industrial world, manufactured goods belong to larger systems of production, distribution, and use. The quiet physical identity of the Apple iPhone, introduced in 2007, recedes in favor of its spectacular screen based interface. Material and immaterial, virtual and real, the iPhone (fig. 1) is one of the

The Bleached Reef. Margaret and Christine Wertheim, the Institute for Figuring; additional collaborators: Lily M. Chin, Ellen Davis, Dagmar Frinta, Evelyn Hardin, Helle Jorgensen, Nancy Lewis, Heather McCarren, Marianne Midelburg, Jill Schreier, Nadia Severns, Sarah Simons, Pamela Stiles, Barbara Van Elsen, Ann Wertheim, Barbara Wertheim, Chinese factory workers, and unknown doily makers. United States, 2007–present. Yarns, beads, baskets, felt, sand

signature artifacts of our time, representing a new paradigm in the field of mobile phones and devices. By attracting a swarm of developers to create third-party applications, or "apps," that extend its function, the iPhone is a site for endless design activity and entrepreneurship. It is an object that communicates in numerous ways—as a physical thing, a virtual interface, a cultural icon, and as a node in a network of other products and services.

fig. 1

While the iPhone incorporates numerous functions—talking, texting, gaming, taking pictures and video, surfing the Web, and more—the Amazon Kindle (fig. 2) focuses on a single activity: reading. Light and thin, the Kindle lies flat and stays open, using buttons to advance through a text, making accessing content on a Kindle more linear and regimented than flipping through a bound volume. The device connects to Amazon's library of digital titles, which users can buy and download seamlessly; this system is vital to the product's success.

fig. 2

Kindle users can make text bigger or activate the device's text-to-speech function to create instant audio books, features which appeal to older or vision-impaired readers. Since the passage of the Americans with Disabilities Act in 1990, the design professions have become more attentive to universal design issues. More recently, the rise of accessibility standards in Web design have prompted designers and developers to help realize the potential of the Internet by making content accessible to all people, including the vision-impaired. Using a raised printing surface, Sean Donahue's experimental *Touch* magazine (fig. 3) communicates to sighted and non-sighted readers. Industrial designer David Chavez has created a prototype for a Braille wristwatch, allowing blind users to check the time silently, without an audio prompt. Even more ambitious is Samsung's Touch Sight (fig. 4) camera, a device that non-sighted people can use to create embossed, 3D-surfaces. The typeface Clearview, (fig. 5) created for U.S. roads and highways by Donald Meeker and James Montalbano, aims to make it easier for all drivers— and older drivers in particular—to read signs safely at night and from a distance.

fig. 3

fig. 4

fig. 5

What happens when communication systems break down? The Etón FR 600 radio (fig. 6) works where the grid fails to function. Designed by Whipsaw Inc., this emergency radio is charged via hand-crank or solar cell, and it serves as a flashlight and USB cell-phone charger as well as a radio. The XOXO laptop (fig. 7), designed by Yves Béhar for the One Laptop per Child initiative, is a low-cost computer designed specifically for the developing world. Planned for a different set of conditions

fig. 6

than the typical commercial laptop, it can function outdoors in extreme heat and humidity, and can be held flat, angled, or like a book, by one person or a group working together.

Not all design projects seek to solve real-world problems. Design can be critical, speculative, or theoretical, shedding light on social or philosophical issues. As critic Peter Hall recently pointed out, "Many objects are designed not to be useful but to make an argument." Anthony Dunne and Fiona Raby's Risk Watch (fig. 8) has a nipple-like face that transmits audio information about local security alerts when held to a user's ear. Reflecting on the role of technology, surveillance, and fear in contemporary culture, objects like this one prefer to comment on the world rather than work out its predicaments. They use design to ask questions and communicate ideas.

Many graphic designers strive to author messages as well as give them shape. Based in the Netherlands, Mieke Gerritzen uses graphics and multimedia to elucidate issues of network fatigue and information overload. Her Celebrity wallpaper, a pattern made from dozens of tiny portraits of famous people, taps the repetitive energy of mass media to generate a dense visual texture. Public-service campaigns deliver arguments in a more direct way. Michael Bierut's Green Patriot campaign (fig. 9), commissioned by The Canary Project, uses the tough idiom of World War II propaganda to promote sustainability. Posted on city buses in Cleveland, Ohio, one poster proclaims, "This bus is an assault vehicle in the fight against global warming." On the Web, videos such as *The Girl Effect* (fig. 10), *The Story of Stuff,* and *L.A. Earthquake: Get Ready* use hard-hitting content and Web links to provide viewers with easy ways to learn more and take action in response to urgent issues.

Journalists, scientists, activists, and artists are using data visualization to cast light on social and environmental phenomena. A map or diagram can reveal patterns and relationships that are harder to recognize in a table of numbers or a long verbal description. At *The New York Times* (fig. 11), visual journalists combine rigorous reporting with interactive technologies and information-design strategies to illuminate and explain everything from U.S. immigration trends to parking ticket hotspots in Manhattan. Approaching information design as a tool people can use, Green Map Systems (fig. 12) has created icons and mapping systems used by environmentalists around the world to document green spaces, biking paths, endangered habitats, and more.

The founders of Worldmapper (fig. 13) have collected data about dozens of global economic factors, from population

fig. 7

fig. 8

fig. 9

fig. 10

fig. 11

fig. 12

Communication

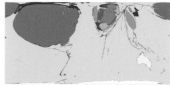

fig. 13

growth to energy use. They feed the numbers into an algorithm that changes the relative size of geographic areas, yielding maps that instantly reveal disparities between the developed and developing worlds. In 1990, only three million people worldwide had access to the Internet; 73% of them were living in the United States and 15% were in Western Europe. By 2002, there were 631 million Internet users worldwide, and use had spread across Asia, South America, northern and southeastern Africa, and the Middle East, profoundly changing the geographic shape of communication.

All fields of design practice, from product and fashion design to architecture and landscape design, rely on systems of media and messaging to develop and promote ideas. Designers comment on the world through objects and images designed to stimulate thought and provoke action. Tools like Twitter (fig. 14) are changing the way journalism is produced and consumed, even as traditional news organizations are using design and technology to reinvent themselves. Too much communication can become its own form of pollution, clouding our lives with its imploring, incessant buzz. Good design helps people cut through the haze and find the information they want as well as surprising them with fresh and unexpected thinking.

fig. 14

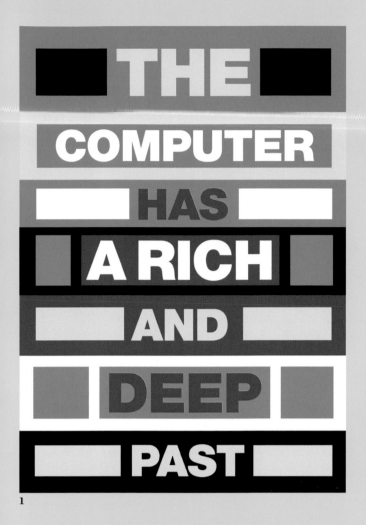

1

PERSONALSPACE
JUNKSPACE
VIRTUALSPACE
CELLSPACE
VISUALSPACE
FREESPACE
PUBLICSPACE
NETWORKSPACE
SOCIALSPACE
COMMERCIALSPACE
WORKSPACE
CYBERSPACE
SMARTSPACE
AUGMENTEDSPACE

2

All Media Wallpaper and Paintings

A graphic designer working in the Netherlands, Mieke Gerritzen explores the cultural impact of mass media through publications, exhibitions, videos, and events. Through her not-for-profit organization, All Media, she mobilizes the bombastic language of tabloid newspapers and hard-sell advertising to create a new kind of billboard that spreads ideas rather than selling products.

For an exhibition of her work at the Mudac Design Museum in Lausanne, Switzerland, in 2007, she commissioned a factory in China to create a series of hand-rendered paintings of her posters. Ordering the paintings over the Internet, Gerritzen provided the manufacturer with digital files that factory workers converted by hand into one-of-a-kind art objects. The painting *Everyone is a Designer* began as a book (published in 2003) consisting of slogans, headlines, and logos about the pervasive grip of media around public and private life. Gerritzen argues that everyone can become a designer by taking charge of communications tools—if not, they risk being designed themselves by the constant barrage of sales and marketing messages.

Gerritzen's Celebrity wallpaper, also presented in her 2007 exhibition, consists of fifty small-scale portraits of famous people, from Saddam Hussein to Mickey Mouse, stepped and repeated to create a dense pattern that enacts the obsessive logic of celebrity, with its relentless broadcast of familiar faces. Gerritzen's pattern is a colorful blur when viewed from a distance; it exposes its crowded cult of personality when viewed up close. Gerritzen, who produces limited-edition silk scarves

based on her patterns, updated the Celebrity pattern in 2009 to include new icons of fame and power, including President Barack Obama.

1–3 *The Computer, Space,* and *Everyone Is a Designer.* Mieke Gerritzen, All Media Paintings. The Netherlands, 2006–7. Canvas, oil paint

EVERYONE
IS A DESIGNER!
MANIFEST
//////FOR THE//////
DESIGN
ECONOMY

3

4 Artificial Biological Clock, concept. Revital Cohen. United Kingdom, 2008. Glass, nickel plated brass, acrylic resin, motor

5 The Bleached Reef. Margaret and Christine Wertheim, the Institute for Figuring; additional collaborators: Lily M. Chin, Ellen Davis, Dagmar Frinta, Evelyn Hardin, Helle Jorgensen, Nancy Lewis, Heather McCarren, Marianne Midelburg, Jill Schreier, Nadia Severns, Sarah Simons, Pamela Stiles, Barbara Van Elsen, Ann Wertheim, Barbara Wertheim, Chinese factory workers, and unknown doily makers. United States, 2007–present. Yarns, beads, baskets, felt, sand

4

5

Artificial Biological Clock

Revital Cohen, who studied under Anthony Dunne and Fiona Raby (designers of the Risk Watch) in England's Royal College of Art's Design Interactions department, designed the Artificial Biological Clock as an object to help us ponder the way emerging technologies and complicated realities fit into our lives. As Cohen argues, the ideal age for childbearing is constantly being challenged today because of blurred perceptions of women's reproductive cycles. Technologies such as in-vitro fertilization and egg freezing, mounting pressure on women to pursue careers, and the use of contraceptive hormones all contribute to distorted readings of the body's reproductive signals. The Artificial Biological Clock "compensates for this increasingly lost instinct . . . given to a woman by her parents or partner." It "reacts to information from her doctor, therapist, and bank manager via an online service. When she is physically, mentally, and financially ready to conceive the object awakes, seeking her attention." Works like this one, known as critical design, are an important part of the contemporary design discourse. They raise debate about the implications of emerging technologies in our everyday lives, using design to explore ethical, cultural, and psychological questions. Cohen's clock comments on how our continued attempt to control time is altering one of our most basic human functions, and acts as a "reminder of the temporary and fragile nature of fertility," causing us to reflect on what has become, perhaps, the overcomplicated nature of contemporary human life.
—*Andrea Lipps*

The Bleached Reef

The Bleached Reef is a small part of a much larger installation known as the *Hyperbolic Crochet Coral Reef,* which is being orchestrated by twin sisters Margaret and Christine Wertheim of the Los Angeles–based Institute for Figuring. The Crochet Reef project was conceived in 2005 by the Wertheims as a response to the devastation of coral reefs worldwide due to the effects of global warming, increasing water temperatures and the acidification of our oceans.

The first sign that corals are stressed manifests in large-scale "bleaching" events, in which whole sections of reef turn white. If conditions do not quickly improve, the corals begin to die. The Bleached Reef is a handcrafted invocation of this environmental tragedy. The Crochet Reef project as a whole has become an unintended world-wide movement that now engages many thousands of women across the U.S., the U.K., Australia, Latvia, Japan, South Africa, and elsewhere.

The distinctly crenulated, or irregular and wavy, forms seen in living corals are examples of a mathematical structure known as hyperbolic space. The discovery that this type of geometric structure could be modeled in crochet was first made in 1997 by Dr. Daina Taimina, a mathematician working at Cornell University. During the course of the Crochet Reef project, the Wertheims and other contributors have expanded on Dr. Taimina's techniques to evolve a new taxonomy of crochet coral species. The resulting woolen ecology is the byproduct of an unlikely fusion of mathematics, marine biology, a traditionally feminine handicraft, environmental consciousness-raising, and collective art practice.

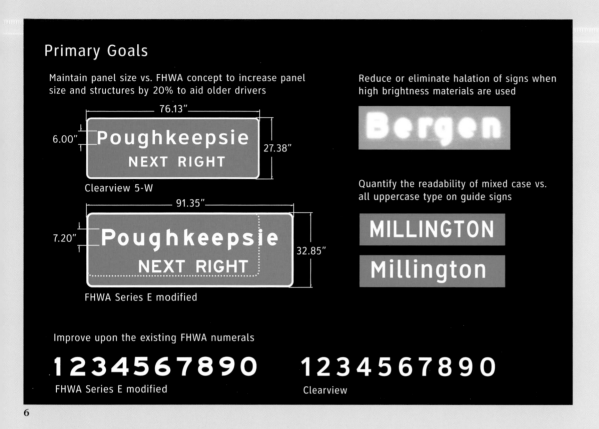

Primary Goals

Maintain panel size vs. FHWA concept to increase panel size and structures by 20% to aid older drivers

Poughkeepsie
NEXT RIGHT

Clearview 5-W

Poughkeepsie
NEXT RIGHT

FHWA Series E modified

Reduce or eliminate halation of signs when high brightness materials are used

Bergen

Quantify the readability of mixed case vs. all uppercase type on guide signs

MILLINGTON

Millington

Improve upon the existing FHWA numerals

1234567890
FHWA Series E modified

1234567890
Clearview

6

ClearviewHwy® Typeface

Few people slow down to consider the design of road signs, yet most of us interact with them every day. Since the 1940s, the U.S. Federal Highway Administration has used a standard typeface, commonly known as Highway Gothic. Graphic designer Donald Meeker, working with typeface designer James Montalbano and a team of human factors scientists and other experts, have spent over fifteen years trying to replace Highway Gothic with something better. Approaching the project with passion and zeal, they have struggled against a far-flung and recalcitrant bureaucracy.

What's wrong with Highway Gothic? The open spaces in the characters, such as the bowl of the lowercase "a," are too small, making the letters hard to read, especially at night, when headlights hit the reflective surface of the sign and make the text blurry. This effect, called halation, causes the cramped open spaces in Highway Gothic to look even smaller, making it difficult for drivers—especially older drivers—to distinguish among different letterforms. Making the letters bigger to accommodate older drivers would address the problem, but it would also mean manufacturing larger signs. Bigger signs would generate more visual clutter as well as enormous infrastructure costs.

Meeker and Montalbano created Clearview, a set of elegant, readable letterforms optimized for distance reading. The characters have enlarged counters, yet occupy no more space than Highway Gothic. After dozens of iterations and rigorous testing, Clearview received interim approval from the FHWA in 2004, and over twenty states are now using it for various applications. The struggle to transform the nation's signage, however, is far from over. The designers are now testing characters for use in dark-on-light conditions and developing a proportional grid system for creating more consistent, logically arranged signs. They released road sign versions of Clearview in Cyrllic, Greek, and extended Latin in 2009.

6 ClearviewHwy® typeface. Donald Meeker and Christopher O'Hara, Meeker & Associates, and James Montalbano, Terminal Design Inc. Human-factors research: Philip Garvey and Martin Pietrucha, The Larson Transportation Institute at Pennsylvania State University, and Susan T. Chrysler, Texas Transportation Institute. United States, 2004–present.

7

8

Etón FR 600 Radio

The Etón FR 600 radio is designed for use in emergency
situations, when access to power may be interrupted and communication is vital to safety. Featuring weather and worldwide
multiband radio channels, the unit also serves as a walkie-
talkie, cell-phone charger, flashlight, siren, and SOS light beacon.
Powered by a solar cell as well as a hand-crank dynamo, the FR
600 functions off the grid and without batteries. The hand crank
uses a barrel-style hinge to fold flat against the front of the unit.
The solar panel, which can power the radio even in overcast
weather, is integrated into a bridge across the top of the device
that also serves as a handle. The designers hope to "mitigate
the emotion of fear" with the radio's large-scale controls and
compact, rugged styling (inspired, in part, by rally cars). The
radio is marketed as a consumer product for outdoor adventure
and home preparedness as well as a tool for rescue workers.

7 Etón FR 600 radio. Daniel Harden and Sam
Benavidez, Whipsaw Inc. Manufactured by Etón
Corporation. Designed United States, manufactured
China, 2008. PC/ABS plastic, elastomer

Etsy

Etsy is an online international marketplace for handmade goods
that connects makers to consumers. Founded in 2005, Etsy taps
into the thriving do-it-yourself community by creating tools that
make it easy for artisans to share their wares. Etsy lets craft-savvy
consumers buy anything from hand-knitted baby booties to jew-
elry, digital prints, and furniture. Products like Rachel Wright's
hand-embellished Maori tattoo shirt or Necklush's looped scarf
are one-of-a-kind products that combine skilled craftsmanship
with visual invention.

From the beginning, Etsy has experimented with its online
interface, offering diverse ways to find and compare goods. Users
can search for products by color or geographic region as well as
via basic categories such as knitting, clothing, or paper goods.
Etsy's "Time Machine" function pulls up recently listed items,
while "Pounce" finds undiscovered shops or ones that have just
made a sale. Once a buyer has made a choice, all sales transactions
are made directly between buyer and seller; Etsy collects a small
commission on each sale. Etsy's Virtual Labs consist of multi-user
tools for education and communication, such as online classrooms
and galleries.

Etsy helps its sellers become self-empowered entrepreneurs
by holding virtual seminars, classes, and community meetings.
As of June 2009, Etsy had over 2.6 million members, including
250,000 sellers. In 2008 and 2009, a period that saw sharp

9

10

11

Furumai

declines in consumption throughout the economy, Etsy's sales actually grew. Buying goods directly from makers turns out to be economical while appealing to people's longing for authentic experiences with objects and the people who make them.

8 Etsy. Founders: Robert Kalin, Chris Maguire, and Haim Schoppik. United States, 2005–present

9 Maori tattoo shirt. Rachel Wright, Toolgrrl Designs. United States, 2009. Cotton dress shirt, hand embellished with black jersey, red embroidery floss

10 Necklush, natural with dark grey print. Stephano Diaz and Troy Mattison Hicks, Necklush/Microfantastic. United States, 2008. Organic cotton, water-based, nontoxic ink

11–12 *Furumai*. Kotaro Watanabe, Kinya Tagawa, and Motohide Hatanaka, Takram Design Engineering, and Taku Satoh, Taku Satoh Design Office. Japan, 2007–present. Paper, water-repellent coating

Furumai, which means behavior or dance in Japanese, is an installation created for the *Water* exhibition at 21_21 Design Sight in Tokyo in 2007. The project consists of paper plates treated selectively with an invisible water-repellent coating. As visitors interact with the plates, beads of water dance about the surface, creating surprising visual effects. In one, drops gather in a baby's eye, while others form abstract, three-dimensional patterns. The designers hope that as people interact with these tiny droplets of water, they will recognize water's myriad manifestations—as tears, rain, and the medium of life itself.

12

LEARN
GIVE
SHARE

the girl effect

THE WORLD IS A MESS.

AGREE or DISAGREE

THE GIRL EFFECT CAN'T HAPPEN WITHOUT YOU
JOIN THE MOVEMENT ON FACEBOOK ›

INVEST IN HER FUTURE NOW
DONATE HERE ›

ABOUT   FACT SHEET   YOUR MOVE   PRIVACY POLICY   TERMS OF USE   PLAY THE GIRL EFFECT VIDEO

13

The Girl Effect Campaign

The Girl Effect is a communications platform rooted in the theory that investing in adolescent girls in the developing world offers the greatest opportunity for change for them, their families, and their communities. When girls win, the world benefits. The Nike Foundation created the Girl Effect with significant financial and intellectual contributions by the NoVo Foundation and Nike Inc.

In many developing countries, impoverished girls are invisible and neglected. They are often denied education after the onset of puberty, and risk being forced into unwanted sexual activity, early marriages and childbearing, and exposure to HIV. If these girls were empowered with educational and economic opportunities and given sovereignty over their own bodies, they would increase their own health and wealth as well as those of their communities. That is the Girl Effect—the powerful social and economic change brought about when girls have the opportunity to participate.

The Girl Effect video was created to inform the public about the power of girls. It is presented entirely through text and music, using minimal means to elicit a powerful emotional response. By stating its premise in simple, direct prose, delivered through a beautifully timed typographic animation, the video demonstrates the power of design as a communications medium. The supporting Web site, GirlEffect.org, makes it easy for any viewer—from grade-school students to government officials—to take meaningful action.

D SEE HER GET A LOAN

14

UNEXPECTED SOLUTION

15

THE REVOLUTION
WILL BE LED BY A
12-YEAR-OLD GIRL

IF YOU WANT TO END POVERTY AND HELP THE DEVELOPING WORLD, THE BEST THING YOU CAN DO IS INVEST TIME, ENERGY, AND FUNDING INTO ADOLESCENT GIRLS. IT'S CALLED THE GIRL EFFECT, BECAUSE GIRLS ARE UNIQUELY CAPABLE OF INVESTING IN THEIR COMMUNITIES AND MAKING THE WORLD BETTER. BUT HERE ARE 10 THINGS THAT STAND IN THEIR WAY:

1 LET'S SEE SOME ID
Without a birth certificate or an ID, a girl in the developing world doesn't know and can't prove her age, protect herself from child marriage, open a bank account, vote, or eventually get a job. That makes it hard to save the world.

2 ILLITERACY DOES NOT LOOK GOOD ON A RESUME...
70% of the world's out-of-school children are girls. Girls deserve better. They deserve quality education and the safe environments and support that allow them to get to school on time and stay there through adolescence.

4 THE FACE OF HIV IS INCREASINGLY YOUNG AND FEMALE
When girls are educated about HIV, they stand a better chance of protecting themselves. But education is not enough. Girls need to be empowered and supported to make their own choices.

3 ...AND PREGNANCY DOESN'T LOOK GOOD ON A LITTLE GIRL
Child marriages are the norm in many cultures where girls' bodies aren't considered their own property. Pregnancy is the leading cause of death for girls 15-18 years old. Girls have a right to be able to protect their health and their bodies.

5 A NICE PLACE TO WORK WOULD BE NICE
If girls have the skills for safe and decent work, if they understand their rights, if they are financially literate and considered for nontraditional jobs at an appropriate age, if they get their fair share of training and internships, they will be armed and ready for economic independence.

6 THE CHECK IS IN THE MAIL, BUT IT'S GOING TO YOUR BROTHER
LESS THAN TWO CENTS of every international aid dollar is directed to girls. And yet when a girl has resources, she will reinvest them in her community at a much higher rate than a boy would. If the goal is health, wealth, and stability for all, a girl is the best investment.

7 ADOLESCENT GIRLS AREN'T JUST "FUTURE WOMEN"
They're girls. They deserve their own category. They need to be a distinct group when we talk about aid, education, sports, civic participation, health, and economics. Yes, they are future mothers. But they actually live in the present.

8 LAWS WERE MADE TO BE ENFORCED
Girls need advocates to write, speak up, lobby and work to enforce good laws and change discriminatory policies.

9 SHE SHOULD BE A STATISTIC
We won't know how to help girls until we know what's going on with them. Hey, all you governments and NGOs and social scientists: You're accountable! We need an annual girl report card for every country so we can keep track of which girls are thriving and which girls are not.

10 EVERYONE GETS ON BOARD OR WE'RE ALL OVERBOARD
Boys, girls, moms, dads. If we don't all rally to support girls, nothing is going to change. Not for them, and not for us. Change starts with you. So get going.

girleffect.org

16

13–16 The Girl Effect Campaign, video, Web site, and poster. Wieden + Kennedy. Animation design and direction: Matt Smithson; additional designers: Julia Blackburn, Paul Bjork, Jelly Helm, Steve Luker, Ginger Robinson, Jessica Vacek, Tyler Whisnand. Production: Curious Pictures and Joint Editorial. Client: Nike Foundation. United States, 2008. Poster: lithograph

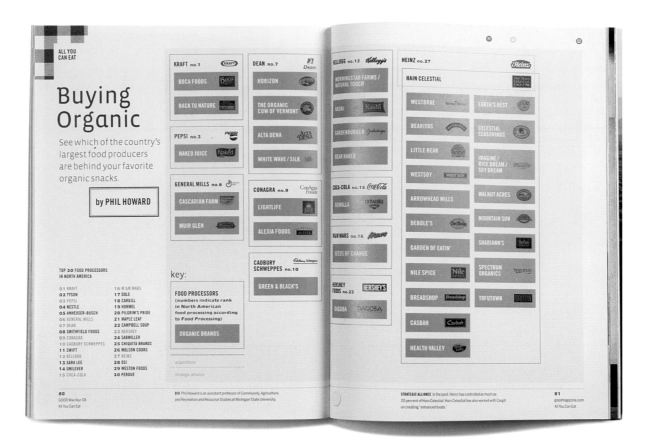

17

GOOD Magazine

Founded by Ben Goldhirsh in 2006, *GOOD* is a new kind of design magazine. In its pages, design is a recurring issue, but not the primary subject matter. Design continually resurfaces as a tool and inspiration for furthering the publication's larger agenda: to make a better world, environmentally, socially, and economically. With stories on social entrepreneurship, new energy technologies, and green mass transit, the magazine appeals to young, educated readers seeking optimistic analysis of the world's problems. Directed at "people who give a damn," *GOOD* is fun to read and fun to look at.

Graphic design is integral to the magazine's editorial success. Design director Scott Stowell created its friendly but hard-hitting look, with its bold headlines and elaborately produced information graphics. Like its writing style, the magazine's visual tone is direct, clever, and crisp. *GOOD* often looks at business from fresh angles, and the magazine has evolved innovative business strategies of its own. When signing up for a subscription, the reader gets to direct the full price ($20) to a not-for-profit organization. Ideas like this make people feel *good* about subscribing to a magazine.

18

17–18 *GOOD* magazine. Scott Stowell with Susan Barber, Robert A. Di Ieso, Jr., Gary Fogelson, Carol Hayes, Serfican Ozcan, Nicholas Rock, and Ryan Thacker, Open. United States, 2006–present. Offset lithograph

19–20 Green Map system. Wendy E. Brawer with Té Baybute, Beth Ferguson, Eric Goldhagen, Yoko Ishibashi, Risa Ishikawa, Millie Lin, Carlos Martinez, Aika Nakashima, Akiko Rokube, Andrew Sass, Alex Thomas, Thomas Turnbull, Dominica Williamson, and Yelena Zolotorevskaya, Green Map System. Designed globally, founded 1995, Version 3 icons 2008

19

Green Map System

Founded by Wendy Brawer in 1995, Green Map System supports local communities around the world, providing tools for charting green living and ecological, social, and cultural resources. Four hundred locally designed Green Maps have been published, promoting environmental change in 600 cities, towns, and villages in fifty-five countries. Adults and youth have created hundreds of additional maps in workshops that help citizens engage with sustainability issues where they live. The maps feature Green Map Icons, a collection of symbols depicting dozens of ecological and social features, from bicycle paths and public libraries to deforestation and brownfield sites. Noted for their simple design and intuitive iconography, these graphic marks are a common vocabulary that unifies Green Maps created around the world.

In 2009, the organization launched the Open Green Map, an interactive Web site that merges open technology, universal design, and local knowledge to create easily accessed maps that invite the public's comments, images, and ratings. This social mapping platform shares its content with multilingual audiences on mobile phones and diverse online formats.

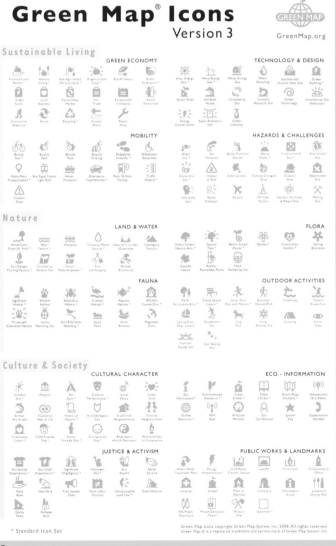

20

21

22

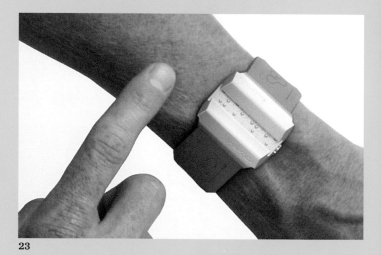

23

Green Patriot Posters

Historically, the environmental movement has been associated with the culture of liberal politics, leading some people to regard global warming as an ideological construct rather than a real and urgent crisis. The Green Patriot Posters project, created by Ed Morris and Dmitri Siegel, seeks to revive and redirect the attitude of World War II propaganda, which employed heroic icons such as Rosie the Riveter to unite people from across the political spectrum around a common cause.

Mass transit makes America stronger by reducing dependence on petroleum as well as by cutting down on greenhouse emissions. In the summer of 2008, Morris and Siegel invited Michael Bierut to design posters that emphasize this point to commuters on buses in Cleveland, OH. Bierut—a Cleveland native who now works in New York City and uses mass transit nearly every day—employed bold copy and simple graphics to proclaim the patriotic value of riding the bus.

In addition to commissioning campaigns by Bierut and other well-known designers, the Green Patriot Posters project invites any designer or concerned citizen to upload posters to its Web site. The initiative is one of several programs produced by The Canary Project, one of the first and only organizations in the United States dedicated exclusively to art and climate change.

Haptica Braille Timepiece

For the visually impaired, reading the time has typically meant either tracing the watch hands on an exposed watch face, which leads to slow and inaccurate readings, or receiving an audible signal from a talking watch, which inhibits a user's ability to check the time unnoticed. In order to provide a more effective user experience, designer David Chavez created the Haptica watch, a Braille timepiece concept that provides a silent, accurate reading. The watch displays a row of four numbers in military-time format. The numbers are written in Braille, placed on dials that rotate in and out of a channel as time passes. Users read the time by running their fingers over the raised Braille display. Based on end-user research with students and faculty at the Braille Institute in Anaheim, CA, Chavez's design negates the stigma of a disability while providing an intuitive ergonomic interface.
—Andrea Lipps

21–22 *Green Patriot* posters. Michael Bierut, Pentagram. Creative directors: Ed Morris and Dmitri Siegel, The Canary Project. United States, 2008. Printed on busmark and polystyrene

23 Haptica Braille timepiece, concept. David Chavez. United States, 2007–9. Stainless-steel case, rubber strap

24–25 iPhone. Apple Industrial Design Team, Apple. United States, 2009. Arsenic-free glass, stainless steel, polycarbonate

26 Kindle wireless reading device. Amazon Kindle Team, a division of Amazon.com. United States, 2009. Plastic, acrylic, aluminum, E Ink®

24

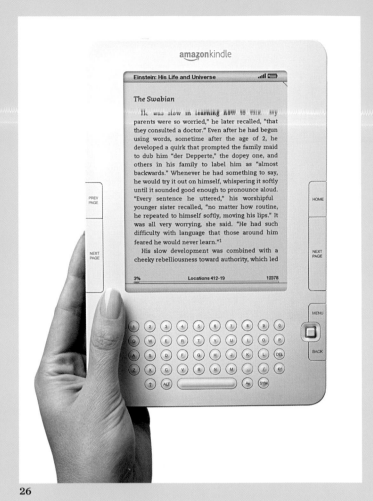

26

iPhone

The design of the Apple iPhone accentuates virtual interface over physical presence. The object itself is a sleek, monolithic slab that recedes in favor of what's happening on the screen. While the traditional cell phone marries a mechanical keyboard with a small screen, the front of the iPhone gives way almost completely to a touch-sensitive surface, which responds to a tap, flick or pinch of the fingers. iPhone is far more than a device for making calls. It combines three devices in one: a revolutionary mobile phone, a widescreen iPod, and a breakthrough Internet device. Introduced in January 2007, the iPhone became an instant design icon. The App store helps users do more with iPhone. Consumers can choose from a vast range of applications in 20 categories, including games, business, news, sports, health, reference and travel. For many consumers, it is a product synonymous with "design."

25

Kindle Wireless Reading Device

In the 1990s, Amazon pioneered the use of digital systems to sell physical stuff. In November 2007, the company introduced its own tangible product, the Kindle. Although commentators used to view electronic books as poor substitutes for the warmth, tactility, and elegance of printed paper, the Kindle hit a chord with consumers, as did Sony's Reader and several other new digital-book devices. The e-book was an idea whose time had come.

Amazon's free wireless Whispernet service allows users to quickly download books, magazines, and blogs from nearly anywhere in the United States. Purchasing new titles is a simple transaction: Customers' Kindle accounts link directly to their primary Amazon accounts. Publications download straight to the device, which never has to be synced to a computer station. The second-generation Kindle, introduced in 2008, is sleeker with an improved interface. The 2009 Kindle DX features a larger screen, native PDF support, and landscape mode to provide a better experience for reading newspapers, magazines, personal and professional documents, and textbooks.

The Kindle employs "electronic paper," a technology created by E Ink in Cambridge, MA. Unlike a typical computer screen, which glows, the Kindle screen is reflective, like paper. Digital ink consists of tiny capsules filled with black and white fluid. An electrostatic charge pushes white capsules to the top layer and pulls black capsules downward, creating a highly readable surface that remains in place until a new charge is received.

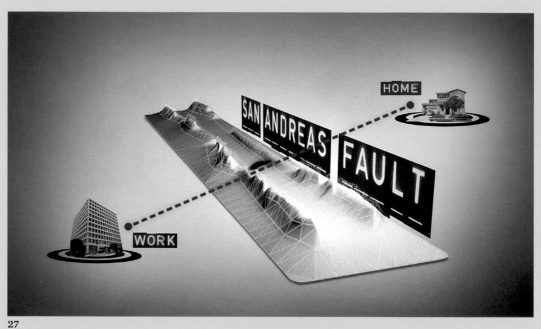

27

L.A. Earthquake: Get Ready Campaign

Users can adjust the size of the text as well as using the text-to-speech feature to create an automated audio conversion.

As of 2008, less than one percent of all book sales in the United States were digital, but the market has been growing rapidly; overall e-book sales increased more than threefold between 2007 and 2008. Because of their convenience and readability, electronic books are being embraced as a new kind of reading experience.

A major earthquake could strike Southern California at any time, causing widespread injury and death, property loss, and disruption of services. It is unrealistic to expect government emergency teams to sweep in and instantly deal with the potential aftermath. Each individual and household must be prepared for this possible disaster.

That's the message of the L.A. Earthquake: Get Ready campaign, a multi-pronged endeavor organized by Designmatters, at Art Center College of Design in Pasadena, CA, in partnership with dozens of public and private organizations. Directed by Mariana Amatullo, Designmatters is a research and advocacy initiative and educational department that engages the Art Center community in social-impact projects.

Designmatters built the campaign around a simulation of a magnitude 7.8 earthquake striking the Southern San Andreas Fault. Scientists predict that such an earthquake could kill 1,800 people, injure 50,000, and cause $200 billion in damage. Nearly three million Californians used the campaign's simulation to drill for disaster at schools and businesses around the state; they documented their experiences online at ShakeOut.org. The short film *Preparedness Now*, designed and directed by Art Center alumnus Theo Alexopoulos, is an animated photomontage that uses raw, direct imagery to bring home the seriousness of the problem. *The L.A. Earthquake Sourcebook*, designed by Stefan Sagmeister, is a richly illustrated collection of expert commentary on the science of earthquakes and their potential social impact. The campaign

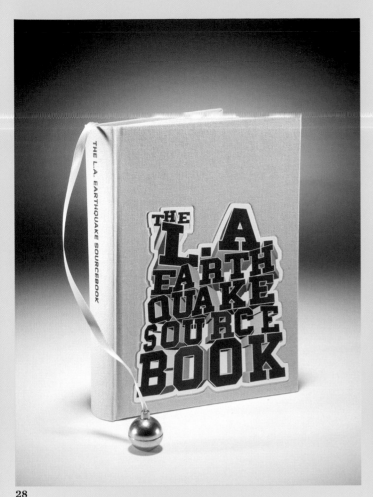

28

Communication

29

also included an educational rally in downtown Los Angeles and an online simulation called AfterShock, produced with The Institute for the Future. The project, which took over three years to implement, mobilized skills from across the fields of graphic and interaction design, film, animation, illustration, and others, demonstrating the essential role designers can play in public education.

L.A. Earthquake: Get Ready campaign.
Designmatters, Art Center College of Design

27 *Preparedness Now* video. Direction and motion graphics: Theo Alexopoulos. United States, 2008–9

28 *The L.A. Earthquake Sourcebook.* Stefan Sagmeister, Sagmeister Inc. Concept: Richard Koshalek and Mariana Amatullo. Printed by Capital Offset Company Inc. United States, 2008–9. Die-cut letter outline on front and back covers, Brillianta cloth cover, ribbon bookmaker with attached bobble

Learning Landscape

Learning Landscape takes a creative approach to elementary math education. Using a grid of half-submerged tires as a setting for math games, this simple system can be built in nearly any part of the world from readily available cast-off materials. The concept comes from Project H Design, a not-for-profit organization that uses design to improve life around the globe. The "H" stands for humanity, habitats, health, and happiness, and Emily Pilloton, founder of Project H, takes a broad view of sustainability and social justice: "We can design 'green' all day long, but if all that results are more bamboo coffee tables for luxury markets, green design is destined to get a bad rap."

Incorporating numbers but not languages or culturally specific iconography, the Learning Landscape is at once universal and locally adaptable. The first Learning Landscape was installed at the Kutamba School for AIDS Orphans in Uganda in 2009. Using chalk to mark numbers on the tires, teachers and students play a variety of games that capitalize on the natural excitement of group competition and physical movement. The tires become an outdoor classroom when fitted with integrated benches.

Learning Landscapes have been installed in Mao, Dominican Republic, as well as in Bertie County, North Carolina, where teachers are creating lessons in geography, language arts, and science as well as math. Plans are underway for a tabletop version of the game (created by the industrial-design firm nonobject) that will be available for retail purchase. Like many Project H endeavors, Learning Landscape is a simple, scalable idea with global implications, developed in direct interaction with local communities.

157 Why Design Now?

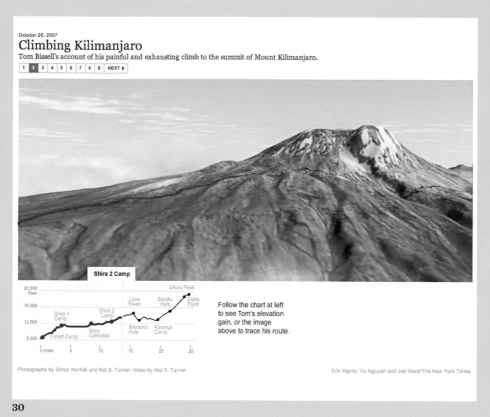

October 26, 2007

Climbing Kilimanjaro

Tom Bissell's account of his painful and exhausting climb to the summit of Mount Kilimanjaro.

| 1 | 2 | 3 | 4 | 5 | 6 | 7 | 8 | 9 | NEXT ▶ |

Shira 2 Camp

Follow the chart at left to see Tom's elevation gain, or the image above to trace his route.

Photographs by Simon Norfolk and Nat S. Turner; Video by Nat S. Turner

Erin Aigner, Vu Nguyen and Joe Ward/The New York Times

30

The New York Times visualization and interaction projects. Steve Duenes, graphics director; Matthew Ericson, deputy graphics director; Matthew Bloch, graphics editor; Amanda Cox, graphics editor; Hannah Fairfield, graphics editor; Xaquín González Veira, graphics editor; Vu Nguyen, graphics editor; Andrew Devigal, multimedia editor; Tom Jackson, senior multimedia producer; Gabriel Dance, senior multimedia producer; research and development: Michael Young, creative technologist; Alexis Lloyd, creative technologist; Nick Bilton, design integration editor; Ted Roden, creative technologist. United States, 2007–present

30 "Climbing Kilimanjaro." Erin Aigner, Vu Nguyen, and Joe Ward, *The New York Times*. United States, October 26, 2007.

31 "Immigration Explorer." Matthew Bloch, *The New York Times*. United States, November 26, 2008.

The New York Times Visualization and Interaction Projects

The graphics department at *The New York Times* includes journalists with strong skills in visualization as well as experts in statistics, cartography, programming, and 3-D software. Graphics director Steve Duenes explains that the people on his staff generally don't call themselves graphic designers. "We're journalists," he says. "We are drawing on the traditions of *The Times* and creating a direction on the Web that employs technology to surprise and engage readers while still clarifying and explaining the world around us."

In the early years of the Web, *The Times* published print graphics online as static images, but now the medium permits complex interactions as well as video, animation, sound, and dynamic content. A 2009 map of U.S. immigration allows users to see patterns over time and place, tracking populations from twenty-three different regions of the world. An interactive 3-D travelogue from 2007 traced Tom Bissell's harrowing climb to the top of Mount Kilimanjaro, coordinating his path with photographs shot along the way and an ongoing account of his rising heart rate and plummeting oxygenation level.

On another floor of *The New York Times* headquarters, interaction designers are rethinking how news can be delivered and displayed in the future. *The Times* Reader changes the layout of the news in response to what device the user is employing. Customized news content can follow specific users from computer screen to phone to television to a print-on-demand kiosk, keeping track of

where readers have left off or where they are geographically. Other experiments use proximity sensors to register the presence of users and to present news onscreen based on a person's identity or their proximity to the device. Concepts like these are being tested and implemented now with live content from *The Times*.

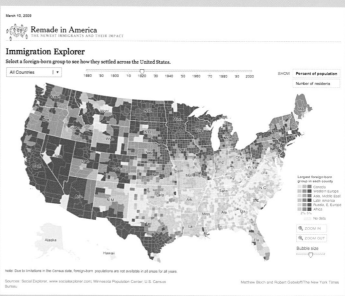

March 10, 2009

Remade in America
THE NEWEST IMMIGRANTS AND THEIR IMPACT

Immigration Explorer

Select a foreign-born group to see how they settled across the United States.

All Countries

1880 90 1900 10 1920 30 1940 50 1960 70 1980 90 2000

SHOW Percent of population / Number of residents

Largest foreign-born group in each county

Canada / Western Europe / Asia, Middle East / Latin America / Russia, E. Europe / Africa

No data

ZOOM IN
ZOOM OUT

Bubble size

Note: Due to limitations in the Census data, foreign-born populations are not available in all areas for all years.

Sources: Social Explorer, www.socialexplorer.com; Minnesota Population Center; U.S. Census Bureau

Matthew Bloch and Robert Gebeloff/The New York Times

31

32   33

OLPC (One Laptop Per Child) XOXO Laptop

Launched in 2005, One Laptop per Child is a global initiative that aims to change the future for two billion of the world's poorest children, who have little or no access to formal education. By providing kids with networked computers, OLPC aims to put the tools of learning directly into the hands of the next generation. This complex undertaking involves coordinating with dozens of world governments and non-governmental organizations as well as developing new paradigms for laptop computers.

The first-generation XO laptop, designed by Yves Béhar, costs $200 and is being used by two million children around the world. The XOXO, also designed by Béhar, was announced in 2008 and is slated for release in 2010. In place of the fixed keyboard/screen combination that has dominated portable computers since the late 1970s, the XOXO consists of two touch screens. These twin surfaces allow the user to fluidly transform the object's function. In laptop mode, one screen becomes a keyboard while the other is a display area. In book mode, the double screens face each other like the pages of a book. In tablet mode, the screens lie flat to become a single surface for collaborative learning. The laptop is built to withstand harsh weather and rough treatment in areas where many kids have no access to schools, desks, or books.

The OLPC concept dates back to the 1960s, when computer scientist Seymour Papert predicted that computers would become a powerful learning tool for kids. He believed that children in poor, rural communities would be as eager and able to embrace digital tools as kids in prosperous areas, and he proved it with on-the-ground experiments in the 1980s. The idea of using computers to help kids "learn how to learn" became a driving principle at the MIT Media Lab, founded in 1985. OLPC is the brainchild of Nicholas Negroponte, founder and chairman emeritus of the Media Lab. The ultimate goal of OLPC is not to distribute any particular laptop, but to give kids direct access to networked computing.

32-33 One Laptop per Child XOXO laptop, prototype. Yves Béhar and Bret Recor, fuseproject. Interface design: Lisa Strausfeld, Pentagram. Concept: Nicholas Negroponte, OLPC. United States, 2008. PC/ABS plastic, rubber

34

Polski Theater Banners

The Teatr Polski in Bydgoszcz, Poland, promotes events with large-scale banners that hang throughout the surrounding neighborhood. Designed by Jerzy Skakun and Joanna Górska of Homework, the banners, coordinated with additional advertising, programs, and publications, establish a brand for each production. Many of the performances address social issues in contemporary Poland. The designers sometimes create startling imagery by suggesting trauma to the banners themselves. For *Return of Odysseus*, a play about emigration, a hand appears to cut through the poster's surface with a knife. For *Terrorism/ Prisoners of Despair*, photographs of holes suggest a skull or masked face as well as destruction wrought by bombs or gunshot. These visual campaigns bring the narrative content of theater to the street via powerful, concise imagery.

35

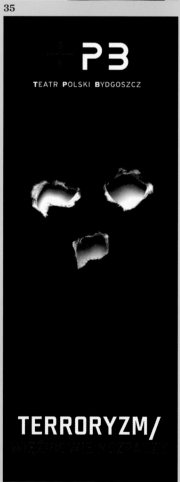

36

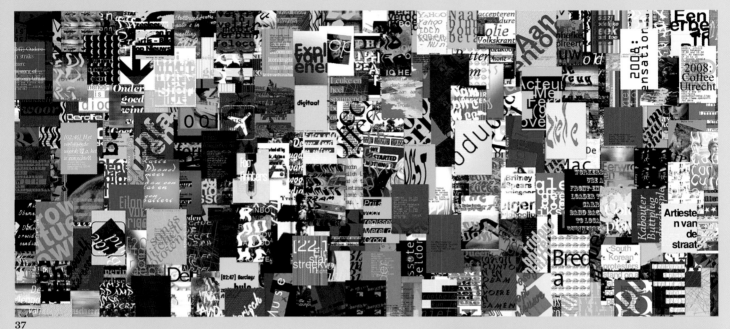

37

Posterwall for the Twenty-first Century

In addition to working with commercial software applications,
the Dutch design collective Lust writes its own code. Members
focus on designing an initial set of rules and then allowing the
visual form to emerge automatically, thus shifting the design
process from the search for an ideal solution to an analysis of
initial conditions and the construction of a system. The end
results of the process are variable and unknown. The Posterwall
for the Twenty-first Century was created for the Graphic Design
Museum in Breda, the Netherlands, where it is projected at the
end of the exhibition *One Hundred Years of Dutch Graphic Design.*
A computer program gathers content from the Internet about
cultural events in the Netherlands and automatically formats
the data into digital posters. By automating such familiar design
principles as repetition, layering, dynamic angles, and contrasting scale and color, the code produces a new poster every five
minutes, yielding 600 unique compositions per day. The resulting pieces are raw rather than polished, using default fonts and
randomly assembled components to comment on the ubiquitous
texture of digital media.

38

39 Risk Watch, "Do You Want to Replace the Existing Normal?" series. Anthony Dunne and Fiona Raby, Dunne & Raby, and Michael Anastassiades. United Kingdom, 2007. Silicone, electronics, MP3 player

40–41 *The Story of Stuff.* Author: Annie Leonard; creative directors: Louis Fox and Jonah Sachs, Free Range Studios; producer: Erica Priggen, Free Range Studios. United States, 2007

40

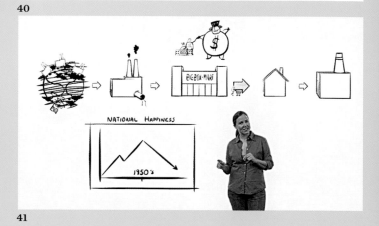

41

39

Risk Watch, "Do You Want to Replace the Existing Normal?" series

Anthony Dunne and Fiona Raby use product design to provoke conversation about contemporary technology and social life. They coined the phrase "critical design" to describe their use of products as a medium of discourse. It is neither a production-oriented commercial practice, nor is it art. Dunne and Raby explain, "We expect art to be shocking and extreme. Critical design needs to be closer to the everyday.... If it is regarded as art, it is easier to deal with, but if it remains design, it is more disturbing. It suggests that the everyday as we know it could be different, that things could change."

Dunne and Raby's Risk Watch is part of a series of pieces called "Do You Want to Replace the Existing Normal?" Rather than tell time, the watch reports information about current dangers, such as the political stability of the country the wearer is in or the current risk of contracting the H1N1 "swine flu" virus. The user presses the object's gray rubber nipple into his or her ear to receive an audio message. The watch employs the "normal" language of design to comment on the cultural effects of secrecy, security, and fear.

The Story of Stuff

The Story of Stuff originated as an informal lecture created by environmental activist Annie Leonard. Honing her performance over a ten-year period, she crafted an impassioned message about how products affect human society and the natural world as they make their way through the cycle of material extraction, manufacturing, consumption, and disposal.

Free Range Studios, a design agency known for producing startling social action videos such as *The Meatrix* and *Grocery Store Wars*, helped Leonard translate her lecture into a film. Together, they created a compact, punchy script around simple, active stories and iconic characters. Rather than present a straight animation, Free Range shot Leonard live in front of a green screen and synced the script with animated black-and-white line drawings that appear behind her in the video. Leonard's earthy, accessible persona combines with the simple animations to bring the piece to life.

The result is an engaging video that has been viewed over six million times on the Web and used in classroom presentations across the country. Although *The Story of Stuff* clocks in at twenty minutes—most viral marketing pieces last five minutes or less— it holds the viewers' attention with captivating tales of greed, waste, and opportunity.

42

Touch Magazine 2/3

Designer Sean Donahue set out to create a magazine that
addresses sighted and non-sighted readers simultaneously. His
magazine, called *Touch*, mixes Braille and Latin characters with
images and text printed with a technique called thermography,
which employs a special ink that swells when exposed to heat.
This inexpensive technology is commonly used by low-vision
communities, but rarely in an experimental way. The magazine's
content addresses issues, innovations, and services related to
sight-impaired users. According to Donahue, his inclusive design
methodology responds to the needs of the visually impaired
within the context of their interactions in and with the sighted
world. The magazine also serves as an inspiration to any designer
wishing to incorporate tactility into work for diverse audiences.

46

Touch Sight Camera

How can vision-impaired people make images of the world around them? Samsung's Touch Sight camera features a lightweight, flexible Braille display sheet in place of the LCD view-finding screen on a typical digital camera. The Touch Sight is designed to be held against the forehead, allowing the camera to become a third eye. This position provides an accurate view of the user's surroundings while also keeping the device steady. When the user presses the shutter, the camera embosses the display sheet with a raised, touchable image. The camera records three seconds of sound with each photograph, serving as a reference and reminder when the user reviews images later. The images and their associated sound files can be shared with other Touch Sight cameras and uploaded to different platforms.

47

46–47 Touch Sight camera, concept. Dan Hu, Fengshun Jiang, Jaehan Jin, Chueh Lee, Zhenhui Sun, Ning Xu, and Liqing Zhou, Samsung Design China, a design center of Samsung Electronics. China, 2008. Plastic, silica, flexible rubber

48 Twitter. Founders: Jack Dorsey, Evan Williams, and Biz Stone. Designer: Douglas Bowman. United States, 2006–present.

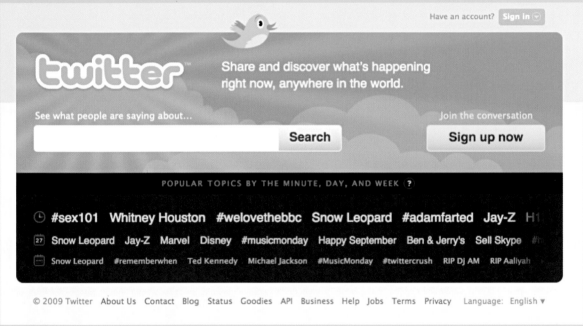

48

Twitter

Twitter is a free social-networking service that invites users to read and send short status messages and updates, called "tweets," that are circulated via many different channels, including SMS, Web, mobile Web, desktop applications, and mobile applications. Unlike email, tweets are intended as ambient communication— the recipient of a tweet is not necessarily expected to respond. Twitter users choose to "follow" other people in the network and receive updates from them. Your followers could know you personally or they could be interested in your point of view on a particular subject.

Sometimes called "micro-blogging," tweeting is defining the next generation of social media. By limiting the length of each message to 140 characters, Twitter created a rapid-fire medium that is used for everything from personal communication to on-the-ground real-time news reporting. Since the disputed 2009 elections in Iran, protesters have widely documented their dissent via Twitter, drawing international attention to unfolding events. While Iranian authorities were able to successfully block text messages sent via mobile phones, protesters found ways to circumvent barriers imposed on tweets.

Twitter was introduced in 2006 as a side project by a San Francisco firm named Obvious. Incorporated as Twitter Inc. in 2007, the service quickly gained notoriety as a popular way to share and explore information on the Internet. It has also become a powerful branding tool, used by companies, celebrities, and politicians to promote themselves, their products, and their opinions.

President Obama's 2008 election campaign used Twitter as well as Facebook and YouTube to build excitement and awareness among supporters. From its playful name, logo, and cheerful bird illustrations to its tidy, customizable user pages, Twitter's interface design embraces simplicity but not austerity.

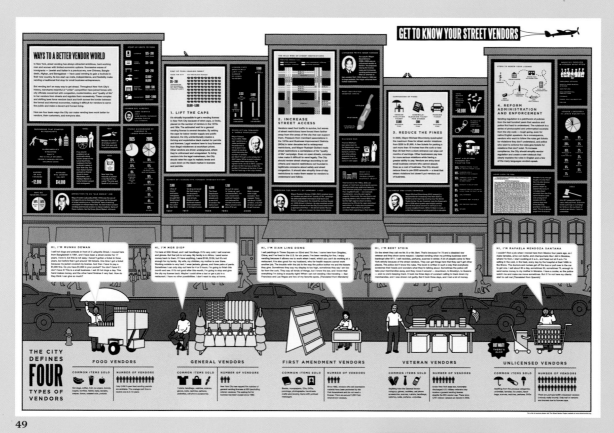

49

50

Vendor Power! Posters

Visual information can be a tool for empowerment. *Vendor Power!* is an illustrated fold-out guide that explains the rules, regulations, and rights pertaining to street vendors in New York City. Produced by the Center for Urban Pedagogy, it belongs to a series of posters called Making Policy Public. CUP invites not-for-profit organizations to submit content ideas and then connects them with graphic designers. Working collaboratively, the designers and organizations create a printed piece that illuminates a complex phenomenon or issue. The posters help particular communities—from street vendors to longshoremen—understand their political rights and opportunities.

Vendor Power! was created by the Street Vendor Project, an advocacy group, and Candy Chang, a designer and artist. Because many of the city's vendors are immigrants, Chang used images in place of words wherever possible. The limited text appears in Arabic, Bengali, Chinese, Spanish, and English. A team of volunteers distributed the posters on foot to thousands of vendors; the publication is also available online. Designed in an engaging, accessible style, *Vendor Power!* aims to help these urban entrepreneurs avoid tickets, understand their rights, and collectively advocate for policy reforms.

49–50 *Vendor Power!* posters. Candy Chang, Red Antenna. Client: Center for Urban Pedagogy. United States, 2009. Offset lithograph

51

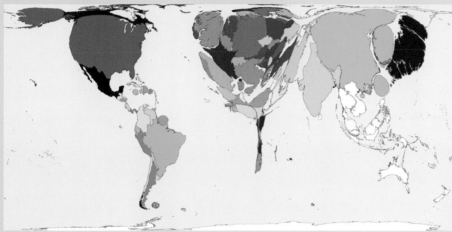

52

Worldmapper

Most maps are built around representations of geographical land-mass. Worldmapper shows us something different. This collaborative team of cartographers from the University of Sheffield in England and the University of Michigan is exploring the uneven effects of globalization. Rather than depict how much land a given territory occupies, each map shows how a social or economic activity, such as emigration or cell-phone use, is distributed across the globe.

Called a cartogram, each map is like a global pie chart. The maps divide the world into 200 territories (191 United Nations countries plus a small number of disputed areas). An algorithm changes the scale of each territory in relation to its dominance in a particular category. The population map, which provides a basis for comparison, scales each territory to reflect its share of the world's total population. This is what different countries might be shaped like if land were evenly distributed to each person on Earth. China and India are the largest territories, and the United States is comparatively small.

Maps of Internet use show a different picture. In 1990, most of the world's Internet users were located in the United States, Western Europe, and Japan, making these regions appear disproportionately large in relation to other areas. By 2007, the geographic picture had changed considerably, with countries including China, India, and Brazil swelling dramatically in size. More than 700 different cartograms can be viewed and down-loaded at Worldmapper.org, where data sources for each map are meticulously documented and explained.

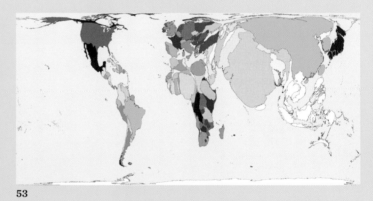

53

51 Worldmapper, Internet use 1990. Graham Allsopp, Anna Barford, Danny Dorling, John Pritchard, and Ben Wheeler, SASI Group, University of Sheffield, and Mark Newman, University of Michigan. United Kingdom and United States, 2005–present

52 Worldmapper, Internet use 2007

53 Worldmapper, world population 2007

Simplicity

Ellen Lupton

A melody with few notes, a sentence with few words, or an object with few parts may appear obvious when you come upon it, but creating simplicity is rarely easy. Design thinking often includes the ruthless yet creative process of weeding out redundant elements. Concise forms and solutions appear everywhere from vernacular technologies to classical temples. Today, as designers strive to make spare use of materials and ground their work in natural processes, the quest for simplicity is shaping design's aesthetic language and its economic, ecological, and ethical purpose.

How does simplicity happen? Many designers study commonplace things and look for ways to merge parts and combine functions. Shigeru Ban's 10-Unit system, created for the Finnish design company Artek, employs a single L-shaped component to construct a series of different products: table, chair, bench (fig. 1). Soft curves modulate the system's basic unit, allowing the pieces to combine into varied and graceful objects. Employing a more severe geometric vocabulary, Cecilie Manz's Pluralis chair (fig. 2) is a single structure whose legs support multiple planes for multiple purposes: seat, table, step. In the Flax Project, Christien Meindertsma studied the traditional craft of rope making in collaboration with Thomas Eyck. Her ingenious hanging

fig. 1

fig. 2

light merges the ancient archetype of the twisted rope with the modern archetype of the electrical cord. As wires disappear inside twisted strands of natural flax, the primeval rope appears to magically electrify the bulbs, which hang from it like postindustrial fruit.

Employing structure as decoration is a longstanding modernist principle. Like a jellyfish, Mikko Paakkanen's Medusa lamp (fig. 3) slowly changes shape, its body defined by glowing fiberoptic ribs. Like apple slices, Ryan Frank's Isabella stools (fig. 4) consist of brightly colored side planes and an exposed front and back, creating a pattern of contrasting conditions: covered and bare, colorful and neutral, soft and hard.

Simplicity affects not just how things look, but how we interact with them. A door with no handle or a light with no switch could present an elegant but bewildering experience. Designers today are developing smoothly functioning forms by examining the conditions of use. The gentle ridges encircling Karin Eriksson's Gripp glasses (fig. 5) help people comfortably grasp the vessels and hold them stable. Jorre van Ast's universal jar tops (fig. 6) and removable table legs yield flexible objects designed to assemble and disassemble. DBA's humidifier (fig. 7) can be emptied and filled as easily as a bucket. The Book LED lamp, designed by Goodmorning Technology, has a lampshade shaped like a book (fig. 8); the covers open and close intuitively to adjust the light's intensity.

Simple forms can be challenging to produce. To create its graceful line of disposable tableware (fig. 9), Wasara had to develop new ways to shape and trim molded pulp, avoiding the bent-around edges typically seen on paper plates and bowls. Meindertsma's hanging lamp exemplifies the widespread revival of traditional craftsmanship, as designers look to slow down production and create fewer products of higher quality. Jetske de Groot's Multiple Family chairs (fig. 10) are one-of-a-kind objects assembled by hand from discarded mass-produced furniture. Seeking quality over abundance, such products offer a grounded, earthly luxury suited to a culture of restraint.

Manufacturers are discovering the benefits of streamlining their production processes. The Danish company Mater, working with skilled craftspeople in workshops and small factories in Vietnam, avoids using toxic dyes and polished glazes in order to protect workers and the environment from harmful chemicals; the result is quiet, spare objects that honor their own means of manufacture. At Muji, the global brand whose name means "no brand," simplified production

fig. 3

fig. 4

fig. 5

fig. 6

fig. 7

fig. 8

processes help unify the company's vast product line. By minimizing packaging, reducing materials, avoiding dyes and finishes, revaluing waste materials, and creating objects that do not change from year to year, Muji embraces an economy of means that is reflected in the company's modest yet pleasing goods, which range from dried mushrooms to CD players and bedroom furniture. Muji wants to make products that are neither the best nor the most desirable, but are instead good enough, leaving people pleased but not sated into complacency. In place of products that are "idiosyncratic + expensive" or "ordinary + cheap," Muji hopes to embody the "naturally low cost of affluence and the inexpensive range of good judgment."[1]

Today, in place of the weary cliché of "timeless elegance," we might speak of relative durability. In place of the cynical strategy of "planned obsolescence," we might speak of planned impermanence. The projects discussed here connect to *our* time, not to all time. Designers engaged with the current state of the world seek to make things that will last for awhile, not forever. If things break, we should be able to fix them. When objects are no longer needed, they should gracefully degrade or regroup into other forms of value. These projects express a fundamental modesty. Limited-edition endeavors like Meindertsma's Flax Project (fig. 11) are grounded in elemental processes of making, speaking beyond the objects themselves to widely held aspirations. Mater's ceramic water jug, DBA's portable space heater, and Muji's seersucker bedding provide alternatives to super-minimal opulence or to sleek high-tech style. They embody an ethical, provisional pragmatism.

As people around the world seek to curb their impulses for overconsumption and waste, they are rethinking how they eat, sleep, work, travel, and learn. What more profound and enduring problem is there than how to bury the dead? Greg Holdsworth, outraged by the wasteful and intrusive funeral business, has created an artisanal, biodegradable coffin (fig. 12) designed not to defy time but to cycle back into the earth. In the United States alone, the funeral industry buries over 90,000 tons of steel, 30 million board feet of hardwood, 3,000 tons of copper and bronze, and 1.5 million tons of concrete every year. Bodies interred in sealed metal caskets in concrete vaults do not truly decompose; instead, they enter a "permanent state of advanced but unprogressive putrefaction."[2] Problems like this one are not only material in nature, but also spiritual and aesthetic. The future cannot solely be

fig. 9

fig. 10

fig. 11

fig. 12

engineered or legislated into submission; it must be designed, and that will require creative thinking—imaginative, poetic, and unexpected—from all segments of society.

1 Kenya Hara, *Designing Design* (Baden, Switzerland: Lars Müller Publishers, 2007): 239–40.
2 Statistics and quote from correspondence with Greg Holdsworth, August 2009.

1

2

10-Unit System

Architect Shigeru Ban collaborated with the Finnish furniture company Artek to design an L-shaped element that combines in various ways to form chairs, benches, and tables. Subtle curves modulate the unit's profile, yielding assembled objects that feature soft, undulating planes and gracefully shaped members. Designed for compact shipping and easy assembly, the pieces are packed ten units to a box, together with attachment elements and instructions. Ten units combine to make a table or chair; twenty units make a bench. An added glass top extends the surface of the table. The box, emblazoned with the message "Art and Tech Forever," celebrates the creative marriage of aesthetic invention and industrial research.

The 10-Unit System is made from UPM ProFi, a durable, weather-resistant composite of recycled wood and paper. Developed by the Finnish paper company UPM, this new material combines plastic polymers with wood fibers recovered from the process of manufacturing adhesive labels. This waste material currently has no other uses. Polypropylene is added to the reclaimed plastic and paper, yielding a PVC-free substance that can be incinerated safely. In 2007, two years before the launch of the 10-Unit System, Shigeru Ban had designed Artek's "Space of Silence" pavilion in Milan, also made from identical units of UPM ProFi assembled into a larger structure. That architectural experiment was the basis for what is now an affordable, versatile consumer product.

AlphaBetter Student Desk

Research on movement in the classroom is showing that having students stand while learning and giving them the freedom to fidget are helping them academically and physically. Realizing that movement is not necessarily a distraction, schools are looking for ways to help their students burn energy and focus attention. The AlphaBetter desk helps them do both. The height-adjustable desk gives students the choice to sit or stand during class, while the companion stool lets them sit down when they need a rest. The swinging motion of the patented Pendulum™ footrest bar allows kids to continuously move their feet to the school-day beat.

While children are twisting and turning to learn, they are also expending calories and excess energy. Having a desk that lets them be active in school helps students stay healthier. It may also enhance academic performance. Being able to fidget has been shown to increase student concentration, especially among students with attention-deficit/hyperactivity disorder (ADHD).

1 10-Unit system, bench. Shigeru Ban, Shigeru Ban Architects. Manufactured by Artek Oy Ab. Designed Japan, manufactured Finland, 2009–10. UPM ProFi (recycled paper and plastic composite)

2 AlphaBetter student desk. Tim Skiba, Sunway Inc. Concept: Abby Brown. Manufactured by Safco Products Company. United States, 2007. Powder-coated steel, MDF, 3-D rigid thermoplastic laminate, phenolic sheet

3 CarryOn collection with porcelain prototypes.
Jakob Wagner, Jakob Wagner Design.
Manufactured by Mater. Handcrafted by Dong Guan
Concord Pottery Co. Ltd. and The Bamboo Factory.
Designed Denmark, produced China and Vietnam,
2008. Porcelain, bamboo

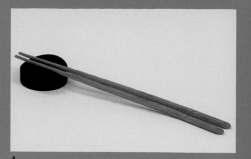

4

3

Angle Chopsticks, CarryOn Collection, and InOut Pitcher

Based in Denmark, Mater is a home-accessories company that supports traditional crafts, local economies, and natural materials. Mater is a member of the United Nations Global Compact, an independently audited framework that helps businesses align their practices with universal values in areas such as human rights, labor, and the environment. By applying creative thinking and ethical standards to product design and manufacturing, Mater seeks to leverage business to engender a more sustainable and inclusive global economy.

Mater worked with French designer Aurélien Barbry to introduce the Angle chopsticks, ergonomic bamboo implements inspired by Japanese *oki* table settings. The InOut pitcher, designed by American designer Todd Bracher, has a minimal barrel form and a beak-like spout. Bracher made the pitcher white in order to avoid using dye and employed a rough finish to avoid the use of potentially toxic glazes. Danish designer Jakob Wagner created Mater's CarryOn collection, a set of white porcelain bowls and plates fitted with nesting bamboo cutting boards for informal dining and serving. Like the InOut pitcher, the CarryOn collection employs white porcelain with a rough finish to protect workers and the environment. All three products are created by skilled craftspeople in small factories and workshops in Vietnam and China.
—*Andrea Lipps*

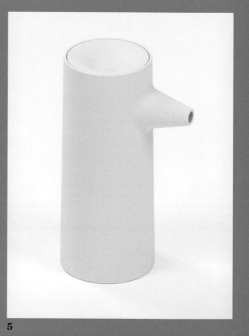

5

4 Angle chopsticks. Aurélien Barbry, Aurélien Barbry Design. Manufactured by Mater. Handcrafted by The Bamboo Factory. Designed France, produced Vietnam, 2008. Bamboo

5 InOut pitcher. Todd Bracher, Todd Bracher Studio. Manufactured by Mater. Handcrafted by Dong Guan Concord Pottery Co. Ltd. Designed United States, produced China, 2007. Porcelain

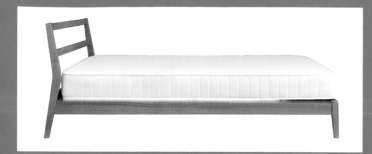

6

7

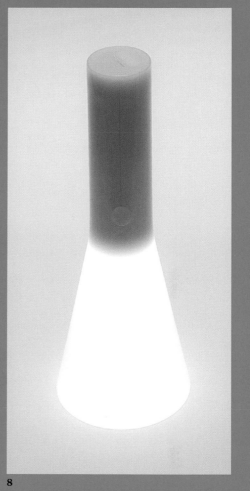

8

Ash Wood Bed, Cotton Bedding, and Torch Light

Muji, whose name means "no brand," is a Japanese company that has become a global purveyor of low-cost, high-quality goods that respect the environment and express a low-key, functional point of view. Economy drives the Muji ethos. By seeking out simple methods of production and basic materials that are not excessively processed, the company creates objects that share a unified sensibility without professing to be stylish and of the moment. Looking at common needs such as lighting, sleep, storage, seating, and dining, Muji has created 7,500 objects suitable to urban living.

      Muji's Ash Wood bed has a curved headboard that supports the body comfortably while reading a book, watching TV, or working on a laptop. The bed can be dressed for summer with Muji's line of seersucker cotton bedding, whose wavy surface results from warp tension during the weaving process. This structural decoration keeps the raised stripes away from the skin, cooling the body during warm weather, while the naturally crinkled surface needs no ironing. Muji's portable Torch light uses an LED to conserve power. Users can set the light on a table or carry it like a torch or flashlight. The milky white shell conveys a soft, warm glow.

6 Ash Wood bed. Naoto Fukasawa, Muji design team. Manufactured by Ryohin Keikaku Co. Ltd. Japan, 2009. Ash wood

7 Cotton bedding (seersucker & double-loop stitch combination). Haruna Morita, Muji design team. Japan, 2009. Cotton

8 Torch light. Yohei Kuwano, Muji design team. Manufactured by Ryohin Keikaku Co. Ltd. Japan, 2007. Polycarbonate, LED

9

Book LED Floor Lamp

The Book LED floor lamp, designed by Goodmorning Technology, is part of a national effort to encourage Danish consumers to switch from tungsten filament bulbs to energy-efficient LEDs. The lamp's shade opens and closes like the cover of a book. As the shade opens wider, the light shines more brightly, and as it closes, it gradually dims and turns off. Made from recycled aluminum, the wide, flat planes of the shade help dissipate heat, a critical function in optimizing the efficiency and lifespan of LEDs. Inside the shade, plastic diffusers create a warm, even glow. This clever design employs familiar imagery and intuitive user interactions to rethink an everyday household object.

10

9–10 Book LED floor lamp. Goodmorning Technology. Manufactured by DTU Technical University of Denmark, Department of Photonics Engineering. Denmark, 2008–9. Aluminum, acrylic, LED

11

Cabbage Chair

The Cabbage chair was created for an exhibition organized in Japan by fashion designer Issey Miyake, who challenged his contemporaries to conceive of new products for the twenty-first century. What types of furniture and objects are appropriate, Miyake asked, for people who "don't just wear clothes, but shed their skin?" He invited Oki Sato of Nendo to find a use for pleated paper, a material employed to process the signature fabric featured in Miyake's garments. Vast amounts of this material are discarded as a by-product of the manufacturing process. The Cabbage chair is a compact roll of paper that the user opens up and peels back, layer by layer, to create a soft and resilient enclosure for the body. Resins added to the paper during the original production process give it strength and memory, while the pleats make the paper springy and elastic. The poetic and practical chair is a direct, minimal transformation of an industrial waste product. Its pod-like skin unfurls to reveal a luxuriant and expansive interior. It has no internal armature, and requires no finishing, assembly, or hardware.

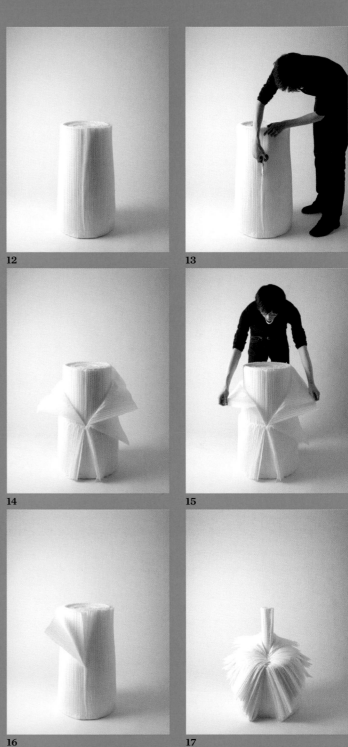

12

13

14

15

16

17

18

19

20

Clamp-a-Leg, Jar Tops, and Nomad Table

Jorre van Ast is fascinated with connections, especially the elemental turn of a screw. This ancient mechanism makes a connection that is at once strong, reversible, and adjustable. Van Ast's Jar Tops are functional plastic lids that screw on to existing glass jars, enabling users to transform discarded containers into new sprinklers, decanters, and jugs. The tops correspond to the twist-off (TO) standard, a worldwide norm for the manufacture of screw-top food jars.

    Clamp-a-Leg consists of a wooden furniture leg threaded into a simple metal clamp, allowing people to quickly transform any flat surface into a functional work surface. Clamp-a-Leg uses less material than a trestle and is easy to ship, store, and assemble. The Nomad table is a high-end, lightweight furniture piece whose legs screw in to the tabletop with a wood-to-wood connection. It is made entirely from wood; using no metal hardware, it returns, in essence, to preindustrial joinery techniques. The Nomad employs diverse woods for their different properties: hard ash for the legs; lightweight balsa, cellulose, and poplar for the tabletop core; and elegant oak veneer for the upper surface. The tabletop is thick enough at the center to receive the legs, and tapers outward to a knife-thin edge.

21

18 Clamp-a-Leg. Jorre van Ast/Studio for Product Design. The Netherlands, 2008–9. Metal, beech

19–20 Nomad table. Jorre van Ast/Studio for Product Design. Manufactured by Arco Contemporary Furniture. The Netherlands, 2009. Honeycomb cellulose, balsawood, thin poplar wood sheet, solid ash

21 Jar tops. Jorre van Ast/Studio for Product Design. Manufactured by Royal VKB. The Netherlands, 2005–8. Polypropylene

22

23

24

22–24 DBA heater and humidifier. Leon Ransmeier, DBA. United States, 2008. Heater: recycled aluminum, heating elements, electronic components; humidifier: recycled polypropylene, RoHS- and EPEAT-ompliant electronic components, high-efficiency ultrasonic transducer

DBA Heater and Humidifier

DBA, a new design company in New York City, is developing a line of functional products for compact, sustainable living. Creative director Leon Ransmeier designs objects and appliances whose reserved, almost anonymous forms neither glorify technology nor try to make it disappear. The DBA humidifier, made of recycled polypropylene, is a cylindrical tank sitting on a low base. Mist escapes from a vent at the top of the unit. A clear removable lid allows users to glance down into the tank to check the water level. The tank lifts off the base and can be refilled as easily as a bucket. DBA's heater embodies similar clarity of purpose. Two wafer-thin heating panels are connected with a bridge that also serves as a handle and a spool for the cord when the appliance is stored.

Operating at the threshold of intuition, these pristine objects explain their own usefulness through physical and visual cues. Made from eco-safe materials, each piece is designed for long use and easy repair. DBA stands for "Doing Business As," reflecting the company's ethos of anonymity. By selling goods directly to consumers online as well as in limited retail settings such as micro-marts and instant shops, DBA seeks to control costs while keeping quality high.

25 Gripp glasses. Karin Eriksson, Karinelvy Design.
Manufactured by Skrufs Glassworks. Sweden,
2008–9. Blown glass

26 Isabella stool, Free Range Furniture collection.
Ryan Frank, Planet G Ltd. Manufactured by
Pli Design. United Kingdom, 2008. Straw, wool

26

25

Gripp Glasses

Karin Eriksson wanted to create elegant drinking glasses that
nearly anyone can use, including people with limited hand
function. Impairments of the hand—which are among the most
common forms of disability—include weakness, shaking, lack of
sensation, and pain from gripping and exertion. Many glasses are
too heavy, wide, or narrow for people with even mild impairments
to comfortably grasp and lift. Some purpose-made products for
the disabled, such as double-handled plastic cups, create stigma
by providing separate tools for different people at the table.
Eriksson's Gripp glasses have an expressed edge near their center
point that provides a stabilizing handhold while imparting
a graceful profile to each object. Eriksson's lightweight, well-
balanced glasses are designed for serving wine, beer, or water.

Isabella Stool, Free Range
Furniture Collection

Ryan Frank is a South-African-born designer working in London,
whose practice is inspired by reclaimed materials, sustainable
systems, and his African roots. His phrase "free-range furniture"
suggests his open, unconstrained way of thinking and his view
of products as domesticated creatures that can be cultivated in
humane and sustainable ways. Isabella, launched in 2008, is a
totem-style stacking stool whose form is influenced by traditional
African seating. Frank created his stools from strawboard, a
formaldehyde-free material made of compressed straw that is an
alternative to wood particleboard or fiberboard. He wrapped
the curving side planes in brightly colored felt, creating a tactile,
comfortable seat, while leaving the front and back surfaces
unupholstered, exposing the strawboard. Isabella stacks to form
a totem structure whose alternating felt and strawboard skins
highlight the seat's iconic form.
—*Andrea Lipps*

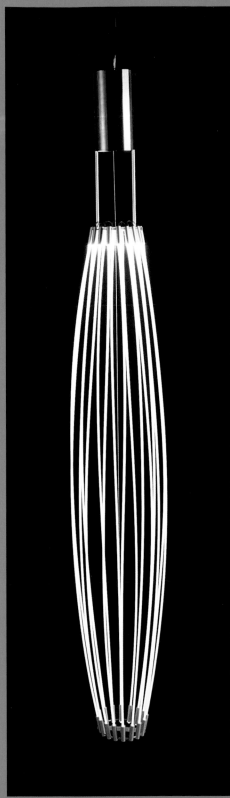

27

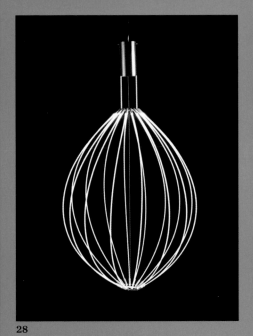

28

29

Medusa Lamp

The Medusa lamp gently swells and contracts, its movement inspired by the motion of a jellyfish. A set of flexible, side-emitting fiber-optic rods, held together at top and bottom, define the volume of the lamp. A high-intensity LED housed in the top of the unit transmits light along the rods. A small motor controlled by a microprocessor causes the ribs to pull up and extend back down, creating a fluctuating shape defined by linear bands of light. Users can choose to halt the motion of the lamp, fixing it in a desired shape. This energy-efficient lamp uses technology to create a malleable, motile form that emulates nature.

30

31

Multiple Chairs #17 and #23, Multiple Family Series

Rather than make new objects from raw materials, Dutch designer Jetske de Groot creates furniture out of things that already exist. Seeking out well-worn chairs, tables, and cabinets, she carefully disassembles each piece and recombines the elements into new pieces that openly declare their mixed heritage and their long years of service. She connects them with visible epoxy bonds that celebrate the act of attachment. In these late-life second marriages, divergent materials, colors, and vocabularies join together, yielding painterly objects whose familiar parts yield surprising wholes. Calling her series Multiple Family, de Groot has created singular, handcrafted objects recovered from the realm of everyday mass production.

30–31 Multiple chairs #17 and #23, Multiple Family series. Jetske de Groot. The Netherlands, 2008–9. Recycled materials, epoxy reinforced by fiberglass

32 Pluralis chair. Cecilie Manz. Manufactured by
Mooment. Denmark, 2009. Solid Oregon pine

33 Return to Sender artisan eco-casket. Greg
Holdsworth, Return To Sender Eco-Caskets. New
Zealand, 2007. Plywood, wool fleece

33

32

Pluralis Chair

Human beings are drawn to flat planes: we sit, sleep, and build on
them; we work, eat, and drink at them. Cecilie Manz plays with
the language of planes to expand the functionality of familiar
objects, from tables and chairs to ladders and shelves. In her
Pluralis chair, three staggered surfaces share legs, merging a
cluster of furnishings into a single artifact: seat, stool, table,
and step. Drawing on the tradition of minimalist art, the chair
contemplates the nature of cubes, lines, and intersections. It
is also supremely functional, offering a convenient place to sit
with a child or set down a glass.

Return to Sender Artisan Eco-Casket

Death is a biological fact, yet many modern customs act in denial
of death while degrading the environment. Coffins typically are
expensive objects designed for permanence in the ground or
made of composites and plastics that release toxins into the air
during cremation.

Greg Holdsworth set out to create a simple, nontoxic, biodegradable casket. Metal and hardwood caskets consume precious
resources, and others are made from wood composites covered
with artificial wood grains or PVC. Many handles and decorative
elements are made from metal-coated plastic, while linings are
typically synthetic. Holdsworth chose instead to use plywood,
a light material with an attractive grained surface. The low sides
of the casket allow bodies to "lie in state" rather than requiring
mourners to peer down into a deep box. Handles are integrated
into the base of the coffin, and a wool fleece mattress provides
a soft, natural cushion that harmonizes with the casket's lightly
oiled finish. Holdsworth describes the casket as "an elegant,
eco-iconic form that honors the deceased and allows their final
footprint to be a small one."

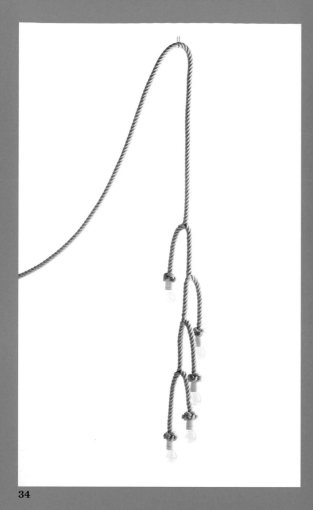

34

34 t.e. 83 hanging lamp. Christien Meindertsma. Manufactured by Ropery Steenbergen for the t.e. collection. The Netherlands, 2009. Flax, porcelain, rubber

35–38 Wasara tableware, compote bowl, maru plate, and kaku plates. Shinichiro Ogata, Wasara Co. Ltd. Japan, 2008. Reed, bamboo, bagasse pulp

35

t.e. 83 Hanging Lamp

Design producer Thomas Eyck commissioned Christien Meindertsma to create a series of products inspired by the traditional Dutch rope-making industry. Meindertsma conceived a rich line of objects using flax, a versatile fiber derived from a plant that grows plentifully in the Netherlands, Belgium, and France. Collaborating with a master rope maker, she used flax harvested from a local Dutch farm to create simple objects for contemporary life. In a series of hanging lights, the rope maker wound strands of flax around the electrical supply cord, combining power delivery and functional support into a single element. The connecting pieces were created in a specialized wood-restoration shop. Other works include a stool that resembles a ball of string, a rug made from a bound length of rope, and a power cord wrapped with rope. Meinderstsma's Flax collection is part of a family of products that Eyck is building in collaboration with contemporary designers, who are working with special materials and skilled craft workers to create limited series of objects.

Wasara Tableware

The phrase "paper plate" usually conjures images of haste and waste, not spiritual enrichment and ecological awareness. The Wasara collection of disposable tableware speaks to traditional Japanese hospitality, which employs diverse plates and bowls to focus attention on individually prepared food items. Wasara's serene, inventive forms enhance the sensual experience of dining while offering the convenience of disposability.

Paper tableware must be made from virgin pulp, owing to the impurities in recycled material. The Wasara collection is made from a mix of reed pulp, bamboo, and bagasse, or sugarcane pulp. Bagasse is a waste product of the sugar-processing industry, while reed and bamboo are fast-growing, non-timber plants.

The molded pulp takes myriad forms, bending and warping to add functionality and beauty to each piece. Designed to stack on the table in sculptural configurations, these paper dishes present a pleasing play of light and shadow. The handle of a coffee cup is also a pouring spout. The undulating edge of a plate makes it easy for a guest to hold it at a party. The texture of the material makes it feel comfortable and artisanal in the hand. Designed for single use, followed by natural decay, the Wasara collection celebrates "ephemeral beauty," a strong current in Japanese culture.

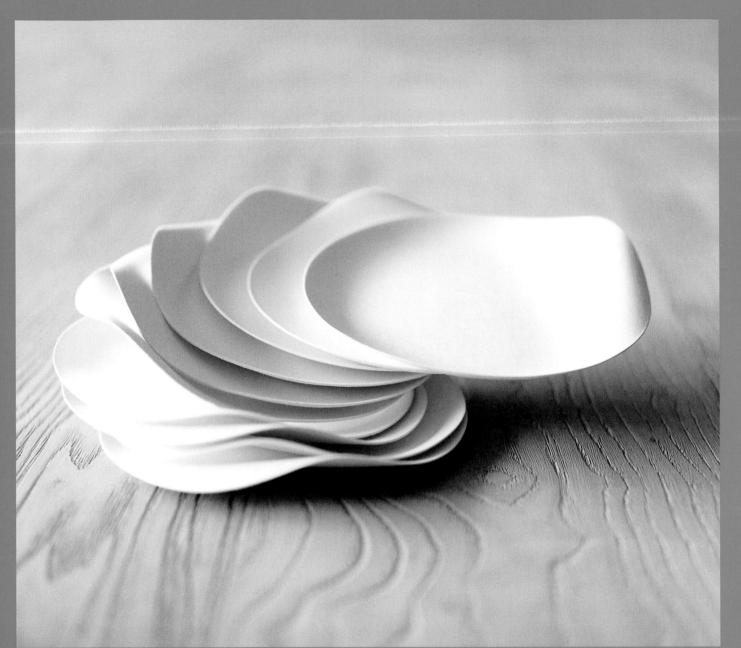

36

37

38

Authors

Ellen Lupton has served as Curator of Contemporary Design at Cooper-Hewitt since 1992. She has contributed to numerous books and exhibitions at the Museum, including *Mechanical Brides: Women and Machines from Home to Office*, *Skin: Surface, Substance + Design*, and the *National Design Triennial* series. Lupton also serves as Director of the Graphic Design MFA program at Maryland Institute College of Art (MICA) in Baltimore. As a leading authority on design education, she has authored books that have become standard texts in classrooms worldwide, including *Thinking with Type* (2004) and *Graphic Design: The New Basics* (2008). A 2007 recipient of the AIGA Gold Medal, she is a frequent lecturer on design topics.

Cara McCarty has served as Curatorial Director at Cooper-Hewitt since 2007. During her twenty-seven-year career, which began at New York's Museum of Modern Art, followed by her tenure at the Saint Louis Art Museum as Head of Decorative Arts and Design, she has written catalogues and articles, built collections, and organized numerous exhibitions that have expanded the way we think about design. Most of her exhibitions have focused on innovation and the overlap between design and technology. These include *Mario Bellini: Designer*, *Information Art: Diagramming Microchips*, *Designs for Independent Living: Products for People with Disabilities*, *Masks: Faces of Culture*, and *Tadao Ando: Architect*. A leading expert on contemporary design issues, McCarty was a Loeb Fellow at Harvard's Graduate School of Design, and has served on a number of international architecture and design juries.

Matilda McQuaid has been at Cooper-Hewitt since 2002, and serves as Deputy Curatorial Director and Head of the Textiles department, one of the premier textile collections in the world. She has organized exhibitions and publications on textiles and contemporary architecture and design, including *Solos: Tulou/ Affordable Housing for China*, *Extreme Textiles: Designing for High Performance,* and *Josef and Anni Albers: Designs for Living*. McQuaid previously served at The Museum of Modern Art in New York for fifteen years, where she curated numerous exhibitions relating to modern and contemporary architecture and design, most notably *Structure and Surface: Contemporary Japanese Textiles* (with Cara McCarty) and *Shigeru Ban: A Paper Arch*. She has lectured and published widely on art, architecture, and design.

Cynthia Smith serves as Cooper-Hewitt's Curator of Socially Responsible Design. Trained as an industrial designer, for over a decade she led both multidisciplinary planning and design projects for cultural institutions. After earning a graduate degree at Harvard University's Kennedy School of Government, she joined Cooper-Hewitt, where she integrates her work experience with her advocacy and activism on human rights and social justice issues. She co-authored *The Politics of Genocide: U.S. Rhetoric vs. Inaction in Darfur* for the *Kennedy School Review*; curated the 2007 exhibition *Design for the Other 90%*; and is working on the next exhibition in the series. Named a "20/20 New Pioneer" by *Icon* magazine, she has served on several international design juries and lectured widely on socially responsible design.

Andrea Lipps is a Curatorial Assistant at Cooper-Hewitt, where she is currently working on the next exhibition in the *Design for the Other 90%* series with Cynthia Smith. Before joining the Museum, she worked in the Architecture and Design department at The Museum of Modern Art in New York, assisting on *Design and the Elastic Mind* and *Home Delivery: Fabricating the Modern Dwelling*. Lipps served as curatorial intern on *Design for the Other 90%* and wrote her master's thesis in design history on twentieth-century post-disaster design, integrating her interest in design with earlier work in international human rights. She has published articles in leading design magazines and teaches in the master's program at Cooper-Hewitt.

Selected Index

Bold denotes project names.

3-D printing, 79

4:Secs condom applicator generation II, 123, *123*

10-Unit system, 169, *169*, 173, *173*

Acumen Fund, 118, 122, 137, *137*

Adaptive Eyecare Ltd., *125*

Adrian Smith + Gordon Gill Architecture, *26*

AdSpecs, 125, *125*

Aerocrine AB, *130*

Aeroponics, 54

Aging, 119, 131, 139, 147

AgriPlast, 73, *73*

AgroResin, 73, *73*

AGV (*automotrice à grande vitesse*) [high-speed self-propelled train], 38, *38*, 41, *41*

Aid to Artisans, 116, *116–17*

AIDS/HIV, 123, 150, 157

Aigner, Erin, *158*

Alabama Chanin 2009 and 2010 collections, 101, *101*

Alar 002, Azha Custom, and Indi 002 wallpapers, 74, *74*

Albert, Dan, *55*

Algae, 23

All Media Wallpaper and Paintings, *9*, 145, *145*

Allsopp, Graham, *167*

Alpaca, 75

Alpaca Velvet, Ditto, Gather 006, and Horsehair Striae 003 Textiles, 75, *75*

AlphaBetter student desk, 173, *173*

Alstom Transport Design and Styling Studio, 41, *41*

Aluminum, 24, 41, 42, 43, 57, 59, 71, 74, 76, 89, 108, 176

Amazon Kindle Team, a division of Amazon.com, *155*

Americans with Disabilities Act, 142

Anastassiades, Michael, *162*

Angle chopsticks, CarryOn collection, and InOut pitcher, 174, *174*

Animation, 156, 162

Apple Industrial Design Team, *155*

Aquaculture, 23

Armadillo body armor and facemask, 126, *126*

Art Center College of Design, 156, *156*

Artecnica, 99, *99*, 116, *116–17*

Artek, 169, *169*, 173, *173*

Artificial Biological Clock, 146, *146*

Artisan manufacturing, 97, 99, 101, 104–5, 109, 112–13, 116–17, 170, 174

Ash Wood bed, Lino Stripe bedding, and Torch light, 175, *175*

Asthma, 129–30

Attar, Tiel, *111*

Azambourg, François, 89, *89*

Bagasse, 77, 184

Bailey, Catherine, 99, *99*, 105, *105*

Bamboo, 52, 81, 174, 184

Ban, Shigeru, 169, *169*, 173, *173*

Bananaplac, 75, *75*

Barendse, Jeroen, *161*

Barbry, Aurélien, 174, *174*

Barford, Anna, *167*

Bayer, Eben, *85*

Béhar, Yves, 142, *143*, 159, *159*

Bellamy, James, *59*

Benavidez, Sam, *148*

Bernal, Alejandro, *2*, 60

Bicycles, 38, 44, 46, *47*

Bierut, Michael, 4, 7, 143, *143*, 154, *154*

Bilton, Nick, *158*

Bio Design Center, 120

Bio-Glass, Bio-Luminum, and Eco-Cem, 71, *71*, 76, *76*

Biomimicry, 17, 29, 32, 92

Bioplastics, 70, 73, 75, 77

BioPower Systems Pty Ltd., 15, *15*, 17, *17*

Bioware packaging, 77, *77*

bioWAVE ocean-wave energy system, 15, *15*, 17, *17*

Biowert Industrie GmbH, 73

Bleached Reef, *140*, 146, *146*

Bloch, Matthew, *158*

Block, Philippe, *59*

Blue Angel, 72

BNIM Architects, 128, *128*

Bodyweight Support Assist, 119, 127, *127*

Book LED floor lamp, 170, *170*, 176, *176*

Boontje, Tord, 116, *116–17*

Bosse, Chris, 28

Bowman, Douglas, *165*

Bracher, Todd, 174, *174*

Braille, 142, 154, 163

Branding, 165, 170, 175

Braungart, Michael, 70

Brawer, Wendy E., 153, *153*

Bright Automotive, 39, 43, *43*

British Council, 116

Broms, Loove, 20, *20*

Browka, Edward, *85*

Brown, Abby, *173*

Brownstein, John S., 122, 132, *132*

Buck, Randall, 74, *74*

Busch, David, *43*

Cabbage chair, 177, *177*

Calera Corporation, 71, 77, *77*

California Academy of Sciences, 15, *15*, 18, *19*

Canary Project, 143, *143*, 154, *154*

Carabanchel social housing, 49, *49*, 52, *52*

Carbon-negative concrete, 71, 77, *77*

Cardboard, 108

Carpets, 94, 99, 104

Carroll, Ryan Michael, 44, *44*

Cartogram, 167

Caskets, 168–69, 171, 183

Castro, Thomas, *161*

Celi, Leo, *133*

Cell phones, *see* Mobile devices

Cellulose, 76, 89, 178

Cement, 71, 76, 77, 86, 113

Center for Integration of Medicine and Innovative Technology, 120–121

Center for Rapid Automated Fabrication Technologies (CRAFT), 79

Center for Urban Pedagogy, 166, *166*

Ceramics, 99, 105, 116, 174

Chang, Candy, 166, *166*

Chanin, Natalie, 101, *101*

ChargePoint networked charging station, 38, *38*, 42, *42*

Charging stations, 38, 42, 44

Chavez, David, 154, *154*

Children's Hospital Boston at the Harvard-MIT Division of Health Sciences and Technology, *132*

Chipchase, Jan, 111, *111*

Clamp-a-Leg, jar tops, and Nomad table, 170, *171*, 178, *178*

Clark, Brad, *128*

Clay, 105, 106, 113

Clean Development Mechanism, 81

ClearviewHwy typeface, 142, *142*, 147, *147*

Clifford, Gari, *133*

Coal, 13

Cobi chair, 71, *71*, 78, *78*

Coffins, *see* Caskets

Cohen, Revital, 146, *146*

Cohn, Donna, 110, *110*

Concrete, *see* Cement

Congestion pricing, 38

Constantz, Brent, 77, *77*

Contour Crafting, 70, *70*, 79, *79*

Cottam, Hilary, *131*

Cotton, 81, 175

Coulomb Technologies, 38, *38*, 42, *42*

Coverings Etc, 71, *71*, 76, *76*

Cox, Amanda, *158*

Cradle-to-cradle, 70–72, 78, 86

Craft, 56, 99, 101, 104–105, 108–109, 116–117, 146, 148–149, 170, 174

Critical design, 146, 162

Cullin, Mia, *83*

Curious Pictures, 150, *151*

Dance, Gabriel, *158*

DBA, 170, *170*, 171, 179, *179*

DBA heater and humidifier, 170, *170*, 171, 179, *179*

De Goey, Heleen, *157*

De Greeve, Maarten, *37*, 46, *46*

De Groot, Jetske, 182, *182*

De Jongh, Ilona, *157*

De Vries, Nathalie, 49, 66–67

Defense Advanced Research Projects Agency (DARPA), 134

De-mining, 126

Denommee, Aline, *83*

Denommee, Dianne, *83*

Desalination, 26

Design that Matters Inc., 120–21, *121*, 135, *135*

Design Without Borders, 121, *121*, 126, *126*

Designmatters, 156, *156*

Devigal, Andrew, *158*

Disabilities, 62, 138, 142, 154. 163–64, 180

Disanayake, Nishan, 33, *33*

Disposable dinnerware, 95, 170, 184

D-Lab, 110

Donahue, Sean, 142, *142*, 163, *163*

Dorling, Danny, *167*

Dorsey, Jack, *165*

Dot Dot Dot Ex Why Zed Design (Pty) Ltd. (...XYZ), 123, *123–24*

Dring, Allison, 92–93, *92–93*

Drury, Kristina, *157*

Duenes, Steve, 158, *158*

Dukehart, Chris, *55*

Dunne & Raby, 162

Dunne, Anthony, 143, *143*, 146, 162, *162*

Dwork, Michael, 95, *95*

Dye photosynthesis, 29, 80

Dye solar-cell PV window, 80, *80*

Dyesol Inc., 80, *80*

Dykers, Craig, 64–5

E Ink, 155

Earth battery, 31

E-books, 142, 155

Echeverri, Alejandro, 60, *61*

Eco-Laboratory, 51, *51*, 54, *54–55*

Ecolect Inc., 72, 72, 84, *84*

Eco-Machine at the Omega Center for Sustainable Living, 128, *128*

Ecovative Design LLC, 85

Index

Education, 56, 62, 104, 125, 133, 137, 148, 150, 156–157, 159

Ehrnberger, Karin, 20, *20*

Electric vehicles, 38, 39, 42, 43, 45

Electronic paper, 155

Elegant Embellishments, 92–93, *92–93*

EMC, 102, *102–3*

Energy Aware clock, 15, *15*, 20, *20*

Energy meters, 15, 20, 31

EnviroMission Ltd., 22, *22*

Epoxy, 182

Ergon GR2 bike grips, 129, *129*

Ergonomics, 123, 136, 154

Ergonomidesign, 129, *129–30*

Ericson, Matthew, *158*

Eriksson, Karin, 170, *170*, 180, *180*

E/S Orcelle cargo carrier, 40, *40*, 42, *42*

ESRI, 102, *102–3*

Etheridge, Dan, *114–15*

Etón Corporation, 142, *142*, 148, *148*

Etón FR 600 radio, 142, *142*, 148, *148*

Etsy, 148–49, *148–49*

Eyck, Thomas, 169, *184*

Eyewear, 125, 129

Fagan, Henry, *59*

Fair trade, 81, 116

Fairfield, Hannah, *158*

Fajardo, Sergio, 60, *60–61*

Fashion, 81, 87, 91, 99, 101, 111

Federal Highway Administration, 147

Felt, 180

Ferracioli, Bernardo, *75*

Ferreira, Claudio, *75*

Fiber optics, 181

Fiberboard, 8

Fibra Design

Sustentável, 75, *75*

Fin Fashion A/S, *81*

Fin spring/summer 2010 collection, 81, *81*

Finnigan, Timothy, *17*

Fitchett, Anne, *59*

FLAKE and Veil curtains, 82, *82–83*

Flat packing, 98–99, 108, 173

Flax, 89, 169–71

Fletcher, Rich, *133*

Flower Label, 72

Foreign Office Architects (FOA), 49, *49*, 52, *52*

Foster + Partners, 26, *27*

Fougner, Martin O., 136, *136*

Fowler, Ryan, *124*

Furniture, 78, 89, 98, 108, 169–71, 173, 177–78, 180, 182–83

Frank, Ryan, 170, *170*, 180, *180*

Free Range Studios, 162, *162*

Freifeld, Clark C., 122, 132, *132*

Fujiwara, Dai, 87, *87*

Fundamental Technology Research Center, Honda R&D Co., Ltd., *127*

Furumai, 149, *149*

Fuseproject, *159*

Fuzun and RubbRe, 83, *83*

Gasoline, 43

Gass, Michael, *73*

Gebbia, Joe, 84, *84*

Geer, Barry, *124*

Geller, Brian, *54–55*

Gensler, *30*

Georgieva, Velichka, *112*

Geothermal energy, 23

Gerber, Egbert, 33, *33*

Gerritzen, Mieke, *9*, 143, 145, *145*

Get-Together, 131, *131*

Gill, Gordon, 26, *26*

Gilson, Robin, *83*

Girl Effect campaign, 143, *143*, 150, *150*, 151, *151*

Glass, 76, 80, 86, 180

Global Innovation Heat Map, 102, *102–3*

Global warming, 13, 26, 143, 146, 154

Gmachl, Mathias, *13*, 29, *29*

GOOD magazine, 16, 40, 152, *152*

Goodmorning Technology, 170, *170*, 176, *176*

GoodWeave and Odegard rugs, 96, 104, *104*

Górska, Joanna, 160, *160*

Graphic design, 145, 150–54, 156–58, 160–61, 166

Graphic Design Museum (Breda, the Netherlands), 161

Green Map system, 143, *143*, 153, *153*

Green Patriot posters, 143, *143*, 154, *154*

Green roofs, 15, 18–19, 76

GreenBox and Product Nutrition Label, 72, 72, 84, *84*

GreenPix Zero-energy Media Wall, 20, *21*

Greensulate, 70, *70*, 85, *85*

Grenidea Technologies Pte Ltd., *73*

Griffioen, Bas, *113*

Grigsby, Matt, *84*

Gripp glasses, 170, *170*, 180, *180*

Grossman, Dan, *157*

Gustafsson, Anton, 31, *31*

Gyllenswärd, Magnus, 31, *31*

H1N1 virus, 120, 162

H2Otel, 51, *51*, 56, *56*

Halation, 147

Hall, Peter, 143

Hammen, Desiree, 112, *112*

Hand impairments, 180

Haptica Braille timepiece, 142, 154, *154*

Harden, Daniel, *148*

Harrell, Myer, *55*

Harshbarger, Stuart D., *134*

Harvard Medical School, 132, *132*

Hatanaka, Motohide, *149*

HDT Engineering Services, *134*

HealthMap, 120, *120*, 132, *132*

Hearing impairment, 139

Heath Ceramics tableware, 99, *99*, 105, *105*

Heath, Edith, 105

Hemp, 83

Highway Gothic, 147

HIV/AIDS, 123, 150, 157

Henschel, Simon, 33, *33*

Hodge, Matthew, 59

Holdsworth, Greg, *168*, 171, *171*, 172, 183, *183*

Homelessness, 62

Homework, 160, *160*

Hope solar tower, 22, *22*

Horsehair, 75

House of Pack Corp., Ltd., *77*

Housing, 16, 52–53, 55–58, 62–63, 66–67

Hugo Industridesign AS, *136*

Hybrid vehicles, 38, 39, 43

Hydrogen fuel, 23

HydroNet: San Francisco 2108, 23, *23*

Hydroponics, 54

Hydropower, 56

Hyperbolic space, 146

IceStone LLC, 71, 71, 86, *86*

IceStone Refined collection, 71, 71, 86, *86*

Ichikawa, Fumiko, *111*

IDEA hybrid electric fleet vehicle, 39, *39*, 43, *43*

IDEO, *118*, 122, 137, *137*

IF Mode folding bicycle, 38, *38*, 44, *44*

Improved clay stove, 106–7, *106–7*

Incubator, 119, 121, 122, 135

Informal settlements, 111

Inora AS, 136, *136*

Institute for Figuring, *140*, 146, *146*

Interaction design, 136, 148, 156–58

Interactive Institute AB, 20, *20*, 31, *31*

Interform, *42*

International Design Development Summit (IDDS), 110

Invisible Streetlight, 16, *16*, 24, *24*

iPhone, 141–42, *142*, 155, *155*

Isabella stool, Free Range furniture collection, 170, *170*, 180, *180*

Isachsen, Leif Steven Verdu, *126*

Island Seat and Cloud Light, Spiral Islands collection, 98–99, *98*, 108, *108*

Issey Miyake Color Hunting collection, 87, *87*

Issey Miyake Creative Room, 87

Iwamoto, Lisa, 23

IwamotoScott, 23, *23*

Jackson, Tom, *158*

John Todd Ecological Design, 128, *128*

Johns Hopkins University Applied Physics Laboratory, 134, *134*

Joint Editorial, 150, *151*

Jung, Younghee, 111, *111*

Kahn, Aamir, *133*

Kalin, Robert, *149*

Karinelvy Design, *180*

Kareline Oy Ltd., 70, *70*, 92, *92*

Karten, Stuart, 121, *121*, 122, 139

Kartono, Singgih S., 99, *99*, 100, 109, *109*

Khoshnevis, Behrokh, 79, *79*

Kibiso, 88

Kibiso Bookshelf, Kibiso Futsu Crisscross, and Suzuji Stripe textiles, 68, 88, *88*

Kieran, Stephen, 57

KieranTimberlake, 51, *51*, 57, *57*

Kindle wireless reading device, 142, *142*, 155–56, *155*

Kirley, Paul, *139*

Kode Design, 126, *126*

Konaris, Thalia, *110*

Kraftplex, 89, *89*

Kulkarni, Unmesh, *113*

Kwame Nkrumah University of Science and Technology, 98

L.A. Earthquake: Get Ready campaign, 143, 156–57, *156–57*

Laboratory for Visionary Architecture, 28

LCA (lifecycle analysis), 84

Learning Landscape, 157, *157*

Leary, Rolfe, *110*

LED technology, 16, 20–21, 24, 29, 30, 31, 176, 181

Lee, Jongoh, 16, 24, *24*

LEED (Leadership in Energy and Environmental Technology), 18, 72

Leirdal, Jørgen, 136, *136*

Leonard, Annie, 162, *162*

Lesniewski, Laura, *128*

Levin, Jee, 74, *74*

Levin, Ori, 35, *35*

Lighting, 16, 30, 34, 108, 169–71, 175–76, 181

Lin, Michael, 44, *44*

Lin 94 chair, 89, *89*

Littrell, Shawn, 30, *30*

Lloyd, Alexis, *158*

Lloyd, Tom, *78*

Loblolly House, 51, *51*, 57–58, *57*

Loofah, 70–71, 90

Loofah recycled plastic composite panel, 70–71, *70*, 90, *90*

Lundevall, Tarald, *65*

Lust, 161, *16*

Luxo, 30, *30*

**M10 kite-power
system**, 14, *14*, 25, *25*

Maas, Winy, *48*, 66–67

Magno wooden radio,
99, *99*, 100, 109, *109*

Maguire, Chris, *149*

Mahaffy, Ian, *37*, 46, *46*

Mahangu, *see* Pearl
millet

Mahangu [pearl
millet] thresher, 98,
98, 110, *110*

Maharam, 75, *75*

Maia, Thiago, *75*

**Maison Martin
Margiela Artisanal
line**, 91, *91*

Makani Power Inc., 14,
14, 25, *25*

Mälarplast AB, *138*

Manassei, Hugo, *131*

Manz, Cecilie, 169, *169*,
183, *183*

Mapping, 100, 102–3, 132,
143–44, 153, 158, 167

**Mapungubwe National
Park Interpretive
Center**, 51, *51*, 59, *59*

Marcelo, Alvin, *133*

Mareguddi, Praveen, *113*

Marincel, Michelle, *110*

Mary Queen of Viet Nam
Church, 114, *114–15*

MAS Design, *44*

Masdar development,
16, 26–28, *26–28*

Masonry, 59

Mass transit, 39, 41, 60,
62, 154

Mater, 174, *174*

McDonough Braungart
Design Chemistry LLC,
71, 78

McDonough, William,
70, 72

McDowell, Steve, *128*

McIntyre, Gavin, *85*

McKinsey & Co., 102,
102–3

Medellín, Colombia, *2*,
50, *50*, 60–61, *60–61*

Medical devices, 121,
123–25, 129–30, 133,
135–36, 139

Medusa lamp, 170,
170, 181, *181*

Meeker & Associates,
147

Meeker, Donald, 142,
142, 147, *147*

Meijer, Joep, *84*

Meindertsma, Christien,
169–70, 171, *171*, 184,
184

Mesa, Felipe, *2*, *61*

Mesh networking, 39

MetaboliCity, *13*, 29,
29

Michael Maltzan Archi-
tecture, 50, *51*, 62–63,
62–63

Michaels, Wes, *114–15*

Micro-blogging, 165

Miller, Matthew, *157*

Massachusetts Insti-
tute of Technology
(MIT), 38, 45, 110,
120, 133, 159

MIT CityCar, 38, *38*,
45, *45*

MIT Department of
Architecture, *45*

MIT Department
of Urban Studies &
Planning, *45*

MIT International
Design Development
Summit, 110, *110*

MIT Media Laboratory,
45, *45*, 120, *132*, *133*,
159

**MIT Next Billion
Network**, 133, *133*

Miyake Design Studio, *87*

Mobile devices,
99–100, 111, 120,
141–42, 154

**Modular prosthetic-
limb system**, 134, *134*

**Modular traffic light
system (MTLS)**, 123,
124

Montalbano, James,
142, *142*, 147, *147*

Mooment, *183*

Morris, Ed, 154, *154*

Mossop, Elizabeth,
114–15

Moussavi, Farshid, *52*

Muji, 170–71, 175, *175*

Muji design team, *175*

Mulder, Roelf, *123*, *124*

Muller, Peter H., *42*

**Multiple chairs #17
and #23, Multiple
Family series**, 182, *182*

MVRDV, *48*, 50, *50*,
66, 67

Mycelium, 70, 85, 133

National Tele-health
Center, University of the
Philippines-Manila, *133*

Negroponte, Nicholas,
159, *159*

Nendo, 177, *177*

**Neonurture car-parts
incubator**, 119, 121,
121, 122, 135, *135*

**New Carver Apart-
ments**, 50, *50*, 62,
62–63

New York City
Department of Trans-
portation, *37*, *46*

New York Times
**visualization and
interaction projects**,
158, *158*

Newman, Mark, *167*

Nguyen, Vu, *158*

Nieuwenhuizen, Dimitri,
161

Nike Foundation, *150*,
151

Ninety Light, 30, *30*

**NioxMino asthma
monitor**, 129, *130*

No Picnic AB, *42*

Nokia Open Studio,
99–100, *99*, 111, *111*

Nongovernmental
organizations (NGOs),
98, 106, 113, 121, 126

Norplasta, *136*

Norwegian Form Foun-
dation, *126*

Norwegian Ministry of
Foreign Affairs, *126*

**Norwegian National
Opera and Ballet**,
49–50, *49*, 64, *64–65*

Norwegian People's
Aid, *126*

Nothwehr, Rollin, *43*

Nuno Corporation,
88, *88*

NYC Hoop Rack, *37*,
46, *46*

Nylon, 108

Obama, President
Barack, 145, 165

Obeng, George Yaw, *110*

Ochsendorf, John, 51,
51, 59, *59*

Odegard Inc., 104, *104*

Odegard, Stephanie,
104, *104*

Ogata, Shinichiro,
184–85

O'Hara, Christopher, *147*

Oil, 13, 40, 42, 70, 94

OLPC (One Laptop per
Child), 142, *143*, 159, *159*

**OLPC (One Laptop per
Child) XOXO laptop**,
142–43, *143*, 159, *159*

Olson, Eric, *139*

Open, 152, *152*

**Orio medical-cord
organizer**, 136, *136*

Orthocare Innovations,
134

Oslo School of Archi-
tecture and Design, *136*

Ove Arup, 19, 20, 21

Oxford Centre for
Vision in the Develop-
ing World, *125*

Paakkanen, Mikko, 170,
170, 181, *181*

Packaging, 70, 73, 77,
78, 85, 92, 173

Padrós, Pedro, *90*

Painted series, 99, *99*,
112, *112*

Palm leaves, 95

Paper, 82, 177

Papert, Seymour, 159

Participle Ltd., 121,
121, 131, *131*

Pearl millet, 98, 110

Pearson, Luke, *78*

PearsonLloyd, *78*

Pentagram, 4, 7, *154*,
159

Pentland, Sandy, 120,
122, *133*

Perez, Richard, *123–24*

Permanent magnet
synchronous motors, 41

Permasteelisa, *20*

Personal protective
equipment (PPE), 126

Peter Rich Architects,
59

Petravic, Robin, 99, *99*,
105, *105*

Phanunan, Ekapoj, *77*

Philips, 30, *30*, 98, *98*,
113, *113*

Philips Bright
Tomorrow Team, *30*

Philips Design, *113*

**Philips LED replace-
ment for the common
lightbulb**, 30, *30*

Photo-catalytics, 92

Photovoltaics, 14,
18–19, 20–21, 80, 128

Pilloton, Emily, 157, *157*

Piranti Works, *109*

PLA (polylactic acid),
70, 92

Plan B Architects, *2*, *60*

Planet G Ltd., *180*

Pli design, *180*

**PLMS6040 compost-
able polymer**, 92, *92*

Plug-in vehicles, 38,
42, 43

Pluralis chair, 169,
169, 183, *183*

Polski Theater banners,
160, *160*

Polycarbonate, 57

Polyester, 75

Polypropylene, 34,
173, 179

Porcelain, *see* Ceramics

**Posterwall for the
Twenty-first Century**,
161, *161*

Pottery, *see* Ceramics

Power Aware cord, 15,
15, 31, *31*

Powers, Daniel, *161*

Practical Action Sudan,
106–7, *106–7*

Prestero, Timothy, *135*

Pritchard, John, *167*

Project H Design, 157,
157

ProSolve 370e, 92–93,
92–93

Prosthetics, 120, 134

Public buildings, 18–19,
59–61, 64–65

Public health, 121, 123,
132–33

Puotila, Mikko, 82

Puotila, Ritva, 82, *82*

Qually, Byron, *123–24*

Raby, Fiona, 143, *143*,
146, 162, *162*

Radios, 109, 142, 148

Rakovska, Rumjana, *112*

Ramage, Michael, *59*

Ransmeier, Leon, 179, *179*

Ranta Carpets, 104, *104*

Rapid prototyping,
70, 79

Rasnow, Brian, *110*

Rau, Thomas, 51, *51*,
56, *56*

Recor, Bret, *159*

Red Antenna, *166*

Redmond, Elizabeth, *84*

Reduce, reuse, recycle
(three Rs), 69–72, 74

Reed pulp, 184

Regenerative braking, 41

Rehabilitation Institute
of Chicago, *134*

Renewable resources,
13, 15, 31, 86

Renzo Piano Building
Workshop, 15, *15*,
19, *19*

ResearchCentered
Design, *163*

Resin, 75, 89, 177

Restrepo, Camilo, *2*, *60*

Restrepo, J. Paul, *2*, *60*

**Return to Sender
artisan eco-casket**,
168, 183, *183*

Return to Sender
Eco-Caskets, *183*

RFID (radio frequency
ID), 133

Rich, Peter, *59*

Richardson, Peter, *32*

Rieck, Alexander, *28*

Ripple Effect, *118*,
137, *137*

Risk Watch, "Do You Want to Replace the Existing Normal?" series, 143, *143*, 146, 162, *162*

Risø DTU, the National Laboratory for Sustainable Energy, *12*, *29*

Robotics, 44, 79, 119, 127

Rocchi, Simona, *113*

Rocky Mountain Institute, 39

Roden, Ted, *158*

Rodriguez, Francisco, *110*

Rofi Industrier, *126*

Rotberg, Jhonatan, *133*

RTI Sports GmbH, *129*

Rubber, 83, 129, 136, 157

Rubber tires, 83, 157

RugMark Foundation, 104

Rugs, *see* Carpets

Ryohin Keikaku Co., Ltd., *175*

SAAS Instruments, *181*

Safco Products Company, *173*

Samarth bicycle trailer, 47, *47*

Sampoorna Chulha stove, Philanthropy by Design initiative, 113, *113*

Samsung Design China, a design center of Samsung Electronics, *164*

Sanders, Mark, 44, *44*

Sarmenta, Luis, *133*

SAS, 102, *102–3*

SASI Group, *167*

Sato, Oki, 177, *177*

Satoh, Taku, *149*

Schoppik, Haim, *149*

Schroeder, Dennis, *139*

Schwaag, Daniel, 92–93, *92–93*

Scott, Craig, *23*

Shigeru Ban Architects, *173*

Ships, 40, 42

Siegel, Dmitri, 154, *154*

Silicon, 24

Silk, 88, 145

Silver, Joshua, 125, *125*

Simone Giostra and Partners, 20, *21*

Sivertsen, Per, 81, *81*

Skakun, Jerzy, 160, *160*

Skiba, Tim, *173*

Skid Row Housing Trust, 50, *50*, 62, *62–63*

Skrufs Glassworks, *180*

SL Rasch, *28*

Slums, *see* Informal settlements

Smart-cartridge construction, 57

Smart Cities, 45, *45*

Smart power grids, 15

Smith, Adrian, 26, *26*

Smith, Amy, 110

Smith, Bruce, *78*

Smithson, Matt, *150*, *151*

Snøhetta, 49, *49*, 64, *65*

Snuza Halo baby breathing monitor, 123, *124*

Social networking, 120, 131, 144, 148, 153, 165

Soil Lamp, 31, *31*

Solar energy, 14, 16, 18, 22, 24, 26. 32–35, 40, 42, 52, 56, 80, 128, 138, 148

Solar Lilies, 32, *32*

Solar rechargeable battery lanterns, *33*, *33*

Solé Power Tiles, 34, *34*

SolPix, 20, *20*

Solvatten AB, 138, *138*

SOLVATTEN solar safe-water purifier, 138, *138*

Spackman Mossop Michaels, 114, *114–15*

Spot guide cane, 129, *130*

SRS Energy, 34, *34*

Stanford University, 77, 120

Stantec Architecture, *19*

Staps, Marieke, 31, *31*

Starkey Laboratories Inc. *139*

Steelcase Design Studio, 71, *71*, 78, *78*

Steenbergen, Ropery, *184*

Stone, Biz, *165*

Story of Stuff, The, 143, 162, *162*

Stoves, 106–7, 113

Stowell, Scott, 152, *152*

Strawboard, 180

Street Vendor Project, 166

Studio Design by Pacific Cycles, 44

Studio Loop.pH, *13*, *29*, *29*

Studio Paakkanen, *181*

Studio Tord Boontje, 116, *116–17*

Sudden Infant Death Syndrome (SIDS), 123

Sudo, Reiko, 88, *88*

Sunlabob Renewable Energy Co. Ltd., *33*, *33*

SunShade, 34, *34*

Suntech, 20, *21*

Sunway Inc., *173*

Surface materials, 75, 86, 89, 92, 94

Sweerts, Margreet, 112, *112*

Swine flu, *see* H1N1 virus

t.e. 83 hanging lamp, 184, *184*

Tagawa, Kinya, *149*

Taimina, Daina, 146

Takram Design Engineering, *149*

Taku Satoh Design Office, *149*

Tarazi, Ezri, 35, *35*

Tarazi Studio, 35, *35*

Temer, Bruno, *75*

Terminal Design Inc., *147*

Textiles, 75, 82–83, 87–88, 94, 104

Thatte, Neha, *157*

Themoteo, Pedro, *75*

theRightenvironment Ltd., 84, *84*

Thomas, Marc, *80*

Thorn Lighting, 20, *21*

Thorsen, Kjetil Trædal, *65*

Threshers, 98, 110

Tidal power, 14

Tile vaulting, 59

Timber, *see* Wood

Timberlake, James, 51, *51*, 57–58, *57–58*, 72

Tolhurst, Michael, *131*

Toneva, Magdalina, *112*

Touch magazine 2, 142, *142*, 163, *163*

Touch Sight camera, 142, *142*, 164, *164*

Trains, 38, 41

Tricycle Inc., 94, *94–95*

Triple bottom line, 98

Trove, 74, *74*

Trubridge, David, 98–99, *98*, 108, *108*

Tryk sustainable sampling tool, 94, *94–95*

Tulane City Center, Tulane University, 114, *114–15*

Tulloch, Sylvia, *80*

Tulusan, Indri, *111*

Twitter, 144, *144*, 165, *165*

Typography, 142, 147, 150–51, 161

Tyvek, 82

UNESCO, 59

United Nations Universal Declaration of Human Rights, 98

University of Michigan, 167, *167*

University of Montana Environmental Studies program, 114, *114–15*

University of Sheffield, 167, *167*

UPM ProFi, 173

Urban design, 16, 26–28, 60–61

Urban farming, 29, 54–55, 113

Urban Landscape Lab at Louisiana State University, 114

Van Ast, Jorre, 170, *171*, 178, *178*

Van Dore, Thomas, *134*

Van Drimmelen, Saskia, 99, *99*, 112, *112*

Van Genugten, Lianne, 34, *34*

Van Niekerk, Becker, 25

Van Rijs, Jacob, 48, *66–7*

Vander Lind, Damon, 25

Veira, Xaquín González, *158*

Vendor Power!, 166, *166*

VerTerra Ltd., 95, *95*

VerTerra tableware, 95, *95*

Vertical farming, 54–55

VerticalVillage, 50, *50*, 66, *67*

Video, 143, 156, 162

Viet Village Urban Farm, 114, *114–15*

Viral marketing, 162

Vision impairment, 125 142, 154, 163–164

Visualization, 15, 31, 100, 102–3, 121, 132, 143, 158, 167

Vulcana LLC, 83, *83*

Wadström, Petra, *138*

Wagner, Jakob, 174, *174*

Wallcoverings, 74, 143, 145

Wallenius Wilhelmsen Logistics, 42, *42*

Wallisser, Tobias, *28*

Wal-Mart, 39

Wasara Co., Ltd., 170, *171*, 184, *184–85*

Wasara tableware, 170, *171*, 184, *184–85*

Waste water, 26, 57, 86, 128

Watanabe, Kotaro, *149*

Water, 23, 35, 122, 137–38, 149

Water heating, 52

Wave power, 14, 17, 40, 42

Web4Dev, 121

Weber Thompson, *54–55*

Weir, Richard, *134*

Well Ausstellungssystem GmbH, 89, *89*

Wertheim, Christine, *140*, 146, *146*

Wertheim, Margaret, *140*, 146, *146*

Wheeler, Ben, *167*

Whipsaw Inc., 142, *142*, 148, *148*

Wieden + Kennedy, *150*, *151*

Wieler, Aaron, 110, *110*

Williams, Evan, *165*

Wilson, Jeff, *110*

Wind, 14, 25, 26, 40, 42, 52

Wingfield, Rachel, *13*, *29*, *29*

Wiseman, David, *124*

Witches' Kitchen collection, Design with a Conscience series, 99, *99*, 116, *116–17*

Wood, 89, 92, 98, 109, 116–17, 173, 175, 176

Woodnotes OY, 82, *82–83*

Wool, 81, 98, 146

World Economic Forum, 102, *102–3*

World Health Organization, 119, 131, 132, 138

Worldmapper, 143–44, 144, 167, *167*

Young, Michael, *158*

Z-10 concentrated solar-power system, 14, *14*, 35, *35*

Zaera-Polo, Alejandro, *52–53*

Zaldívar, Elsa, 90, *90*

Zamora, Christina, 105, *105*

ZenithSolar, 14, 35, *35*

ZM Architecture, 32, *32*

Zōn hearing aid, 121, *121*, 139, *139*

Cooper-Hewitt, National Design Museum is grateful to the following organizations and individuals for their permission to reproduce images in this book. Every effort has been made to trace and contact the copyright holders of the images reproduced; any errors or omissions shall be corrected in subsequent editions.

Numerals indicate figure numbers, except where indicated.

Title Page: © Sergio Gómez. **Introduction:** © Mieke Gerritzen: p. 8. **Energy:** © Loop.pH: frontispiece; © ZenithSolar: 1; © Makani Power: 2; © BioPower Systems: 3; © Interactive Institute: 4–5; © Tom Fox, SWA Group: 6; © Koninklijke Philips Electronics N.V.: 7; © Jongoh Lee: 8. **Energy Entries:** © BioPower Systems: 1; © Tim Griffith: 2; © Renzo Piano Building Workshop: 3; © Nic Lehoux: 4; © Tom Fox, SWA Group: 5; © Interactive Institute: 6; © Simone Giostra & Partners/ARUP/Ruogu: 7; © Simone Giostra & Partners/ARUP: 8; © EnviroMission: 9–10; © IwamotoScott: 11–12; © Jongoh Lee: 13–14; © Makani Power: 15; © Adrian Smith + Gordon Gill Architecture: 16; © Foster + Partners: 17–18; © LAVA (Bosse Walliser Rieck) with MIR: 19; © LAVA (Bosse Walliser Rieck) with Atelier Illume: 20; © Loop.pH: 21–22; © Samuel B. Freeman: 23; © Koninklijke Philips Electronics N.V.: 24; © Carl Dahlstedt: 25; © Marieke Staps: 26; © ZM Architecture Ltd.: 27–28; © Sunlabob Renewable Energy: 29–30; © SRS Energy: 31; © Lianne van Genugten: 32–33; © ZenithSolar: 34. **Mobility:** © Glen Jackson Taylor: frontispiece; © ALSTOM Transport/F.Christophorides: 1; © Coulomb Technologies Inc.: 2; © MIT Media Lab, Smart Cities: 3; © Pacific Cycles Inc.: 4; © Bright Automotive Inc.: 5; © No Picnic AB: 6. **Mobility Entries:** © AGV Italo Train of Nuovo Trasporto Viaggiatori S.p.A.: 1; © Coulomb Technologies Inc.: 2; © No Picnic AB: 3; © Bright Automotive Inc.: 4; © Pacific Cycles Inc.: 5–6; © MIT Media Lab, Smart Cities: 7–8; © Ian Mahaffy: 9; © Glen Jackson Taylor: 10; © Vahe D'Ala: 11–13. **Community:** © Rob't Hart: frontispiece; © Duccio Malagamba: 1; © Jiri Havran/Snøhetta: 2; © Iwan Baan: 3; © MVRDV: 5; © James Bellamy: 6; © Rau, Amsterdam, in cooperation with Powerhouse Company, Rotterdam: 7; © Halkin Photography LLC: 8; © Weber Thompson Architects: 9. **Community Entries:** © Duccio Malagamba Fotografía de Arquitectura S.L.: 1; © www.arquima. es - Alejanddro García & Francisco A. García: 2; © Sergio Padura: 3–4; © Weber Thompson Architects: 5–9; © Rau, Amsterdam in co-operation with Powerhouse Company, Rotterdam: 10–12; © Peter Aaron/Esto: 13; © Halkin Photgrphy LLC: 14–15; © KieranTimberlake: 16; © James Bellamy: 17–20; © Sergio Gómez: 21; © John Octavio Ortiz Lopera: 24–25; © Iwan Baan: 27–29, 32; © Michael Maltzan Architecture: 30–31; © Jiri Havran/Snøhetta: 33–34; © jens.solvberg.com: 35; © Snøhetta: 36; © MVRDV: 37–39, 41; © Rob't Hart: 40. **Materials:** © Nuno Corporation: frontispiece; © Matt Flynn: 1; © Behrokh "Berok"

Khoshnevis: 2; © Ecovative Design LLC: 3; © Rolex Awards/Jess Hoffman: 4; © Coverings Etc: 5; © IceStone LLC: 6; © Steelcase Inc.: 7; © Ecolect: 8. **Materials Entries:** © Biowert AG: 1–2; © Grenidea Technologies Pte Ltd.: 3; © Trove: 4–6; © Matt Flynn: 7–8; © Fibra Design Sustentável: 9; © Ofer Mizrahi: 10; © Coverings Etc: 11–13; © Matt Flynn: 14; © Bareket Kezwer: 15; © Steelcase Inc.: 16–17; © Behrokh Khoshnevis: 18–20; © Thomas Bloch: 21; © Dyesol: 22; © FIN: 23–26; © Woodnotes: 27–29; © Vulcana LLC: 30; © Ecolect: 31–33; © Ecovative Design LLC: 34–36; © IceStone LLC: 37–38; © Issey Miyake Inc.: 39–40; photo: Frédérique Dumoulin, © Issey Miyake Inc.: 41–42; © Nuno Corporation:43–44; © Matt Flynn: 45; © Well Ausstellungsystem GmbH: 46; © Christophe Fillioux: 47; © European Confederation of Linen and Hemp: 48; © Rolex Awards/Jess Hoffman: 49-50; © Marina Faust: 51–52; © Matt Flynn: 53; © Elegant Embellishments Ltd.: 54–56; © Tricycle Inc.: 57–59; © Theodore Samuels: 60. **Prosperity:** © U. Roberto Romano: frontispiece; © F S Rodríguez-Sanchez: 1; © Philips Design: 2; © David Trubridge: 3; © Jeffery Cross: 4; © Areaware: 5; © U. Roberto Romano: 6; © Witches' Kitchen: 7; photo: Louise Te Poele, © Painted: 8; © Nokia Corporation: 9; © McKinsey & Co.: 10. **Prosperity Entries:** © Alabama Chanin: 1–2; © McKinsey & Co.: 3–4; © U. Roberto Romano: 5–7; © Jeffery Cross: 8–10; © Practical Action–Sudan: 11–14; © David Trubridge: 15–17; © Singgih S. Kartono/ magno-design: 18; © Singgih S. Kartono: 19; © F-S Rodríguez-Sanchez: 20–21; © Nokia Corporation: 22–25; photo: Louise Te Poele, © Painted: 26–28; © Philips Design: 29–31; © Spackman, Mossop + Michaels: 32–34; © Witches' Kitchen: 35–37. **Health:** © IDEO: frontispiece; © American Honda Motor Co. Inc.: 1; © Next Billion Network: 2; © John Brownstein and Clark Freifeld: 3; © Design that Matters: 4; © kodedesign.com: 5; © Starkey Laboratories Inc.: 6; © Particple Ltd.: 7; © IDEO: 8. **Health Entries:** © Dot Dot Dot Ex Why Zed Design (Pty) Ltd.: 1–2, 4; © Modular Traffic Light Systems–Barry Geer: 3; © Biosentronics CC: 5–6; © Centre for Vision in the Developing World: 7–8; © kodedesign.com: 9–10; © American Honda Motor Co. Inc.: 11–12; © BNIM: 13; © Farshid Assassi: 14; © Ergonomidesign: 15–21; © Particple Ltd.: 22–24; © HealthMap: 25; © Next Billion Network: 26–27; © HDT Engineering Services: 28–29; © Design that Matters: 30–31; © Inora AS: 32–33; © IDEO: 34–36; © David Wadström: 37–38; © Starkey Laboratories Inc.: 39–40. **Communication:** photo: Francine McDougall, © The Institute for Figuring: frontispiece; © Apple: 1; © Amazon.com Inc. or its affiliates: 2; © Sean Donahue: 3; © Samsung Electronics: 4; © Meeker & Associates Inc.: 5; © Whipsaw Inc.: 6; © fuseproject: 7; © Francis Ware: 8; © The Canary Project: 9; © Nike Inc. and its affiliates: 10; © The New York Times: 11; © Green Map System Inc.: 12; © SASI Group (University of Sheffield) and Mark Newman (University of Michigan): 13; © Twitter: 14. **Communication Entries:** © Mieke Gerritzen: 1–3; © Revital Cohen: 4; photo: Aaron and Cassandra Ott, © The Institute for Figuring: 5;

© Meeker & Associates Inc.: 6; © Whipsaw Inc.: 7; © www.etsy.com: 8; © Rachel Wright: 9; © Necklush: 10; © Takashi Mochizuki (original artwork created by takram design engineering for the *Water* exhibition at 21_21 DESIGN SIGHT, directed by Taku Satoh): 11–12; © Nike Inc. and its affiliates: 13–16; © Scott Stowell/Open: 17–18; © Green Map System Inc.: 19–20; © The Canary Project: 21–22; © David Chavez: 23; © Apple: 24–25; © Amazon.com Inc. or its affiliates: 26; © Designmatters at Art Center College of Design: 27–28; © Project H Design: 29; © *The New York Times*: 30–31; © fuseproject: 32–33; © Joanna Górska & Jerzy Skakun: 34–36; © Lust: 37–38; © Francis Ware: 39; © Ann Leonard and Erica Priggen: 40–41; © Sean Donahue: 42–45; © Samsung Electronics: 46–47; © 2010 Twitter: 48; © Center for Urban Pedagogy, The Street Vendor Project, Candy Chang: 49–50; © SASI Group (University of Sheffield) and Mark Newman (University of Michigan): 51; © SASI Group (University of Sheffield) and Mark Newman (University of Michigan): 52–53. **Simplicity:** © Greg Holdsworth: frontispiece; © Artek OY AB/Artek.fi: 1; © MOOMENT: 2; © Saas instruments: 3; © Ryan Frank: 4; © Karin Eriksson: 5; © Royal VKB: 6; © Ransmeier Industrial Design: 7; © Goodmorning Technology: 8; © Wasara Co. Ltd.: 9; © Jetske de Groot: 10. **Simplicity Entries:** © Artek OY AB/ Artek.fi: 1; © Safco Products Company: 2; © Mater A/S, Denmark: 3–5; © Ryohin Keikaku. Ltd.: 6–8; © Goodmorning Technology: 9–10; © Masayuki Hayashi: 11–17; © Jorre van Ast: 18–20; © Royal VKB: 21; © Ransmeier Industrial Design: 22–24; © Karin Eriksson: 25; © Ryan Frank: 26; © Saas Instruments: 27–29; © Jetske de Groot: 30–31; © MOOMENT: 32; © Greg Holdsworth: 33; © Thomas Eyck: 34; © Wasara Co. Ltd.: 35–38.

Cooper-Hewitt, National Design Museum is particularly grateful to the following individuals and organizations for their assistance and support during the preparation of the *Why Design Now? National Design Triennial* exhibition and catalogue.

Curious Minds

Vito Acconci, Marc Alt, Mariana Amatullo, Kurt Andersen, Shigeru Ban, Michael Bierut, Tim Brown, Wendy Brawer, Blaine Brownell, Chris Collins, Andrew Dent, John Frane, Elizabeth Guffey, Hunter Hoffman, Lorraine Justice, Reed Kroloff, Amory Lovins, James Ludwig, Geoff Mamlet, Robert Moorhead, Chris Neidl, Julia Novy-Hildesley, Peter O'Toole, Phil Patton, Hadrian Predock, Beatrice Ramnarine, Tom Revelle, Terry Riley, Timothy Rowe, Sven Shiers, Henry Siegal, Suzanne Tick, Tessa van der Zouwen, Cathy Veninga, Susan Yelavich, Yasmina Zaidman

Curatorial Thanks

Tuija Aalto-Setälä, Dr. Martti af Heurlin, Eliisa Anttila, Julian Beinart, Staffan Bengtsson, Maria Benktzon, Lena Berglin, Wendy Brawer, Sissel Breie, Giada Bufalini, David Carlsson, Robin Chase, Lars Dafnäs, Dickson Despommier, Frida Eriksson, Karin Eriksson, Peer Eriksson, Wendy Feuer, Odile Hainaut, Elisabeth Halvarsson-Stapen, Corwin Hardin, André Heinz, Ted Hesselbom, Eric Holterhues, Veikko Hyvönen, David Iida, Mark Z. Jacobson, Tahmineh Javanbakht, Magnus Jonsson, Richard Julin, Ilkka Kalliomaa, Johan Karlsson, Harri Kilpi, Aila Kolehmainen, Ton Kooymans, Søren Krogh, Mirkku Kullberg, Barbro Kulvik, Ewa Kumlin, Håkan Långstedt, Tapio Laukkanen, Carolina Laverde Vasquez, Suzanne Lindbergh, Sara Lönnroth, Susan Lundgren, Margarita Matiz Bergfeldt, Perry L. McCarty, William McDonough, Alicia Mejia, Tina Midtgaard, Eva Moksnes Vincent, Heidrun Mumper-Drumm, Kuni Murayama, David A. Muyres, Camilla Norrback, Aslaug Nygård, Christina Öhman, Maureen Orth, Permasteelisa, Julian Posada, Mikko Puotila, Juliana Restrepo, Claes Rickeby, Anna Romboli, Daniel Sachs, Laura Sarvilinna, Roger Schickedantz, Mike Schragger, Antti Siltavouri, Paul Simonetti, Carina Sjögren, Mårten Skogö, Mattias Ståhlbom, Anne Stenros, Per Stotz, Teemu Suviala, Beate Sydhoff, Kerstin Sylwan, Krister Torssell, Anssi Tuulenmäki, Anne Uuttu, Maria Vallin, Alexander van Slobbe, Susanna Wallgren, John Waters, Robert Weil, Carin Whitney, Kerstin Wickman, Anders Wilhelmsson, Camilla Wirséen, Sue Zielinski, and the many other individuals who have been generous with their time, information, and assistance.

Design Team

Book design: Pentagram: Michael Bierut, Yve Ludwig
Installation and graphic design: Tsang Seymour Design: Catarina Tsang, Patrick Seymour, Naomi Freedman, Candice Ralph
Lighting design: Jeff Nash Lighting Design

At Cooper-Hewitt

Communications and Marketing: Jennifer Northrop, William Berry, Laurie Olivieri
Conservation: Lucy Commoner, Perry Choe, Sarah Scaturro
Curatorial: Sarah Butler, Laura Camerlengo, Darvia Douglass, Bareket Kezwer, Devon Lawrence, William Myers, Sunette Viljoen
Development and External Affairs: Caroline Baumann, Sophia Amaro, Debbie Ahn, Deborah Fitzgerald, Kelly Gorman, Kelly Mullaney, Barbara Roan
Education: Caroline Payson, Madeline Diaz, Shamus Adams, Mei Mah, Erin McCluskey, Alexander Tibbets
Exhibitions: Jocelyn Groom, Matthew O'Connor, Mathew Weaver, and the installation crew
Finance: Christopher Jeannopoulos
OFEO: Janice Slivko
Publications: Chul R. Kim
Registrar: Steven Langehough, Melanie Fox, Wendy Rogers, Bethany Romanowski, Larry Silver